REMEMBERING THE FUTURE

I0625451

Reflections on Ugandan Culture in Changing Times

Edited By Christopher Conte
With Hilda Twongyeirwe
2023

The Copyright © by Christopher Conte

All rights reserved

No part of this publication may be altered, reproduced, distributed, or transmitted in any form, by any means, including, but not limited to, scanning, duplicating, uploading, hosting, distributing or reselling, without express prior written permission of the editor, except in the case of reasonable quotations in features such as reviews, interviews, and certain other non-commercial uses currently permitted by copyright law.

ISBN: 979-8-218-19322-5
Library of Congress Control Number: 2023909811

Cover Design by CoCreate (Kampala, Uganda)
Cover Photograph by Parisa Azadi
Back Cover Photograph by Florence Kyohangirwe

Published by:

Christopher Conte (available online and as an ebook)
Silver Spring, Maryland, USA
www.ugandamemories.com
(Copies available in soft cover and ebook formats)
and
IBUA PUBLISHING (Africa)
Kampala, Uganda
www.ibuapublishing.com

Contents

Introduction

Remembering the Future is a successor to *Crossroads: Women Coming of Age in Today's Uganda,"* *which* was published in 2015. In both books, a diverse array of writers examine culture through the prism of their personal lives. While *Crossroads'* all-female lineup of writers explored tensions between values they learned when they were growing up and their aspirations as adults, *Remembering,* whose authors include men as well as women, delves more into the past and how culture has changed. Their main method was to seek out the views of earlier generations. That seems an obvious strategy for a project designed to explore changes in a culture, but these writers had a special interest in exploring the past: For many Ugandans today, the search for identity is complicated by abrupt interruptions in their culture that began with colonial occupation (1894-1962) and has continued under the influence of powerful western institutions and media. The fact that in Africa culture traditionally has been passed on orally rather than in writing, adds urgency to the effort to seek the wisdom of elders now.

As a westerner who has seen my own culture waver under the weight of its past and its internal contradictions, I find these writers' stories compelling portraits of a fascinating society that is not well known in much of the world. But more fundamentally, I am moved by the writers' depth of feeling and insight in capturing issues that are unique in many ways, but also are characteristic of the human experience everywhere. Culture is the milieu in which we exist, the oxygen of our personal and social lives, and seeing it described frankly and with such sensitivity in its many dimensions – joyful, tragic, ironic, funny and bittersweet – is an enriching human experience. Ugandans may be particularly well suited to the task. Their own exposure to foreign influence and internal diversity makes them astute observers of their own and other cultures.

The essays here were produced independently, without any overall message in mind. There is no overarching or unifying theme. Each chapter is, in effect, a snapshot designed to capture an issue the writer finds important. Since, as a collection of separate narratives rather than a single story, the various chapters may appear to be random, I will offer a few words to help you navigate them.

In the first three chapters, Edna Namara, Linda Orando and Wobusobozi Amooti Kangere set out to explore the unsettled nature of gender relations today, but they ended up with much more: *A Bride's Farewell Song* by Namara offers a compelling profile of the stoicism that defined earlier generations; Orando's *Goria Ubuntu* probes an old-school patriarch's ideas about leadership; and Kangere's *A Tale of Two Matriarchs* sums up the "thing or two" his powerful grandmother taught him about being a man. In the end, the three chapters offer compelling portraits of distinguished elders people who would make stellar role models for people of any time or gender. The fourth chapter, renowned Ugandan journalist Joachim Buwembo's discussion of the enduring power of clans as a basis for social organisation, also may seem narrowly focused at first, but Buwembo notes that the elders were onto something important when they designed a social system that brilliantly tied every person to each other and to the whole society. Do we pay enough attention to that need today?

The book next turns to reflections on forces, some external and some internal, that profoundly interrupted Uganda's cultural evolution. In his *Journey Through the Ateker Land of Karamoja*, A. K. Kaiza masterfully traces the upheaval brought by colonization and its legacy. Kaiza's case study of Karamoja, which he describes as the region of Uganda that most successfully resisted colonial domination only to encounter misfortune and mistreatment in post-colonial days, encapsulates much of Uganda's history. Next, Journalist Buwembo turns his wit on deconstructing another cultural disaster in *And Money Made Men Mad*, and Caroline Ariba's *If it Takes a Village, What Happens When the Village Dies?* tracks the devastating consequences of the money economy, its underlying values and population growth on small farmers and their villages, the bedrock of Ugandan society for millennia leading up to today. Joseph Elunya Sr., shares with Ariba a sense of nostalgia about growing up in a village. His *Of Healers, Quacks . . . and Confusion* is a fascinating but true parable of village society caught between competing organising principles. It also is a fascinating tale of cultural blending and the triumph of pragmatism.

The next set of chapters look at different responses to cultural dissonance. Regina Asinde's searing *Dance of Death* describes how the growing burden of living up to her tribe's religious beliefs ultimately led her to abandon her religion outright, while Aliker P'Ocitti recounts in *Our Justice or Their Justice?* the inadequacy of both traditional and modern systems of justice to bring peace and reconciliation for a brother who joined a rebel army. Achelam D. Kinyera depicts the struggle between innovation and preservation in *The Words Died in My Mouth*, a charming but bittersweet tour of the rise, fall and transformation of the dozens of languages spoken in Uganda, and then Buwembo returns for a third instalment in his triptych of contributions: *Radio Katwe: From Drums to the Internet*, a description of how Ugandans have deftly used changing communications technologies to manoeuvre the appearance of divisive, partisan politics on their cultural scene.

The book concludes with two essays that describe a cultural peace of sorts. Stephen Ssenkaaba's *Wakaliwood: Uganda's Answer to Hollywood* describes the reappearance and transformation of spirits and demons from Ugandan folklore in modern movies, and Flavia Nassaka's *A Healing Tradition* explores how a traditional healer's ideas live on in the work of her son, a noted psychiatrist and educator.

The book ends with a story by Edna Namara, but you'll have to read it to see why it struck your editor as a fitting capstone to this exercise in remembering – and making memories the foundation of the future.

I hope you find these stories as fascinating, uplifting, memorable and relevant whatever your culture is as I have.

Christopher Conte
June 2023

Goria Ubuntu

By Linda Orando

The battle of the sexes
Coming soon to a studio near you
Ladies and Gentlemen,
If they all be trash, who be the trash cans?

Eish! A beg,
my kinsmen

How be it that two sides of a coin face off like a standoff between midnight and noon?
It is like the clock with two hour hands that couldn't decide which tick to tock first
Or like the thread strands of a plaited twist come undone in a sinister plot to sow discord
As if the obvious was hidden before their eyes like the belt under the beer belly of a drunk!
Who lights a fire under the sun during summer or takes a cold shower in the winter night?
Look, the egg just dropped out of the cradle of her nest and waits to shutter smackdown.
Excuse me Mr. Masculine Sir, Madame Feminine Ma'am, 1 hate to interrupt, but the baby is crying!

ON A RECENT ERRAND into town, I witnessed a confrontation the likes of which I doubt earlier generations would have seen. As our rickety old van sat idle at the taxi stage, a passenger, a 40-something woman, grew increasingly impatient. The 20-something driver was dawdling, no doubt in hopes that more fare-paying passengers would appear. The mama finally lost her patience and demanded to be let out. In an instant, the driver revved his engine, and the van lurched forward. Soon trees and pedestrians were passing by in a blur. But the woman, indignant at being ignored, insisted that the driver stop and let her dismount. The man spat a nasty female stereotype at her.

"Ono naye talina amagezi. Empty airhead." She retorted with a blow to his sense of manhood: "N nsobola n'okusuzza gwe. I can even house and feed you." Did it occur to the mama that this young man could be her son or to him that the woman could be his mother?

Such confrontations have become unfortunately common. Hardly a day goes by that I don't encounter nasty exchanges between men and women, especially on social media. One especially nasty fight broke out in 2018 when a tweet with the provocative hashtag *#Men Are Trash* triggered a nasty Twitter war featuring misogynistic attacks by men and vows by women to "dismantle the patriarchy."

In Uganda, as in many sub-Saharan African societies, patriarchy remains entrenched in spite of the gains that women have made in politics, education and civic life. In rural areas, women still can't make decisions that affect their lives, control their finances or gain full education because of demands on their time and labour at home. Urban women have fared better; some can own real estate, get quality education and enjoy greater social freedoms, but gender-based violence and limitations on self-determination in personal relationships are still common, especially among the poor. Among the urban elite, patriarchy manifests in a far more nuanced way; while women thrive in professions that were once dominated by men, they experience an imbalance in power in their personal relationships with men who cling to outmoded notions of masculinity to justify misogyny.

The resulting battle between men and women appears everywhere, from social media to the privacy of our homes. Amidst endless disagreements about how to share domestic duties, many career-driven women fear losing their marriages if husbands deem them insufficiently submissive, while some professional men suggest condescendingly that less-educated women make better wives. While most men support women's rights and equity in the abstract, they resist sharing power with their wives. The problem is so pervasive that marriage itself sometimes seems endangered; divorce, once a rarity, is now becoming more common, and some women are raising families on their own, either because they don't think they need men or because their men flee when they become pregnant.

Have we just become, as I frequently hear my elders say, a bad-mannered generation? Or are we missing something fundamental – a key ingredient for creating a good, modern society?

I decided to take my questions to Kwara Asan Odoi, the patriarch of my family clan. He might seem an odd choice to consult on gender relations since many women trace today's problems to traditional patriarchy. But an almost primal need led me back to him. I figured he might help me understand how we got to where we are today. Besides, I figured that before we turn our backs completely on our patriarchal traditions, we should make sure we know what we are rejecting.

Driving east from Kampala toward Kwara Asan's home feels like seeking the source of the rising sun. As you leave the city behind, the calm green of the countryside soothes the senses. Many city dwellers make this trek regularly to escape the chaos of urban life and visit their ancestral homes. For me, the trip runs 225 kilometers to a place on the Tororo-Mbale highway that local people know simply as Mile 8. There, a dirt road branches into an expanse of savannah leading to Asinge, where my great-great-grandfather settled his family. Along this road, the surroundings are almost completely devoid of the small huts one often sees in rural eastern Uganda. But eventually, one comes to a scene that looks like a picture in a storybook: A gallery of 11 bungalows spread neatly over three acres of land. A few nostalgically reflect the earthen, rustic feel of thatch that typifies traditional village housing, but most are replicas of urban-style homes, with city comforts like tiled floors, piped water and electricity.

I have been to this place before, of course. But now I see it in a new light. As an architect, I have become conscious of the way our man-made environment reflects our social lives. In the city, each of these homes would be hidden behind a big wall, probably topped with sharp glass or razor wire, with a steel gate to keep passers-by from entering or even seeing what lies behind it. But here, the houses are surrounded by small lawns and separated only by little flower hedges and trees that offer a visual accent but do not block neighbours' views of each other. The homes are connected by a network of winding paths stemming from a central spine that links the whole complex to the main road. At the heart of this little village is a gazebo called "the Rwakitura" after President Museveni's home in Mbarara. Here, it is a place where residents of this small compound gather to make merry and share meals on holidays. The place is quiet when I arrive, but just imagining it filled with adults talking and children playing gives me a warm feeling.

Kwara Asan Odoi, the last surviving son of my great-grandfather, is waiting for me. Technically, he is my granduncle, the brother to my biological grandfather. But everyone in the family calls him "Grandpa." Lines gather around his eyes and ears, but I sense a young soul trapped in the body of an old man. He is animated. Every word is alive with energy despite his aged voice. His strides are gallant, and he shows he still has a flair for drama.

He quickly picks up my fascination with the complex, and after we dispense with the formalities, he explains it by offering me a history lesson. The story begins with my great-great grandfather and namesake, Orando, who moved his family here from West Budama, which is east of where we now stand. They brought with them the ways of their old village, where people lived close to one another. The land was clan-owned, so there were no assigned plots other than the individual households. People worked it collectively and shared the produce. This wasn't just a matter of economics; it also served to maintain family bonds and create a structure for growth and continuity. As sons grew older and found wives, the patriarch would tell them where they could build homes for their families close to their parents' homes, so that the extended family would remain tightly knit. Over time, it was not unusual for family clans to grow this way into entire villages.

My grandfather's message is clear. Although the settlement I see before me seems unusual to me, a millennial, it is a modern rendition of traditional society – one family's celebration of its cultural roots and the bonds that tie its members together even though a changing economy has led them to acquire larger homes and more modern lifestyles. But our discussion subsequently makes clear that the settlement is much more than that: It is the embodiment of the values that those early settlers brought with them. I sum them up as Goria Ubuntu. Goria is our clan's totem, a local species of weaver bird. Ubuntu is a Zulu word for the universal bond between people based on sharing – a principle that Grandpa describes as "being one" or "unity." Goria Ubuntu underlies our clan's approach to many things, including food, marriage and social security, our symbiosis with nature and, most importantly, our commitment to advance not just individually but collectively across generations and genders.

Kwara Asan describes how Goria pursued these goals in the old times.

Whenever an adult male brought home a wife, she lived first with his family in their household for a season. Female in-laws taught her their ways of cooking and caregiving, relationship norms, and all other values of the new family. Once she was well assimilated, her husband built a hut, known as a 'simba,' for his family next to the main house. The women set up a kitchen for the new wife identical to the one in the main house. They gave her pots and pans and then cooked the first meal with her, which the whole family shared in the main house. In the ensuing days and months, the new wife prepared meals herself but continued to send a portion of the food to the main house. As the tradition developed, people could have meal after meal together in the different homes of siblings who were settled in the compound. That is how the spirit of togetherness and oneness was established in every home.

Society, in short, was an extension of family. Every uncle was your father, your cousins were your siblings (unless you married them), every nephew was your son, and every niece was your daughter. "There was no such thing as 'uncle' – That is a dot com thing," Kwara Asan says, trotting out his favourite term for my generation. "So you should not be calling me 'grand uncle.' Call me brodeKwara – Grandpa."

Much more was at issue than names. Recalling his own grandfather, Orando, Kwara Asan says,

He urged us never to quarrel, and he encouraged those in the family who had 'better pockets' to cater for others. So if I was buying two pounds of meat for my mother, I'd have to buy the same portion for the other households.

Why? Because of the tradition of eating together from one another's homes. It would have been awkward for children to eat greens in one household and then eat beef in another household.

This is the family my grandfather knew from the time of his birth. Strolling around the compound, he talks more about his childhood. It was a time, he says with a chuckle, that his daily apparel consisted of little more than a loin cloth – "Not like the napkins . . . sorry, 'diapers' . . . you people talk of."

Boys would range over great distances with the family's cows, feeding themselves on an assortment of wild berries and fruit. On their way home they would milk the cows, delivering the product to their mamas at sundown. Girls prepared the meals. Late in the evening, the old folks told tales around the fireplace. No one missed this event, just as people don't miss TV and radio today. While the plots and characters always changed, the stories back then were laced with lessons about how to behave.

As I listen to the old man's account, the scenery before my vision fades to hues of black and white. The modern houses slowly morph into grass-thatched houses. The trees dwindle in size and stare back at me with their lips shut. Kwara Asan recalls a time when he was 12 that his father, Onyango Thomas, gave him a good smacking on his bare bottom because he had attempted to dodge school. The old man might have been assuaged since his son was trying to attend a community church service, but the underlying reason for his transgression eliminated any possibility of easy redemption: He was curious about the nature of the blood that ran through the veins of the white missionaries. Was it as green as the veins he noticed through their skin? His father had no time for such questions. "If you don't go to school, in the future," he would warn, "you'll be the one slaughtering chicken and buying malwa (local brew) for your brothers when they get jobs." This warning proved more effective than all the beatings the boy ever got.

Onyango Thomas had three sons – Valerian (my biological grandfather), Martin, and Odoi, the boy who grew up to become our Kwara Asan. When the time came for their schooling, only the boys were sent to school. To pay their school fees, their father rented some land to raise more cotton for cash. Here the story takes a familiar path – one that outrages modern women and social reformers.

> *Who were the labourers? The girls – my sisters and their mothers. They would go communally and clear these gardens. When we (boys) got to the August holidays, we would join them and clear the gardens. They would continue with the planting while we returned to school, but in December, we would join them in picking the cotton. At the end of the season, the cotton was sold, and guess whose fees would get paid? Ours. So Martin, Valerian and I would receive the money through the labour of the girls.*

People today may see this as giving the boys an easy life, but what seemed like preferential treatment in days past served a practical purpose. Onyango had a lean purse; educating the boys was a priority since in the economy of those days they would have greater earning power than the girls would. But that's not as unfair as it sounds. When the boys finished school and got jobs, they were expected to pitch in to support the family and educate their younger siblings. Eventually, the importance of girls in the changing economy became apparent, and the importance of educating them came to be recognised. "Unity was not just about everybody living together, each in his own house," Kwara Asan says. "In practice, we were each of benefit to one another."

Onyango's sons learned this principle well. That was clear when Kwara Asan's older brother, Martin, finished his education and got a job teaching college in Mbarara. His first salary payment was 210,000 Ugandan shillings. Grandpa remembers the moment well.

> *He told me to come and asked, 'What do I do?' God wants you to give him a tenth, but Martin first thought of his parents and allocated money to his father, mother and the other mothers. The remainder he gave to me. It was the most pocket money I had ever received. I grabbed it and prepared for Saturday to distribute it accordingly. It was not a question of 'mine' but 'ours.' We are still trying to keep this tree [our family] straight.*

The bond between the two brothers – and the family's commitment to unity – became even clearer later. Valerian had moved away; some say because strife between his two wives shattered the peace of the family, but Kwara Asan says he went in search of land where he could establish a large farm. By the time Kwara Asan had finished his own education in public health, he was playing an active role in running the family compound. The family lived with cows in their home, as was the custom, but he had learned that the animals could spread tuberculosis to humans, so he helped build a new family home. He also built a house in the compound for Martin. And he provided for the education of his younger sister, who became a nurse.

Then a new challenge arose: Demonstrating the sense of "oneness" between them, he set out to find a wife for brother Martin.

> *"I had to look for a woman who would not be just a wife to the man but a mother to the home. She had to be educated and have a good background, because we had seen how uneducated girls could be so difficult. So after the survey, I recommended two ladies to him. One of them interested him. Valerian and I engaged the parents of the girl on his behalf because he wasn't around.*

Martin married the girl his brother found for him. Today, we know her as Grandma Mary. She had been educated by nuns, and Kwara Asan credits her for instilling a sense of discipline and respect for knowledge in the whole family. "She was positively aggressive," he says with an admiring chuckle. "She was a no-nonsense lady. She did not tolerate familiarity and misbehaviour. Her 'yes' was 'yes,' and her 'no' was 'no.'"

Mary not only governed the home and raised her children. She helped supplement their income with proceeds of her own cotton growing. Along with her husband, Martin, she imbued the spirit of Ubuntu in their children. Perhaps the best proof of that is how the next generation turned out. Martin's oldest son, Fred, completed his education and became a successful lawyer, but he stayed involved in family matters. *"As he started earning more money, he educated his siblings – first George, then together with George they educated Charles, who in turn joined them in supporting the rest of the siblings — Jane, Felix and Christine. They kept pulling together to raise the girls."*

After visiting the home of a colleague who had died and finding the man had lived in a humble grass-thatched structure, Fred came home to build the first modern house in the compound. It was for his siblings, who were now finding jobs of their own in the modern economy and would need a place to lodge whenever they came on holiday. The brothers also rebuilt their father's house to similar standards. Eventually, one after the other, this next generation got married and built more houses for their own families, as well as the gazebo at the heart of it all.

My grandfather and I now survey the results. The compound now consists of 10 cottages, the latest ones reaching the outskirts of the family land, just as my grandfather said families in old times expanded to become villages. Kwara Asan points to one of the compound's homes that he says has seven rooms. With the land starting to get full, he tells me, the family soon may have nowhere to grow but up; in fact, plans are afoot to build the compound's first storied house.

I look at the umbrella trees in the compound. They must have seen much over decades running up to this day, silent witnesses of the comings and goings of the family and the man who has become its overseer. Thinking about the many people who shaped what I see, I picture a team of acrobats forming a human pyramid. My grandfather and his brothers climbed on their fathers' shoulders. When they finished school and got jobs, they pitched in to educate their siblings, who took their place in this structure, each of its members supported by – and supporting – one another. Ubuntu.

Finally, I raise the question that brought me here in the first place. What does the patriarch think about the troubled relations between men and women today? His answer may satisfy neither advocates of feminism nor believers in patriarchism. *"In my day,"* he starts . . .

> *. . . the value of men was to build homes and train their sons. The need for that discipline has never ended. The man had to provide for the family. Every family had to have at least one cow in the home and breed more to grow wealth. How would a home with a lazy man be wealthy? He had to work hard to prepare the garden and provide food for the home. It was not for the man to go drinking irresponsibly from the proceeds of the harvest because then he would never develop or educate his kids. A man's role was to bring about development.*
>
> *The wife, on the other hand, was the manager of the home. You could say that she was the permanent secretary. The minister dictates policy on an issue, but the actual implementation is done by the permanent secretary. When she [married and came to her husband's*

family], it was said that she had gone to 'make a home.'
She would genuinely do that. It was not a punishment.
It was a normal thing, and everyone respected her role.

Kwara Asan disavows any notion that women are somehow less important than men. When God says that a woman must 'submit' to her husband, he says, *"He didn't mean that the woman has got to be a servant of the man. They must work together."*

He does argue, though, that there must be a leader – and that is a responsibility God gave to men. I will admit to feeling a bit uneasy when the conversation turns to arguments about leadership, God-given roles and a woman's obligation to submit. But I relax when Grandpa cites the Bible, which says we are all "children" in the eyes of the Creator. In Kwara Asan's telling, Adam comes across as a whiner who failed to live up to his manly duty. "Adam failed to work with Eve -- that is why we were all punished," he explains, wryly adding that the man took the coward's way out by blaming Eve for his failure. *"Adam relinquished his leadership when he ate the fruit and then afterwards told God, 'It's the woman you gave me.'"*

As if he needs further proof that his version of patriarchy does not require women to be passive, Kwara Asan offers another story about his older brother.

I remember a time of commotion in this home when my brother was away teaching in Mbarara and his wife (Grandma Mary) was left with the children. She was the ultimate disciplinarian. When the children came back after school, they were given a range of chores from fetching water to cleaning and tending to the cows, irrespective of whether they were boys or girls. My parents did not like this very much; to them, the notion of a boy fetching water was unthinkable because this was a woman's role. When Martin came back, he defended his wife. He said, 'This is the woman who produced these children. If she wants to beat them to death, let her beat them! They are her children, and she knows best how to raise them. You leave her alone to do whatever she wants.'

Of course, Martin was exaggerating for effect, but his statement makes the point. A woman was all-powerful in her realm. Kwara Asan believes today's problems between men and women arose because women's empowerment has been accompanied by a new sense of competition. It began in schools. *"There were fights, and the challenge from the girls was, 'Illoya gi ngo? What do you defeat me in? In brains, we are together.'"* The competition got even more intense as women started to make inroads in the job market, he says.

> *When some women were put in higher positions, instead of thanking God for it, the mindset was, 'Uhuh, they used to think we cannot do anything, but we can do everything.' Back in the day, the man, being stronger, found the woman to be vulnerable and unable to defend herself against threats, so that is why she was told to stay behind while he went out to be at the front line. But now that we are both at the front line, the problem is that the wife says, 'I am like you. Onsinga ki! What do you beat me at?'*

Kwara Asan recalls such an exchange he once heard in his workplace. It was so much like the one I heard from the Mama who was angry about the taxi driver's disrespectful behaviour. *"I even heard my boss, who was a doctor married to a husband who was also a doctor, say, 'That man mishandles me, but we were in the same class and I was beating him. If he wants anything, we shall fight.'"* I detect in my grandfather no wince, disdain, discomfort or even sense that it was unusual that his boss in the workplace was a woman. Her gender was irrelevant to her working relationship with him.

We have a brief diversion to debate how significant men's greater physical strength is today. Under Grandpa's ribbing, I am forced to concede that if a snake fell out of a tree into our path, I would run like crazy rather than face the enemy. I choose not to dwell on that point. Instead, I latch onto my grandfather acknowledgment that men share responsibility for the competitiveness that has come to pollute male-female relations.

> *Unfortunately, this competition has also spilled onto the men who say, 'If I allow this one to go, next time she will boss over me.' Because of this, in many cases, I have seen men do everything to keep women from rising. These are the stupid men who think this way. . . Okay, not stupid, but ill-informed.*

So, both women and men who look at relationships through competitive eyes are missing the point. Cooperation, not competition, ensures a society's success. Building a family and a society requires collective effort in the workplace and at home. *"Where the mother has put down her foot on something, the father reinforces. When I fail, the mother would chip in,"* says Kwara Asan.

Ubuntu is more than a family affair. Kwara Asan recalls a time his older brother found himself in a boundary dispute with neighbours. Martin didn't call in the lawyers. He didn't build a fence. He didn't fight. Instead, he simply went to talk with the neighbours. "He told them to plant the mark stone where they saw fit, and that was the end of the matter," my grandfather recalls. It wasn't the only such instance in our family history. Later, Martin's son, Albert, decided to raise mango trees as a commercial venture but was concerned that the neighbours would undermine his business by helping themselves to his produce. So he gave them all mango seedlings to plant for themselves. Problem solved.

Don't be selfish because when the community benefits, your interests are protected. Everyone around here knows us to be friendly. In fact, when there is a threat, neighbours are the first people to rise to our defence. Nobody here robs us because we add value to the lives of our neighbours. Also, when there is a drought and people run out of food, we share with them a little here and there. Sometimes we sell and just top up for them a little more at the end of the day. So there is harmony in the village.

Ubuntu should apply even wider – to the whole population, he adds.

The knowledgeable people should sit with these people and guide them. Political leaders are only interested in their stomachs, so they are not guiding people. People don't have the knowledge, and if at all it's there, it's half-baked. People are not [behaving badly] because they want to. It's simply because they lack the knowledge.

Before he retired, Kwara Asan served for a time as a district health officer in Gulu. In that job, he interviewed many job applicants.

When I was interviewing people who had applied for some professional positions, I asked them, 'Why do you want to become a health officer?' They would answer, 'Because I want to serve my country.' This is very good, but I would say, 'Yes, you want to serve your country, but how about the one who is cultivating cotton that is exported and brings foreign currency into the country? Aren't they serving their country too?'

Platitudes don't satisfy my grandfather, who suggests that the applicants didn't understand what makes a society succeed. They "just wanted the jobs for money," he concludes.

Our stroll has become a long, enlightening trek into the past. Now the bungalows are more than a curiosity. They fill me with a sense of nostalgia for the history they hold. I feel connected to them, as if they, too, want to ask the question that now looms before me: "Where do we go from here?"

As Kwara Asan prepares to answer, something about his countenance changes. His youthful soul takes a sabbatical. It is almost as if a golden opportunity has been presented to an Oracle that had been long silenced by the events of the century. *The holy scripture says, 'My people perish because of a lack of knowledge,'* he notes. *"Education is at the centre of the whole thing."*

It's clear he isn't just talking about going to school or getting a degree. Those are just means to the ultimate end – knowledge. To him, education has many facets. He reminds me of how a public health official taught the family to stop living under the same roof as their cows. He recounts a trip he made to Israel and was impressed that people there, through knowledge, could grow crops in a desert. He says the family no longer pays or seeks bride price because they have been educated to understand that the practice, carried on through negotiations and haggling, amounts to "selling" girls and treating them like "slaves" – a denunciation as strong as I have heard from anybody. Finally, he mentions how Grandma Mary, educated as a girl by nuns, went on to teach a new generation to value knowledge over property and to live their lives with discipline and strong principles. Mary, he says, was an emancipated woman who used her empowerment through education to benefit the whole family instead of "throwing the baby out with the bath water," as he believes many of the "dot-com" generation of women do in the wake of their "empowerment."

Once again, his words lift a burden I have felt. Education enables us to find our way through complicated situations and adapt to changing circumstances. My mind flashes to my own father. I was told that he might not have been enthusiastic initially about having four girls and just one boy, thinking the girls would have limited earning potential as adults. But he changed his mind after visiting some other countries where women were making big inroads in careers and the economy. Suddenly, he started encouraging his daughters to watch martial arts movies (one of his loves) and telling us we could accomplish anything we dared to dream. It was not purely by chance or my own sense of ambition that I have a professional career today.

To exercise his leadership, Kwara Asan continues, a man can't just issue orders and expect blind obedience. He must be exemplary. He emphasises the word "exemplary" by reminding me that its root is "example." A man's first duty is to set a good example. This is a woman's duty too. She is not limited in developing her skills and using her talents any more than a man, though like a man, she, too, has responsibilities. The problem with the new emphasis on equality, Grandpa says, is that it leads people to forget a more fundamental truth: "Unity is best."

Kwara Asan also leaves me feeling appreciated as a woman. His philosophy suggests I have ample room to pursue a career but can make my contribution in other ways as well. Carrying a baby for nine months, suckling it for maybe three years, making a home and, like Grandma Mary, working to help supplement the family income are no small things, he says. They are achievements. While I celebrate the opportunities women – including me – now have, I find myself thinking of some of my women colleagues at work, who sometimes voice hidden frustrations not about being denied opportunities but about having ones they aren't sure they want; they even admit that they would prefer spending their time at home rather than doing things like inspecting foundations being laid at dangerous construction sites far beyond the city. Women, like men, are lucky to have many ways to contribute.

As we say our goodbyes, Grandpa notes that our conversation reflects his current role in life – to give advice. But he also issues a challenge to me and my generation.

> *Now, if you are not united, the legacy will stop at Odoi, Valerian and Martin. Then people will say, 'The homes we used to see here, those people who used to have these homes, these people who became local chiefs, who even married two to three wives – as soon as death struck, the children separated and went into property fights for land. [Will people say] that they hate one another even more than the locals who are near them?' Will the homes have been deserted so that you just find bush?*

Pondering these questions, I look one last time at the calm and harmonious group of homes standing together on the small swath of savannah. Is it a monument to a time gone by or a model for how we might preserve the best of our culture in today's world? Can we still find social solidarity and overcome the selfish impulses unleashed by individualism?

Amidst an orchestra of chirping birds, a gentle breeze rustles leaves – reminders of what the trees have witnessed. Perhaps it is a promise of how much more serene our relationships can be if we just get them right. As I return to the city, an image of the pyramid of athletes with the strongest and heaviest at the bottom and the lightest and smallest at the pinnacle dances before my eyes.

A Tale of Two Matriarchs

By Wobusobozi Amooti Kangere

ONCE AS I STARTED to drowse while riding a rickety old bus after a long, tiring day, a video of a Kadongo Kamu song – Buganda's answer to American country music – grabbed my attention. Kadongo Kamu music often consists of dramatic tales spun with poetic twists and comedic timing. Despite my fatigue, I was instantly sucked into this modern successor to the lost tradition of fireside oration and storytelling.

The song narrated a man's visit to a friend, ostensibly to collect an overdue debt. The friend divines his visitor's intention and adroitly launches into a traditional Kiganda greeting to distract him. Kiganda greeting is a lengthy ritual. It begins with enquiries about the night (or day, depending on the time), followed by a litany of questions that must be reciprocated until the initiator is exhausted. Kiganda etiquette does not permit interrupting a greeting.

Our host stretches the greeting to comic lengths. *"Did the night pass in peace? How are the people at home … the neighbours … the animals … this uncle … that auntie … this relative … that friend … the rains … the drought? What news of the lake? What news of the road?"*

The visitor is flabbergasted. But he becomes concerned when the ploy finally runs its course and the host collapses into a chair, his face a picture of desolation. *"Why are you upset?"* the visitor asks, forgetting his mission.

The melodrama takes a new turn. The friend rises slowly, palm held limply to his cheek, and launches into a verse lamenting the loss of his wife. Her head has been eaten by the city. She has started wearing trousers. She returns home whenever she pleases, refuses to do housework, demands they hire a maid, and no longer cooks traditional dishes. She even has the temerity to deny him his "marital rights."

Just then, a woman's head peeps through a doorway. She listens and then vaults onto the stage, launching a verse of her own with theatrical gusto. Her husband is hardly ever home. He spends too much time in bars and wastes all his money on younger women. He doesn't buy her clothes anymore. There is no food in the house. She is tired of looking ragged and old.

The plot thickens. The visitor, now turned arbitrator, sits man and wife down and counsels them with a verse of his own. He laments the reach of western influence and destruction of tradition so mournfully that the host's wife is moved. She disappears into the back, reappears in traditional garb, and kneels before her husband as Kiganda custom dictates. He, in turn, apologises and vows to mend his ways. They embrace. Peace is made!

Our visitor leaves triumphant. He probably will never get his money back, but who cares? He has saved a marriage. Half the bus is abuzz with jubilant chatter as if he has scored a goal in a football game.

I pretended to be unmoved, but the song sparked a neuron or two in my brain. I was reminded of a report a lawyer friend once told me he was writing for a study on divorce trends in Uganda. When divorce rates increased by approximately 10% in the 1990s, it was said that post-war trauma and economic stress could be blamed for the tear in our social fabric. But between 2005 and 2015, when Uganda was arguably swimming in a golden era of sorts, that percentage jumped by 40 points. What happened?

Modernity is always the go-to answer. Nearly every year I was in primary school, teachers made us debate the proposition "*Modernisation has brought more harm than good.*" In secondary school, they made us write essays on "*How western influence is destroying African society.*" One would think the answer to his quandary is obvious. We have become more modern. But is that the whole story? Was everything rosy and glorious before the white man came to our borders? Who is to say when every account of precolonial times is disputed since our history before western contact was never written down? It exists only in the memories of grey heads that received accounts from other grey heads who, in their own way, passed on versions that favoured their ideological or religious leanings. How do we measure the true value of a lost heritage when its guardians and curators left no tangible records?

Some years back, I found myself in the audience of a spiritual elder who challenged many notions I had received about pre-colonial Africa, including the popular belief that men had all the power and women had none. According to this elder, society in those days viewed the two genders as twin strands of the divine energy that creates and sustains life on this planet, so every level of spiritual and secular authority was thought to have a masculine and feminine form. Typically, the masculine strand of power was exercised as secular–or "administrative"–authority, while the female strand was exercised through spiritual–or "ritual"–authority. In the court traditions of Buganda, Tooro and Bunyoro, kings ascended to the throne with their sisters. More notably, the highest office in the kingdoms was not the king's throne, it was the office of the Queen Mother. Thus, in Bunyoro, the Queen Mother presided over the ritual marking a prince's ascension to becoming a King, but the High Priest conducted the actual public enthronement ceremony. Similarly binary practices marked the rise to authority of clan heads and heads of homesteads.

This elder's version of events resonated with my experience of the women in my family. I had always found it hard to accept the modern narrative that women were door rugs in precolonial Africa. Both my grandmothers were raised in that era yet they were towering personalities. My father's mother, Atwooki, was a fierce woman who had been a warder in the men's section of Masindi Prison. She had the type of voice that shook walls when she spoke. Legend had it that the toughest inmates cowered when she barked at them. I could not, for the life of me, picture her being anyone's doormat. Every time we stayed in the house my father had bought for her, it was clear that she was the boss under that roof. Even my father had to fall in line when she put her foot down on any subject.

My mother's mother, Chaachi, was the opposite of Atwooki in personality. She was genteel and soft-spoken but there was no doubt she was the boss in her household too. My grandfathers both died before I was old enough to form meaningful bonds with them, but I was old enough to see that neither man embodied that tyrannical beast that men of that era were supposed to represent. They were respected as heads of households, but the women in their homesteads were not submissive by any measure. Nowhere in my memory could I find the type of passive woman described in modern literature about their era.

Of course, children see the world differently from adults. There's always the possibility that my younger self missed some nuance. The only way to know for sure what it was like to live in that era was to ask my only surviving grandparent, Chaachi. So I embarked on a 300-

kilometre journey to her home in Ibanda, a district in western Uganda, to record as much of her life story as I could while her memory was intact.

Born in 1917, Chaachi was 102 at the time I interviewed her. She was the oldest living person on either side of my lineage. She had lived through much of the colonial period and all of the post-independence era to date. More importantly, she was raised by an aunt who was already a legend in their region, Nkore, when British colonists and missionaries first arrived. This aunt went on to play a leading role in helping the British to rule and the Christian faith to gain acceptance in the region. As the only living person who had been raised by this remarkable woman, and been her confidant, Chaachi was a walking trove of memories that went back to days before Britain disrupted African life.

Kibubura

High up on his perch, his neck towering above the white feathery clouds floating at his chest, Ruyonza watches life stir as dawn reaches Ibanda and its surroundings. Below this great hill, a whistling milkman pedals a creaking Roadmaster bicycle towards his first morning delivery. A farmer plunges a mud-caked hoe into brown loam as a choir of birds chirps in the trees. Children in brightly coloured uniforms shuffle heavy feet over muddy roads, dragging sleepy bodies to classrooms. An ageing trader pushing slow steps toward his shop stops to greet every person he passes; most people here take haste for rudeness, and the merchant can't afford to lose a single potential customer – especially now, since his youngest child will be starting university next year.

At the main road cutting through the town centre, passengers clamber up to the rusty door of a battered bus that leans ominously to one side. It's the first bus of the day to Kampala, the capital city. In the scramble to claim seats, young men and women dig elbows into each other's sides, forcing elderly travellers to stand aside with bitter frowns at the brazen disregard of the privilege their greying heads deserve. For the young, there is no honour in being left behind. Life in the city has cured them of bondage to inconvenient proprieties.

To Ruyonza, Ibanda town must seem serene. From his lofty position, the smoky trucks trudging up steep inclines to fetch produce or firewood from farms are like ants crawling up a mound. I don't think he sees the pockets of people letting penned chickens and goats out to graze or laying grain on sheets of patched-up sacks to dry in the sun. They would be too small for him; he would see just a green carpet and rolling hills – undisturbed tranquillity. But inside Ibanda, things are not so placid.

Like most towns that find themselves suddenly elevated from trade outposts to commercial hubs, Ibanda is changing quickly. The trading centre that once had just two lanes has expanded into a sprawling labyrinth with eight streets. One now has to be careful when crossing roads; boda bodas shoot out from everywhere at perilous speed, just like their cousins in Kampala. I have been warned not to use certain paths after the sun has dropped from the sky; people get beaten up for phones and money nowadays.

Scenes from a time when Ibanda's pioneers were first setting camp in this valley fill my imagination like a montage against the backdrop of new buildings mushrooming everywhere, their cement talons clawing away at the green blanket. I picture these pioneers huddling together over a fire in the night and then rising before dawn and setting off to collect earth, wood, grass, reeds and food. By noon, they finish making circular bases for their huts, then fortify them with mud and wattle walls bound to frameworks of thin reeds. By evening, they are crowning the huts' conical roofs with grass thatch. These people are refugees fleeing a civil war that has engulfed the region we now call western Uganda. They were led here by a woman whose story has fascinated me since childhood – doubly now that I am an adult, for I have been told constantly that women in her time were nothing more than chattel. Her name is Kibubura.

Kibubura is a legend in Nkore kingdom. She is remembered as the first female Chief in Nkore (though I suspect that there were others in more distant times), a fearless reformer who championed girls' education long before it ever became a social cause, and a devoted convert who helped Christianity become a force in the region's spiritual sphere. But to my grandmother, Chaachi, she was aunt, mentor, mother and father, all in one form – the woman who took her in when her parents were both gone.

Memories of her public life have gradually faded over the years. But I can still remember a time when her name was spoken with reverence everywhere in these parts. Her life may have taken a completely different turn had it not been for a fateful crossing of paths with another historical figure, Omukama Kabalega of Bunyoro.

History remembers Kabalega as a hero who resisted the British invasion for eight years until his gun arm took a bullet during a defiant last stand on the northeastern shores of Lake Kyoga. Even his captors, who greatly loathed him, admired his spirit. But little is said of the havoc his warring wracked on the region. In my grandmother's story, he is remembered as the man who drove her family from their home.

Around 1870, Kabalega won a short but bloody battle of succession for Bunyoro's throne, then turned his sights on restoring Bunyoro's boundaries to their former glory. His first target was Tooro, a province that had seceded and declared itself a kingdom during the reign of his grandfather, Kyebambe Nyamutukura. War was coming to Kibubura's home. Her father was the governor of Mwenge, a centre where princes went to be schooled in the art of ruling before Tooro's secession. Kabalega was keen on bringing it under his heel.

When Kabalega arrived in Mwenge with his troops, one of his first acts was to seek a bride to cement his conquest. It was customary for kings to consolidate alliances with powerful families in the provinces. One would expect Kabalega to pick Kibubura or her elder sister Kishokye for his harem. Instead, he went for their youngest, Ntama (Chaachi's mother).

The version Chaachi received says nothing of how this happened, except that Kabalaga placed a ceremonial crown (orukwanzi) on Ntama's head, and she was promptly taken to his harem. In my mind's eye, I see Kabalega strolling across a grassy plain with a few of his men, inspecting the lands he has just conquered, when his eyes catch sight of a young gazelle coming from the well. She throws her head back daintily as she laughs at something a peer has said, waterpot balanced gracefully on her delicate neck, undisturbed by the rocking of her head. The King is struck. He approaches the party of young women and asks her name and her people. The next day, he turns up at her father's gate to claim her for his own.

Kabalega was not a man easily refused. People who disagreed with him often ended up with gutted entrails or exiled. But for some reason lost to memory, Kibubura's father was willing to risk everything to prevent this match from happening. He ordered Kibubura to rescue Ntama from Kabalega's harem and flee the kingdom. She must have been some character to be trusted with such a challenging mission. A king's harem was a well-guarded place, but Kibubura somehow managed to whisk her sister away that night and flee to the neighbouring kingdom of Nkore.

According to Mzee Kibeherire, Chaachi's last surviving nephew, Kibubura left Mwenge with three sisters (Kishokye, Kazana, and

Ntama) and a large party of men and women fleeing Kabalega's war. He says that Kishokye and Kibubura jointly led the party but Kibubura, though younger than Kishokye, was the more feared and respected. The party arrived in Nkore during the reign of Omugabe Ntare V, who let them settle in a part of his hunting grounds that would later come to be known as Ibanda. Some accounts claim that Ibanda was already settled when Kibubura and her group arrived. The family account holds that it was virgin land.

Whatever account you choose to believe, the remarkable thing about this story is that Ntare V, a ruler renowned for being one of the greatest warrior-kings in Nkore's history, granted Kibubura and Kishokye the right to govern Ibanda. Either there must have been a precedent for women holding secular authority in Nkore, or the sisters and their party held some strategic value for the kingdom. Ntare's successor, Kahaya II, would maintain their position and develop even closer ties with them. He too came to rely on Kibubura as his father had.

From my grandmother's description of Kibubura, I suspect her personality had a hand in Ntare's decision. "*He respected her,*" Chaachi tells me. "*She was one of the few people who stood up to him without fear. When she received instructions she did not agree with, she would go to his court and explain why she would not obey them. He came to trust her as a friend.*"

When Nkore fell under British control and Ibanda became a formal chieftaincy in the colonial administration, Kahaya II insisted on appointing Kibubura as its first chief despite great resistance from his advisors. Many at court wanted her position, but she was an indomitable force. She survived every plot and relinquished her post only when age had withered the fight in her spirit. Ironically, her ceaseless self-determination is reminiscent of Kabalega's. They might have made wonderful allies.

My favourite story about Kibubura involves a clash she had with the British administrators in Nkore. The British did not share the lay folk's love for Kibubura. "They tried to sideline her when they were creating Ibanda County," Chaachi says, "but the king insisted on making her the chief." It was in this intense atmosphere that a racist "sub commissioner" (a euphemism for tax collector) called Harry George Galt comes into the story. He was very unpopular for being harsh to the natives – including Kibubura, who wasn't impressed with British shows of power.

The official story has it that one day when Galt was coming from a tax-collecting mission in Fort Portal, a town on the fringes of the Rwenjura mountain (now Rwenzori), he stopped to rest in Ibanda. He had pushed the porters who carried him on their shoulders long and hard without rest. They were too tired to continue. But Galt was impatient. He ordered them to pick him up and continue down the road after a brief rest. They defied him. In the ensuing scuffle, a resident who came to intervene hammered him with a stone that killed him. To kill a British officer was unheard of. The authorities immediately blamed Kibubura.

My cousin, Aruho, swears by a different story. He claims that Galt had ordered one of his porters to summon Kibubura to his camp for a sexual liaison, but a resident, insulted by his audacity, stoned him to death. Whatever the truth, Kibubura and her superior (the district chief) were arrested and held accountable for Galt's death. During the trial, Kibubura outreasoned them and secured their release, returning to Ibanda a hero for defeating this British plot. Residents didn't get off easy, though. They were punished by being forced to build a monument of stones on the spot where Galt was killed. It still stands to this day. Residents called it Amabare ga Galt – *Galt's stone pillar*.

By all accounts, Kibubura was popular with both the King and the common folk, but none of the stories I'd heard accounted for the source of her power until I interviewed Canon Samuel Bishaka, a long-term friend who was a contemporary of my grandfather Anania. The Canon's guardian was Kibubura's successor after she resigned, so he too grew up hearing stories that offered insights into how Kibubura came to be such a powerful figure.

According to Chaachi's account, Omugabe Ntare respected Kibubura and Kishokye because they were royals. But the Canon noted that Kibubura and Kishokye were revered priestesses in the traditional spiritual system that prevailed before Kibubura converted to Christianity. So great was their prowess that the king relied on them for protection from witchcraft, which was a huge problem at the time. Her reputation as a grand priestess grew so widespread that people began migrating to Ibanda to live under her protection. Ibanda's original name was "*Ibandiro rya Kibubura*," which translates to "Kibubura's shrine." It only became Ibanda because the British had difficulty pronouncing its full name.

I find this account a more plausible explanation for Kibubura's power than her royal blood. In the collective consciousness of the period, prowess in the spiritual arts carried more currency than royal blood. Certain priesthoods exclusively held by women often came with secular authority as well; the provinces of Buruli and Musendamu in ancient Bunyoro, for instance, were traditionally governed by women from such priesthoods.

If true, this account would explain why the British went to great lengths to get Kibubura fired. After the beatings they'd received from influential priestesses like Muhumuza wa Nyabingyi, they were suspicious of anyone who wielded that kind of power.

In her final years as Chief, Kibubura became one of the first Christian converts in Ibanda. Because she was the Chief, missionaries would come to her for permission to operate in the region, and she would ask them all sorts of questions about their faith. Eventually, she grew to like it because it was simpler and less demanding than traditional faiths, so she invited them to set up the first church and school in Ibanda. She poured her indomitable spirit into growing its membership, winning her new friends and allies. For her efforts as a pioneer for girls' education in the region, a dormitory at the first girls' school in the region – Mbarara Girls Boarding School – was named in her honour. Today, a school at the upper end of the town bears her name: Kibubura Girls School.

To think that this woman did all this at a time when such things were supposed to be impossible for women is a powerful reminder to take everything you hear with a pinch of salt. This was a woman who governed a country, made friends with kings, survived British plots to unseat her, and retired with a one square mile estate in her name. If that is not power, what is?

> *"She was always making mats and giving them out as gifts to visitors," Chaachi recalls. "She had important friends in many places and would often send them gifts. Such was the reach of Kibubura's influence that she was friends with leaders of other kingdoms even though she was only a county Chief. She would often send letters and gifts to kings of places as far off as Buganda [roughly 350 kilometres from Ibanda], Karagwe [northwestern Tanzania], and [after Kabalega's capture and deportation] nearby Bunyoro. And those leaders would send her gifts and letters in return."*

Chaachi

My grandmother, Chaachi, is a tiny woman with the spirit of ten lions. Standing at roughly 5'4", she is diminutive in size and small in build. She carries herself with regal grace in everything she does and will never let anyone rush her. Those who mistake her frailness for weakness quickly learn their place. Her tongue is sharp and witty. If ever I had any wit, it comes from jousting with her. She is a font of wisdom.

Even at her great age, Chaachi's memory is sharper than mine. She remembers the names of all the friends she has met and asks after each one. As she speaks, I can see the clear imprint of Kibubura in her. I now understand what Canon Bishaka meant when he said "*Chaachi is Kibubura.*" Listening to her tell it, I see the imprints of that great woman's life in every inch of Chaachi's face and in my sisters and cousins.

For as long as I have known Chaachi, she has always read her Bible thrice a day. She also has always made mats and given them to her visitors. When I arrived to interview her, I found her reading her Bible in bed, absorbing the morning's verses through thick reading glasses a tad too big for her head. Soft hums emanated from her throat. Beside the bed was a small table with a flask, an empty teacup, and a plate with banana peels and breadcrumbs; she had just finished her breakfast. The light was dim. She had to hold her Bible up to a window that opened on a matooke garden where her late husband was laid to rest alongside three of their five sons. She looked up through the glasses without lifting her head, and invited me to take a seat and pour myself some tea. Then she went back to reading.

The room was small – about twelve-by-ten feet. Its light-brown walls had remained unchanged since she moved in some three decades earlier. The house was built for her by her only daughter – my late mother, Kobusingye. The floor had been repaired recently. An air of newness wafted from renovations made by Nankunda, her youngest son's daughter, who had recently refurbished the house with new furniture and electricity, perhaps following a tradition that started with Kibubura.

I was reminded of an incident that is one of my favourite stories of how Chaachi could unleash the ten lions in her. Nankunda, who had passed her exams, was denied a place at Kibubura Girls School. Ostensibly it was full. That would have been nothing irregular; popular schools always have greater demand for slots than supply. But sometimes, "full" can mean "make us an offer if you want a spot." I don't know which definition applied in this case, but the decision was doomed the moment the news reached Chaachi's ears. She was weaving mats — a task she never stopped until she had met her quota for the day, even if she was entertaining guests. But on this day, she promptly dropped everything she was doing, dressed up, sent for her walking stick, trekked the full six kilometres to the school, went straight to the Headmistress' office, and gave a stern lecture on how the school she was running came into being. Chaachi was about 91 at the time. A slot was found.

At the foot of Chaachi's bed lay a bundle of treated grass blades, which she used to weave the mats she was widely known and admired for producing. I spied some blades dyed purple and cream – the colours of the mat she gave me when I joined Makerere University 15 years earlier. I prize that mat, a reminder of the myriad lessons Chaachi passed on to me in conversations over the years. She pointed to an unfinished mat in the corner and told me she had to stop weaving because her sight was failing. "If God allows, I'll complete it," she said. The gentle resolve in her voice reminded me of my mother – whenever she started something, she didn't stop until it was done. I could see now where it came from.

Before we started our conversation, Chaachi led us in a thanksgiving prayer. She gave thanks for being blessed with 12 grandchildren even though she was the only surviving child from her mother's womb. Our greetings and prayers done, we were ready to start.

"My birth name was Nyamwiza," Chaachi said. "It's a name given to girls who come after twins. I never saw my twin sisters. They died before I was born.

I was named Egransi Tophas at my christening. Chaachi is a nickname given to me by an aunt because I loved going to church. My father came from a village in Mpororo called Nshenyi, and my mother was from Mwenge, in Bunyoro. They met here in Ibanda.

I nearly died when I was still a babe suckling at my mother's breast. I had fallen ill with pneumonia. This disease killed many infants in the old days because traditional healers had no reliable cure for it.

One day, my heart stopped beating. My mother, who knew something about traditional healing methods, having been raised by a sister who had been a priestess, tried everything she could to revive me. She placed a fire next to my chest and head and pumped breast milk into my mouth until her breasts were dried. She even sent for cow's milk late in the night. But nothing worked. My body remained motionless. I was declared dead.

The custom back then was never to bury anyone without preparing a meal [a ritual last supper of sorts]. But in this case, it started to rain heavily before they could begin preparing one. Since the cooking was done in small huts separate from the main house, they had to wait.

All the while, my mother, Ntama, kept adding things to my blanket to make me warm. She refused to give up on me. She used her body to make me warmer, even when told to accept what had happened and let me be.

Fortunately, the downpour continued through the night, into the next morning, and all the way to the next evening. My mother kept checking on me. Then she felt my heartbeat and called her sister, who confirmed that I was alive.

Later, my mother took me to live with one of her sisters to wean me off breast milk so that I could become independent. I stayed there until I was old enough to walk. That is when I was taken to live with my father at his place in Kyaruhanga [near Ruyonza]. By this time my mother had left my father and gone to live in Ibanda with her elder sister Kibubura, so my father's first wife, Samali, looked after me.

Samali was a good woman. She had only one daughter with my father, so I became her second. She loved me so dearly that when my father died, she cried, knowing that we were going to be separated. He died at Ruyonza, where he went to graze his cattle. I don't know what killed him. After my father died, my sister and I were each given a cow. The rest of the herd was given to Samali, who returned with them to her people. I reconnected with them recently when I was reunited with some of my father's relatives in Kazo.

What I remember most about my childhood is that I loved going to school. My aunt Kibubura was friends with the missionaries, so she put me in school as soon as I was old enough to go, but my father took me out when I was in Primary Two. I was completely devastated. I cherished going to school more than anything else.

Most parents in those days preferred to educate boys over girls. They would say that a girl wasn't going to become a leader in the clan or government, so what use was education going to be to her? Someone later told me that my father didn't share that view. He saw education as a good thing that could help our people. He had even put one of my elder cousins from my mother's side in school. She was studying nursing in Mulago when I started primary school. But when she got pregnant, my father got angry. It was an abomination for a girl to get pregnant out of wedlock. It brought shame to the entire family. That was his reason for taking me out of school. He feared that I might get pregnant too.

The tradition in those days was that girls were educated by their mothers at home, and boys by their fathers. Women would instruct their daughters in domestic tasks according to their family's line of work. If it was a farming family [Bairu], they were taught how to farm. If they were cattle keepers [Bahima], they were taught how to milk cows, look after calves, and cut grass for fodder. Farmers [Bairu] mainly grew millet; they would grind it on a large stone [orubengo]. Everyone in the household worked together and ate together. Children sat apart from adults. Each group ate from one plate.

Boys lived in the same huts as their fathers. They would receive instruction by working with the men in their respective trades. When a boy was old enough and his father was satisfied with his character, the father would give him a piece of land on which to build his own hut, and a cow to start his own life. And once the boy had accumulated enough property (cows if he was a herdsman; crops if he was a farmer), his father would seek a wife for him and make the initial negotiations with the girl's father.

Girls in those days stayed at home until a man came to marry them. Women did not go out to meet men as they do today. If no one came to ask for your hand, you stayed in your father's compound. The men would be told that "so and so" had a daughter and she had this or that kind of character. Men who were interested enough would approach your parents without speaking to you. If your parents accepted, you would be married. There was no room for rejecting a man your parents had accepted. It sometimes happened among Bairu, but never among Bahima. A Muhima man would disown his daughter if she refused to marry the man he had selected for her. That would dishonour the family.

Men did whatever they could do with their hands in those days. Bairu planted millet, potatoes, cassava, and matooke. Sometimes Bairu would exchange food for milk, but Bahima sustained themselves on milk mostly. They didn't like hard foods. For breakfast, a Muhima would eat food kept from the previous night and wash it down with milk. Bairu ate their breakfast with porridge.

My people were cattle keepers who sold ghee from their cows to get money. We never ate lunch. We only ate breakfast and dinner. Meat was rare. Bahima abhorred the killing of cows, so we only ate meat when a cow had died. The only time a cow could be slaughtered was for a big occasion like a wedding. Bairu sometimes hunted wild animals, but Bahima would not touch them. They only ate cow meat, and they ate it roasted. Only Bairu made sauce out of meat. No one ate pork back then. I don't know when people started eating it; pigs were regarded as disgusting creatures.

I got married to Anania Katanywa in 1945. I was around 28 years, which was very old for the time. Girls in those days usually got married between 12 and 17, depending on what their parents decided. I took long because I was very strong headed. Most men were afraid that they would not be able to handle my spirit.

It was Kibubura who gave me away. That role was normally performed by a man, but my father had died by then, and Kibubura, who had been looking after me, had no husband. That is why Anania had to go to her for my hand: she was the head of our household.

Anania jokingly called her Tatazara [father-in-law] because she had been tough on him. She had sent him away the first time he asked for my hand because he was poor and she didn't think he could give me the life she wanted for me. But when he came back a second time, she took pity on him and set the bride-wealth at one cow. When he brought it, she instructed him to sell it and use the money to pay for our wedding. They became really good friends after we married.

At first, we lived in Kazo, where Anania worked as a head man on road works connecting Kazo to Ibanda. His land was in the middle of the bush, so he was constantly afraid that something could happen to me and that there would be no one to help me. The population was very small back then. Most people preferred to stay together in one compound, but he had some disagreements with his people and preferred to stay alone.

During my first pregnancy, I fell seriously ill and nearly died. That scared him deeply. As soon as I was able to move, he took me back to Ibanda and asked Kibubura to keep me there because his land in Kazo was in the wilderness and he didn't want me to fall sick again. She tried to keep her word, but once I was fully recovered, I insisted on returning to my husband. One day he appeared out of the blue with his mattress, a mat, and his grazing stick. He said his business in Kazo had failed. He had decided to sell his land and move to Ibanda. So Kibubura gave us this land to start a new life. That is how we ended up settling in Ibanda.

Around that time, he fell badly ill and was taken to Bunyoro for treatment. He could not work for a long time after his return. That was very tough on him. He did not like being idle. He was always doing something to keep himself occupied. Later, he went to Tooro and learned how to make chairs. He would sell them to get money for sugar and other things we needed in the home.

After some time, he befriended some medical doctors and learned from them how to dispense drugs. That is when people started calling him "Doctor." He began treating patients on his own. One day, someone complained that he was not a qualified doctor. It caused some controversy, but his patients defended him. I told him to stop giving people injections. I didn't want him getting into trouble. We both had good knowledge of traditional herbs, so I urged him to start dispensing those instead. That's how he started selling herbal medicine. I would help him prepare the herbs, and he would dispense them.

Life was not so good, but it wasn't that bad either. Some parts of married life were hard, like having little money and struggling to make ends meet, but we managed to pull through. We always had something to eat. And we managed to put our children through school.

We both had to do all sorts of jobs to pay for our children's education, but we also had help from friends. We would make sure they completed primary school, and if they didn't perform well enough to earn a bursary [scholarship], our friends would help with the fees for secondary school. Your mother was helped by Canon Bishaka. He paid some of her fees and got her a place at Bweranyangi Girls Secondary School.

In the days of our parents, it was not common for girls to go to school, but I made it a must for every girl in my household to get an education. I would think about how much I liked school but was forcibly removed, so I made sure that no girl under my care would be denied the opportunity to study. The colonial government played an important role in helping people change their attitude towards educating girls. They informed people that boys and girls were of equal value, and the church added its weight to this message too. This helped change people's attitudes towards educating girls.

Anania and I had a good relationship. He was a very caring man, so we never quarrelled. We were very good friends; we listened to each other's concerns. One time when I fell sick from eating common salt, he walked several miles to find high-grade salt, which was being sold only on magyendo – the black market [illegal vendors were the surest way to buy common goods in the 1970s because domestic goods had become scarce during Idi Amin's economic war against Asians]. Anania would go out of his way to get me goods and clothes from the black market. He did not want to see me using inferior products again. He never wanted me to suffer.

Anania never raised a hand to beat me. If either of us had angered the other, we would speak about it openly and settle the matter amicably. I had warned him when we were getting married that I never wanted to be beaten. I was prepared to never marry again should this marriage fail.

I cared for him very deeply. I did not want to die before him. Who would look after him? He appreciated that very much. Before he died, he called me to his bedside and thanked me for taking good care of him. He asked to speak to our youngest son's wife, Christina, as well. She had helped me a lot with his care when she joined the family. He was too ill to do anything by himself. Christina came, and he thanked her too. He breathed his last a few minutes later.

A Question of Character

I am seated in the shade of a large tree on the gentle slope of a well-trimmed hill, eyes fixed again on Ruyonza's crest. Birds coast the easy breeze. Questions are turning in my mind, but the words to give them shape still elude me. I look at the great hill for clues to pursue, but his mute form offers no suggestions. The sound of footfalls jolts me from the reverie. It's my cousin, Derrick Aruho, coming to tell me it's time for our next interview, Canon Samuel Bishaka and his wife, Naome.

It's a short climb from the tree shade to the Bishaka residence, but I reach the top out of breath. Although the hill is a dwarf in Ruyonza's shadow, it makes Kampala's star hills – Namirembe and Lubaga – look like flat plains in comparison. The houses constituting the Bishaka compound are well-spaced and fastidiously kept. The canon and his wife are waiting for us on their porch.

At 110 years, Canon Bishaka is the only person I know who is older than Chaachi. He and his wife have been married for more than 80 years, nearly as long as Makerere University has been open. He knew my grandfather and Chaachi since they were young children. He speaks fondly of them.

"In all my years as a Canon, I never once heard Chaachi or Anania say there was trouble in their home," he says. "Chaachi was a very committed Christian, just like Kibubura. When Kibubura would find children talking in church, she would take up a cane and threaten them. Chaachi would do the same. They were both strict disciplinarians. It isn't surprising that she took after Kibubura in many ways. No one spent as much time with Kibubura as Chaachi did. She got her strength of character from her aunt."

His wife tells us many stories about growing up with Kibubura as a childhood hero. Everyone talked about her when I was young," she says. "I slept in a hall named after her when I was at Mbarara Girls Boarding School. But even when I went on to Gayaza High School [roughly 319 kilometres away from Ibanda], she was the talk of the school there as well. She was known all over the country."

I spend most of the interview trying to get more information and new insights into the lives of the women of days past, but the canon and his wife keep steering the conversation toward character and faith and away from historical events. Only later will it dawn on me that my journey was never about history at all. It had always been about character.

Until now, Kibubura had only been a name in family tales and Chaachi was a doting grandmother. Now I see them in a different light. I see matriarchs who steered their families through difficult times. They endured migration from homes where they had some standing, made names for themselves in their new homes and survived droughts, severe losses of cattle, land-grabbing by the regional leaders, deaths, and colonial subjugation.

The image strikes a chord. Chaachi may not have sent mats to kings in distant lands as her aunt did, but she won friends all across the country; she became a celebrity in her own right — a wise person who would hold court every moment of the day with dignity. Her large spirit and quiet charisma have always made people warm to her easily. Once, when she came to live with my family after my mother had fallen terminally ill, she quickly became the most popular member of our household. A steady stream of people – congregants from the local Anglican church, neighbours in our community, people who had grown up in Ibanda and emigrated to Kampala – came to see her. It's as if we were hosting a mayor.

On the many occasions when I have visited her in Ibanda, I have seen all kinds of people — from clergy leaders, local politicians and public servants to relatives and family friends living in places distant from Ibanda — come to pay their respects or seek advice. To this day, my siblings and I all have friends who will break their itinerary when travelling in the region to stop by her home and pay respects. People are drawn to her.

In Chaachi's world, it was presumed that a person of sound character would have the sense to resolve disputes arising from personal misunderstandings. Chaachi's father didn't remove her from school to assert males' prerogative over females; he did it to protect her character and the family's name. A marriage's collapse was interpreted as a family's failure to equip their sons or daughters with strong character. Her aunt Kibubura wasn't trusted by kings and cherished by commoners because she had some "blue blood" in her veins; she was trusted because of her strength and moral rectitude. For both women, personal power was a function of their personalities. It gives me some pride that society recognised their merits and enabled them to succeed, each in her own way.

Somehow, we are failing to meet that test today. The world we have built for ourselves may be more advanced in technology and personal comfort, but we are creating a dangerous environment for relational, mental and physical health. We lack balance. When the characters in the Kadongo Kamu complain about each other, they aren't really railing against modernity. They're bemoaning the loss of character. Institutions and relationships are not struggling because new technology has changed our approach to life; they are struggling because the aspects of character that custom was meant to uphold are fading away. You can see the contrast in the different behaviour of my generation and that of my grandparents.

This story began with a question — I wanted to find out why the elder women in my family did not conform to the stereotype of "the suppressed African woman" of their era. But it ends with more than that. I have learned many lessons.

My grandfather, Anania, died when I was twelve. I never knew much about him. He was a quiet and aloof figure who spoke only when spoken to. Now I see much more. I picture him – thin, very dark and tall, bent over a piece of wood outside his house, patiently shaping it into a table or chair. When he is through, he walks around the entire town looking for someone to buy it. If he fails, he will go to the next town and the next and so on until he gets money to buy a few grams of salt. No doubt it's a grossly unequal exchange, but he finally gets home with a smile, knowing that his wife will not have to eat salt mined from a well nearby and then fall sick again. His feet burn from sustained friction with tire sandals. His legs ache from walking all day. He probably has eaten very little. But he has done his job. He is happy.

Are we?

A Bride's Farewell Song

By Edna Namara

THE KIGA PEOPLE OCCUPY five districts in southwestern Uganda – a land whose steep mountains and cold temperatures have earned Uganda the nickname "The Switzerland of Africa." You might think the austere terrain would keep people apart, but to me, the inhabitants of this beautiful land are one family – a tribe. They live in scattered towns and sparsely populated districts but remain united by a common heritage and culture. I think of my ancestral home, now called Rukiga District, as a son of the town of Kabale, a sibling of Rubanda and grandchild of Kigezi, who also produced Kanungu, Rukungiri, Ntungamo and Kisoro — many names, but a single family.

The Bakiga (the "ba" pluralises the root name) are industrious, as the many small gardens thriving in hand-built terraces skirting the hills attest. They have a dry sense of humour – so dry it sometimes gets them in trouble. In everyday chatter, for instance, a Mukiga (the "mu" is singular) might swear, "Nshwere maawe," which literally means, "I will marry my mother." Such remarks lead some outsiders to believe the Bakiga are vulgar. But the statement is not really an endorsement of immoral behaviour; it is a wry way of saying that something is so abhorrent as to be unthinkable.

More difficult to shake is the kiga reputation for being strict disciplinarians. The time was that daughters who got pregnant out of wedlock were led to a cliff overlooking a high waterfall and thrown to their deaths – a brutal lesson for other girls who might be tempted to stray from society's strict moral code. The practice stopped in response to a wide outcry, but the memory still haunts some Bakiga girls.

A more endearing aspect of Bakiga character is their honesty. Many people today believe that a tinge of lies is okay in dating relationships. But Bakiga believe lies make lovers wear cosmetic lives. So they choose to be completely open and straight-forward. In the not-so-distant past, a Mukiga man might just walk up to a woman and say, "Ndeenda ku kushwera – I want to marry you." No dilly dallying. The matter would be settled there and then. The ladies, being part of the same society, often would agree; they knew that was the way things were meant to be.

Such forthrightness can be as misleading as Bakiga humour. It masks one of the most striking traits of these people: They are a romantic lot. You may not believe this at first, but by the end of my story, you will get my point.

Paradoxically, even though Bakiga courtships in days past used to be short, their marriages lasted till death did them part. That's the opposite of what happens today. These days, people can take as long as ten years looking for Mr. or Miss Right. They believe this enables them to make the best choices. Yet their marriages often last less time than their years of dating. To Bakiga elders, this is absurd. In their day, a typical couple would have at least four stout children in the time it takes modern couples to decide whether to tie the knot, and the Kiga parents would have bonded to each other while making these children ready for the future.

Many modern women say that the old way of marriage was devoid of love – that it enslaved, overworked, and used women, treating them as mere vessels to transport men to their pleasure apex. I find this point of view too harsh. Yes, life was hard in the old days. Women bore many children; it was not unusual to see a woman carrying one child on her back, a second on her chest, and a third in her belly, with older children trotting ahead of her. Names like Korugyendo, ("Born on a Journey"), Kamuhanda ("Born by the Path") and Kemisiri ("Born in the Garden") demonstrate that women used to work right up to the time they went into labour and gave birth without hospitals or professional medical help, relying on traditional remedies and local birth attendants to serve as midwives. Many old women today are shocked at contemporary stay-home housewives who seek the services of maids for fear of being overworked.

Elders shouldn't judge their daughters too harshly, though. Today, corporate women each day must run through full work programmes, respond to dozens of emails, write reports and prepare for the following day, take children to and from school, return home to cook for the family, prepare clothes for the children to wear the next day, lead the children through their homework, see to younger kids, iron clothes for their husbands, and manage any number of unforeseen issues. It's not exactly an easy life.

Just as women today enjoy some benefits in return for their hard work, Bakiga women reaped rewards to offset their many challenges. For one thing, their marital families treated them as daughters. A new bride customarily had a three-month period of staying indoors – "pampering" (kwaraama) – after entering her new home. She would be kept away from dust, rain and extreme sunshine so her skin could become lighter, tender and smooth. This was her time to care for herself and blend in with the new family. This period was akin to what today is called the honeymoon, but there is a big difference. Modern honeymoons do not orient brides to their husbands' people;

instead, couples spend the first days of their marriages in faraway places irrelevant to the future they will face as couples. This alienates brides from their husbands' people and interferes with the process of blending into their new families. Maybe this also contributes to hardships widows face today, such as having their land grabbed by in-laws when their husbands die.

In days past, families would give new brides names of endearment during the kwaraama period, like Kyatukwire (Brown), Kyashemera (Perfect), Kyakwera (The Light-Skinned One), Bagambagye (Soft-Spoken), Bayorooba (Agile), or Kiringaaniire (Proportional). These names expressed genuine family affection. When this period of introduction was over, young brides usually started off as apprentices to their mothers-in-law and sisters-in-law, further helping them find their bearing in their new families.

Today, one of the most criticised Bakiga practices is widow "inheritance." To a modern person, the notion that a man would inherit his deceased brother's wife is demeaning – a concept tantamount to treating women as property. To Bakiga, it was simply a matter of taking responsibility to care for a brother's widow and her children. By tending to her sexual desires, the man prevented promiscuity and undercover adultery. It also enabled a widow to continue fending for her children without disrupting their lives. Granted, such arrangements sometimes were devoid of love, but it was hoped that love would grow with time as the new partners met their responsibilities. It generally worked. Such marriages usually endured.

Now that there is no more widow inheritance, many widows stay unmarried for fear of rude and heart-breaking comments from relatives and society – comments like "Look, she is the one who killed her husband," "She had already teamed up with [a new husband]," "Man grabber," or "Gold digger." Widowers do not suffer such abuse. Society allows men to get new wives when they lose the first ones –

even in cases when a first wife suffers a long, terminal illness. Maybe today's couples should take a leaf from some earlier concepts that worked well.

When I was growing up, I used to hear old women singing a type of song they learned years earlier as younger women. Girls used to sing it on the day they entered married life. They called it "The Bride's Farewell Song" (Okugabuka). I have always been haunted by its mournful tone. Why would a woman express such sorrow on her wedding day? I recently travelled to the village of Noozi, about two miles northeast of Rukiga District Headquarters, to ask an aging woman, Sokodina, to sing it for me and reflect on what it meant to her. She is an aunt to my husband. She has been my good friend for years – even before I married into her lineage.

Sokodina's home sits near a brook that snakes its way through a narrow valley between two steep, volcanic hills. Homes with white roofs dot the hillsides, their gardens green with matooke and sorghum growing on terraces that protect the soil from run-off water. It is not easy to make the steep climb to reach her. After driving with friends up a winding road that parallels the stream, a few friends and I eventually had to leave the vehicle and let our feet take us the rest of the way. Had I been clad in a tight skirt, I might have had to remove it to gain enough leg room to jump over brooks on the way up. The stream frequently bursts its banks. When it does, outsiders have to give the raging waters three or four days to subside before they can reach homes higher up the hill.

Sokodina's home is on an incline, securely beyond the reach of the temperamental water. On the day we visited, sorghum plants lay low on their sides in gardens, forming a green carpet. Women were helping the plants back to their feet lest the entire bloom be lost to the hailstorm that battered them the previous day. We climbed through two garden terraces to reach her home. Sokodina, 78 years old, initially smiled at us, presuming we were stray passers-by, but she chuckled when she realised we were her visitors. Beaming, she opened her sitting-room door to usher us in.

Her home was clean and neatly kept. Neither the folds on her forehead nor her toothless front gums dimmed her smile. Her cheeks revealed a beauty emphasised by hollows akin to dimples. She was excited, a mixture of bliss and awe. She was wearing a two-piece outfit: A sky-blue dress with patterns of black lines running randomly downwards and a matching exterior piece that complemented the dress. The dress stopped below the knees, revealing a kikoyi, a cloth wrap tied from her waist but only visible below the edge of the dress. This is an elegant dress style among the Bakiga.

"Mwebare kwija," she welcomed us. "I hope there is no problem." Soon after, her nephew, Kacanga Vian, who is 50 years old, and her friend Prisca, who is 72, came to greet us. They took seats and became part of us. Later we learned the three of them were planning to go to a meeting at church.

We assured her there was no problem and that we would be swift. "We only came to speak with you about the changes that seem to be happening in the marriage institution dating back to what your memory can recall."

"Of what interest would the old way of life be for you modern women?" she said, clapping her hands in delight.

"We believe the old ways had good attributes that are no longer in practice. Maybe they could help people today."

She shook her head. "Oh no! What help? Everything has taken a complete U-turn." As she spoke, words struggled to come out because of her missing teeth. Her pink tongue roamed the inside of her mouth. "I believe there were strong values that held marriages together, but they might be considered irrelevant by the current generations," she continued.

"Maybe they are still relevant," I replied. "Marriages of your days were crowned with old age, grey hair and charismatic generations founded on a strong legacy."

"Surprisingly, our marriage planning used to take a short time," she noted. "I remember my courtship took a short time. When my husband declared his intentions to me, I was so scared. I did not know anything that goes on between a man and a woman because in those days, chastity was a virtue to kill for."

"A virtue to kill for?" I asked.

"Yes! There was no carnal knowledge between a man and woman before marriage. When my husband proposed to me, I realised he was serious, I told him to come meet my parents. He knew the implications. He went to Buganda, in Kampala, to work so he could get money to pay bride price to my parents. During our days, bride price was a token of appreciation that every groom-to-be would pay to the girl's parents before taking away their daughter. After four months of working in Buganda, my suitor returned and married me."

"How did he propose to you?"

"Hmmm. He met me coming from the well once and offered to carry the pot for me, but I refused. Then he said, 'Tindazaana, ndeenda ngu obe omukazi wangye.' He wanted me for a wife."

"Why didn't you allow him to carry the pot?"

"It would have been interpreted as loose and bold behaviour by me. I did not want to expose my family to ridicule, and I did not want my chastity to be questioned."

"Had you known him enough to marry him?"

"I had not known him at all, but I knew the home where he came from. I trusted that he would be a good husband. Both of us knew it was up to us to make it work. And it did work out."

"So what do you think is different these days, looking back to the times of your courtship?

"Many things. During those days, society did not encourage pre-marital sex. When my husband proposed, he was almost sure he was going to take a virgin. That was a good practice and even protected girls from many sex-related problems, such as diseases and early pregnancy.

"On the marriage night, a plain white cloth would be spread strategically on the consummation bed, and if there was a red stain indicating the breaking of virginity, the husband would take a goat to the girl's family as a gift for keeping his bride chaste. Of course, this was not done in secrecy. If the girl's family did not receive a goat, they knew their daughter was not a virgin. I have heard that some girls do not bleed even when they are virgins. In our days, that was never considered. If that is true, some girls suffered silently. To protect our image and save our clan members from ridicule, we kept ourselves pure.

"And in our days, money was not worshipped the way it is today. When my husband returned, he had only money to buy one cow and three goats for my bride price. That was all his savings. Even though it was minimal, he proved when he paid it to me that he could solve many other challenges in our marriage. So he won my confidence and support. These days some couples do not make a strong commitment because they believe happiness comes from money."

"What do you think about the issue of bride price today in comparison to those days?" I asked. "Critics of marriage traditions frequently object to the notion that a man or his family have to pay the bride's family for the right to marry her."

Surprisingly, Sokodina suggested the problem isn't tradition but how it has been corrupted. "These days, a bride is up for sale. The highest bidder takes the bride. This makes the marriage take on a commercial label. When my husband told me he had gone to look for money to earn for his wife, our marriage began then. I shut emotions for any other, and I am sure he felt the same. Much as our courtship was short-lived, we grew deeper in love [because we were] detached from materialism.

"The fact that our marriages took place between people who were alike and whose villages were close to each other meant there was respect and communal support. These days, people leave their homes, and we hear they have gone to Kabale town, Kampala, and even overseas. A girl can bring in a man from overseas. The homes of his and her parents are far apart. They never commune. The cultures are entirely foreign to each other.

"I hear that for some muzungus, marriage is a contract," she adds, scoffing at the idea that something as sacred as marriage could be reduced to a piece of paper and a legalistic arrangement. "So, why would anyone [today] be blamed for terminating a marriage after a few years?"

Vian interjected that couples in the old days trusted in the wisdom of elders. Marital misunderstandings were brought to the elders, who would preside over cases and counsel both parties.

"But there were other support systems," Sokodina said. "In the days leading to marriage, elderly women would take the girl through lessons and explain that marriage was not a bed of roses. Living tight in a love bond is very difficult. It can never be smooth sailing. Under all circumstances, there must be a listener and a talker. You cannot both listen and talk at the same time, as that would bring incoherence. A battle where both parties seek to win is a battle forever.

"If my husband came home drunk, he would chase me out. I remember once he said he had heard a voice of a man in the kitchen, and he demanded that I produce the man there and then. He slapped me, and I felt my face go numb. It was as if a streak of lightning had passed through my face. I spent days feeling the numbness. It so happened that the man was our son, who had been chatting with me by the fireside."

"How did you handle the situation?" I asked. "Did you take him to the elders' meeting?"

"Oh no. We would only report cases that were too much for us. Four days later, after sensing the heavy air at home, he came to the garden and dug with [me and our children] all day. As he dug, he was keen to be part of our conversation. I felt a connection binding me to him, a release of the rage that was seated in my heart. In a marriage, there are times when one must act stupid. We never had formal training in cognitive skills, but we made rudimentary judgments to solve some of our problems. Occasionally acting as a fool to trample on the wisdom that will chop your family life is a brave action. Bakiga women went into marriage ready to stay."

She then told me the story of her grandmother.

When I was a little girl, I used to hear my grandmother humming a song. It was so common on her lips that eventually I too learnt it. The song had a powerful, pensive message. I confronted her and asked why she loved that song, which did not bear a positive message. She laughed, sat me down with her and started singing all over again. Then she explained the context in which it was sung.

The song was sung the night she left her home to get married. She had earlier been in a garden with her mother and younger siblings when her brother came and urged her to stop digging and respond to an urgent summons from her father. Her father was asthmatic, so she ran home with the approval of everyone in the garden. Her mother had dug up some roots that might quell the seizure.

She ran fast, leaving behind her brother, who was only briskly walking. The garden crew stayed behind. They were terror-stricken, worried that the head of the family might be at the verge of death.

At home, the man presumed to be dying was in the company of three others. She took a step back, but she decided to ask the father why he had sent for her.

Her father ignored her question and ordered her to wash her legs.

'Let Leonarida give you instructions,' her father ordered. Leonarida was her mother's friend. She led grandmother to a reed enclosure that acted as their bathroom. She gave the girl a little bowl full of ash.

When my grandmother asked what the ash was for, Leonarida told her in a hushed voice, 'To pluck out that pubic hair. Go on,' she urged her.

My grandmother did as she was told. Soon, she was clean-shaven, with open pores in each place where the hair had been plucked.

'That place is going to be the centre of relevance from now on,' Leonarida advised her. 'One of those men seated out there will always want to touch and use it. He will be disturbed if you ever allow [that hair] to grow wild. You hear?'

My grandmother could only manage a nod.

Leonarida continued with her instructions. 'Remember, he is not your brother. He is likely not to tolerate your shortcomings – bear that in mind. So be very careful, do not disrespect him or his people. Do whatever he tells you, even at short notice. Do not answer or question him. Do not be surprised if he slaps you. It does not mean he hates you. It could simply be a point of correction. It could even be just a habit. This should not unnerve you at all. Never give back in words or action. Remember, you are leaving your home here and going to his home. One more thing: Inform him when you see blood. Now you go and get your second dress from the house.'

Grandmother was confused. She was disturbed by the rapid shift of events. She was meant to join the rest back in the garden. She was meant to provide a curative portion to her father. Now, all this was irrelevant.

The men in the company of her father were marriage suitors. She had greeted them. One had made a good grip on her hand. He had scratched hard in the middle of her palm, which made my grandmother think he was not of sound mind. But these were short-lived signs. By night, that man was her husband. She was married at the tender age of 14 and found herself in a new place among people she didn't know. She died 65 years later at the age of 79 years. Her husband had died three years earlier at age 93. Both died still bound in that matrimonial union that had been established in just three hurried hours. The marriage had given them six sons and four daughters with two lost pregnancies. Talk of acceptance of the task in your hand. Marriage is total acceptance of your partner. She lost the will to live when her husband died. One day she said she was seeking the good company of her husband, and then she closed her eyes and died.

I took her back to her wedding day – and to the song.

Although Grandmother protested the marriage, her father and husband-to-be had already arranged for many men to carry her on a stretcher hoisted on their shoulders. That was the culture then. On her way to her unfamiliar destination, she sang the song commonly sung by brides of those days. It was a sad song.

'Ba Kanyanya, hmm	*My dear brothers*
Mugumeho, uuhm	*Good-bye*
Musigaregye uuhm	*Stay well*
Nyowe nagyenda uuhm	*I am out of here now*

I pictured her seated in the stretcher as the men carried her up and down a winding mountain path.

I am leaving a strange home, uuhm
I am not sure to cope, uuhm
The rude remarks, uuhm
Displeasing remarks, uuhm,
Weird like stale pots, uuhm uuhm.

Oh, my well-groomed brother, uuhm,
Decent and clean brother, uuhm
I have gone, uuhm.
But I won't manage that home, uuhm
Goodbye, my brothers, uuhm
Have lovely days, uuhm
Have lovely nights, uuhm,
Please bear with me, uuhm
when things go sour, uuhm
I will return home, uuhm.

I am very sceptical
Of a good life in the yonder home, uuhm
I am not sure how to live in another home, uuhm.
I am scared of their words, uuhm
I am scared of their attitude, uuhhm.
I am scared of how I will be received, uuhm.
What can I do right, uuhm
In the home of a woman not my mother? uuhm
Where the man is not my father, uuhm.

Dear brothers, I am leaving home now, uuhm.
Farewell to you all, uuhm
But I will return if things turn out unbearable,
uuhm.

The bride would continue singing until she reached her new home. As she sang, the people from her new home would respond by welcoming her.

We are glad to receive you, Kyakweera.
You are very welcome.
Please join us in our home, Kyakweera.

The men would be wearing ceremonial garlands on their heads, gyrating in the courtyard as they unanimously welcomed the bride. The sisters-in-law would ululate as the bride repeated her dirge.

Aaaayyyyiiii, aaaayyyyiiii. Here she comes, here she
is!"
We are glad to receive you,
Our Kyakweera,
Our Kyatukwiire...
Welcome to our home
Aaaaayyyyiiii, aaaayyyyiiii

Back and forth, the bride would sing her refrain.

I feel as if I am going to be mauled uuuuuhuuumm,
I feel so sad, uuuuhhuuumm,
Leaving my home, uuuuhhhmmm
I feel weak, as if I am going to be speared.
Uuuuuhuuumm.'

The singing continued as they reached what would be the bride's house, where the groom would be waiting. When they arrived, the mood changed. The groom raised his voice above the rest and chanted as his people kept ululating.

Come in, come in my love,
Come into this home.
We have waited too long for you.
Welcome – the door to my home.
Welcome – the door to my heart.

Here comes my mesmerizing bride,
Here comes the most beautiful woman.
Please come,
You are welcome to this home.
I know you will make me a strong home.
Has anyone ever seen a bride so beautiful?

Other men jumped around excitedly, singing,
She has come,
She has come.
Our bride, she is amidst us.
She who will build this family is here.
Welcome homemaker!

Ululations would continue and end with a celebration of local brew and mountains of food.

And that, Sokodina concluded, is how new brides would be led to their new homes. She glowed with delight – at both the memory and the fact she had been able to share it.

Before we left, she sang the dirge one more time. Once again, I was transported to that day years back. I imagined the young girl singing as the men carried her, shoulder high, all the way from her parents' home to her marital one, her lyrics perhaps giving those carrying her the energy to keep moving until they delivered her to her new home, where everybody danced and sang for her.

Then my mind turned to images of a modern wedding where the bride and groom are ushered into a limousine to sit alone, listening to contemporary music stars singing love songs as they drive away from the home where they will build their lives together.

A lot has changed, indeed.

The Once – and Future? – Clans of Buganda

By Joachim Buwembo

IN 2021, 65-YEAR-OLD Ronald Muwenda Mutebi II, the reigning king of Buganda, precariously climbed a ladder to the top of a 65-foot pole, where he placed the final three of 52 concentric rings that would hold the thatched roof of the reconstructed Kasubi Royal Tombs, the burial ground of the kings of Buganda. The magnificent structure, designated by UNESCO as a World Heritage site and popularised by the BBC as one of Africa's top architectural marvels, is made from natural materials that reflect the close connection between Buganda's people and nature. But its most striking features, the 52 rings, reflect their close attachment to each other: Each ring represents one of the 52 clans that have been a bulwark of Buganda society for centuries.

The last century and a quarter have been a time of great upheaval for Buganda, a former kingdom that represents about one-quarter of the land area and population of today's Uganda. In 1894, the British colonialists usurped its independence and folded it into a "protectorate" that included four kingdoms and more than 50 indigenous communities. During the ensuing 68 years of colonial rule, bureaucrats from the kingdom, acting at the behest of the British rulers, entrenched their civil service system throughout the colony in a way that many found to be arrogant. In 1966, four years after Uganda gained independence, the new government banished Buganda's King, known as the Kabaka. The kingdom was restored in 1993 as a "cultural institution" with no political power, but Baganda (people of Buganda) continue to chafe under continued tensions with the government of Uganda and with non-Baganda, who resent their outsized economic, cultural and linguistic influence.

Clans have largely escaped controversy over the festering "Buganda Question." Collections of thousands of extended families, clans were the building blocks of most African nations, and have proven to be among Uganda's most resilient institutions. They are a major reason Baganda remain passionately loyal to their kingdom to this day, almost 130 years after it was stripped of its governing role. At football matches in Kampala's Namboole, Wankulukuku and Kitende stadiums, for instance, Buganda's anthem invariably evokes more enthusiasm than Uganda's national anthem. Ugandan government officials say such "sectarian" sentiments undermine national unity, but before we discard the clans along with everything else that is old, Africans living in modern systems that were unenthusiastically imported from Europe and the North would be wise to consider the long history of the clan system and what it can teach us about social cohesion, resilience and how governments maintain the loyalty of their people.

The traditions of Buganda go back more than 1,200 years. In the last six centuries, the number of clans in Buganda has increased from a mere handful to today's 52. Each clan, identified with either a plant or animal totem, is believed to be descended from one family, so all clan members have long considered themselves brothers and sisters. In this patrilineal society, children take the clans of their fathers, and the clan leader is seen as the father of all. In days gone by, these "fathers" also represented clan members in the Kabaka's court and the kingdom's legislature, called the Lukiiko.

This system linked each person in Buganda to nature (through his clan's totem), to other clan members (names identified people's clan affiliation), and to other clans (through the "fathers" who served at the highest levels of government). The Kabaka sat atop this structure as the custodian of culture and all customs. Significantly, his other title was – and remains – Ssabataka, which means head of the clan leaders.

Clan customs are slow to change, but the clan system proved adept at absorbing new people. As the kingdom grew over centuries by conquest and assimilation, large clans in conquered territories were admitted into the Buganda system intact, and members of weaker groups were absorbed into existing Baganda clans. This enabled people to maintain a sense of identity rooted in history while enjoying full status – including a political voice – in Buganda.

The clan system was refined further about 600 years ago when a charismatic leader known as Kintu became Kabaka. A myth popular with children holds that he descended from heaven with his bride, Nambi. But historians believe he was a rebel prince who fought and killed a tyrannical king named Bemba, who was his brother. At the time, the kingdom was called Muwawa. The clan leaders ratified Kintu's accession to the throne, and the kingdom came to be called Buganda, which means "brotherhood" or "bundle."

The clan leaders went on to devise an ingenious system to guarantee that power would be shared: They selected Nambi, a woman from the Ngeye (colobus monkey) clan, to be Kintu's wife, and stipulated that henceforth the crown prince, unlike all other Baganda, would take his mother's clan. Nobody, not even the king, can marry his own sister (clanmate) since that would amount to committing incest, so the crown prince would have to marry a commoner from a different clan. This meant his son, the next crown prince, would belong to a different clan than the king, thus guaranteeing that no clan would monopolise the throne.

The custom continues to this day. In 2011, when a new crown prince was born, the royal family announced only that the boy's mother was from the Nsenene (grasshopper) clan without disclosing her identity. The next king's clan was all Baganda needed to know. People rejoiced at the news. Although the new prince's mother clearly was not the Kabaka's officially wedded wife, even Buganda's Catholic and Anglican bishops showed unrestrained excitement. (All Baganda, men and women, refer to the Kabaka as "Baffe," meaning "our husband." Until the 20th Century, Kabakas refused to join any foreign religion for fear that doing so would divide their subjects. Today, most Baganda are emotionally more attached to their culture than to "modern" religions.)

As Buganda grew economically and geopolitically in the 19th century, masaza – local governmental units akin to counties – increasingly took on administrative functions like tax collection and infrastructure development. Eventually, chiefs of the masaza replaced clan heads in the Lukiiko. This power shift was underscored in 2022 when, after opening the new legislative session, the Kabaka gave a shiny limousine to each of the 18 county chiefs.

Despite these political changes, the clans' role in preserving culture continues to be strong. This was especially evident during the 27 years when the kingdom was banished and the Kabaka lived in exile. Without any overt campaign, Baganda continued to observe clan rules, the most basic of which involve the naming of children and the treatment of clan members as brothers and sisters. In almost every home in Buganda during those 27 years, there used to hang a notice, often handwritten, proclaiming that every child and grandchild therein belonged to the named clan. The "induction" of children into their clan continues quietly and fervently in Baganda homesteads to this day.

Although the clans have lost their political power, the importance of culture – their province – should not be underestimated. I personally experienced its strength four decades ago when I relocated from my hometown, Entebbe, to Kampala to begin my university education. The two places were only twenty miles apart (they have since merged into one urban expanse thanks to widespread, unguided construction), but they maintained different cultures. Entebbe, a civil service community, was more cosmopolitan, with residents coming from different ethnic communities; most communicated in English. Kampala, on the other hand, was the centre of the Buganda kingdom, and most people there spoke Luganda. When I reached Kampala, I was surprised to find that strangers would react as soon as they heard my name. Someone might say, "You are my kojja (maternal uncle)," for instance, while another would greet me by saying, "You are my brother (paternal cousin)." The Kabaka had been overthrown, and a republican Constitution banning kingdoms like Buganda had been adopted a decade and a half earlier, yet there I was being identified not just by the community I came from but more deeply by my clan.

Baganda have not held national leadership for more than a year since the country gained its independence in 1962, but they believe in their clans even more now than they did 40 years ago. I know because I talk to them, from the lowest to the highest in their community, and they talk to me.

The clan system traditionally played an important role in protecting the environment. Lwera, a large expanse of wetland west of Kampala, is one monument to their influence. From a distance, the wetland looks like a large green carpet extending for miles. Its water is more visible up close, especially during the rainy seasons, but in dry as well as wet seasons, it and other swamps like it hold far more water than the region's lakes – including Africa's largest lake, known for more than a thousand years as Nalubaale but named Victoria by the European explorers and colonial agents. Lake Victoria is a wide basin, but its deepest point is only 80 metres, and its average depth is a mere 60 metres. In ecological terms, that isn't much water. Uganda's water cycle – and hence, its environment – is generally supported by its wetlands more than the famous lake.

Lwera's wetlands are home to the lungfish, or Mamba, which is the totem of the kingdom's largest clan. The biggest taboo a Muganda can commit would be to eat a clan's totem, so members of the Mamba clan – about every sixth Muganda – do not harvest lungfish. Nor do Baganda of other clans, most of whom are related to someone from the Mamba clan through marriage or through maternal relations; for them, eating or cooking the fish for anybody else would contaminate the utensils in their homes.

Because of this reverence for the Mamba, the wetlands in Buganda remained pristine for centuries. Even in later years, when papyrus reeds from the wetlands became popular for making carpets, the environmental impact was limited because only Nubian women, who were originally South Sudanese, used the reeds (the Baganda themselves used dry banana fibre for carpeting).

The protection of the lungfish is not an isolated incident. Environmental protection based on culture was common in the Buganda of old. Almost every clan traditionally had a large chunk of territory where its totem, generally a plant or an animal, was preserved. These large sites, usually hills with forests, were holy ground; nobody – not clan members or anybody else – messed with them. Indeed, forests and wetlands meant so much to the Baganda that when the British effectively took over Uganda, the occupation contract they negotiated took particular care to preserve forests and wetlands. The specific forests and wetlands set aside were identified as Buganda's territory in the agreement stipulating how the entire kingdom would be carved up. It was understood that future adjustments in allocations would only involve land designated for individuals and institutions, not the protected places.

Today, reverence for the lungfish has waned, and economic buccaneers frequently violate modern state environmental protection laws. Mining for sand in the fragile ecosystem, for instance, has made a nightmare of the maintenance of the Kampala – Masaka highway, which leads to Rwanda and Tanzania. The road keeps sinking, and engineers of the Uganda National Roads Authority have been frustrated in efforts to stabilise it; the highway has a way of collapsing under the weight of traffic carrying Kampala residents to visit their native villages and families during festive seasons.

Some may dismiss the clans' role in environmental protection as happenstance – a result not of science but of mystical cultural values concerning totems. The Baganda did not write down their knowledge, instead passing it on by word of mouth and through legends, so the science of the clan system was not documented, and its logic can only be judged by its results. But while the underlying logic may be uncertain, the fact remains that deeply held values – like reverence for the natural world and a sense of kinship with others – proved for many years to be more powerful than modern-day government regulation.

(By the same token, we can't say whether the logic of the prohibition on same-clan marriages resulted from an appreciation of the advantages of genetic diversity, but the effects – political stability and social cohesion – endure; maybe "social scientists" someday will be able to explain that remarkable nexus too).

Sadly, the clan-based protection of nature is largely a thing of the past. The natural areas that were preserved at the time of the colonial takeover generally aren't protected anymore – a symptom in part of clans' declining influence. The colonial-era agreement that led to the protection of environmentally important areas has become obsolete, and wetlands and forests have become fair game for all manner of land grabbers. Environmental destruction, much of it arising far beyond Uganda's borders, is happening on a scale Buganda's ancestors could not have imagined. Remarkably, Uganda, known for its rich forests and green hills, could become water stressed in the coming two decades or sooner.

Another example of modern ignorance of the importance of culture came in 2022 when the government of Uganda allocated a square mile of land to Akon, an African American musician and entrepreneur, to build a city based on a cryptocurrency he created and named for himself. If that project comes to fruition, the futuristic city will arise on forest land where clans performed key rituals for centuries.

Today, there is little evidence of protection for the places critical to the water cycle that supposedly "primitive" cultures consciously preserved for centuries before western-inspired "civilisation" was forcefully introduced. The uneducated forefathers who successfully preserved nature must be turning in their graves to see Ugandans now being taught about environmental protection by outsiders who have been busy polluting and ruining the environment in Europe and America since the 1800s, when the Ugandans knew better.

The clan system may have some life in it yet, though. It proved its mettle during the 27-year banishment period. Because the clans are genetically and spiritually based, no known force, except maybe time, can destroy them. Consider this: In the printing industry hub based on Nasser and Nkrumah Roads in Kampala, printers can forge anything from IDs to currency, foreign passports, visas, land titles, and even High Court rulings with all the required seals. But they will not, for any price, forge a simple Buganda Kingdom Certificate printed on cheap manilla board. The certificates, which are embroidered with all the 52 clans' insignia, are used as a modest fundraising tool for the kingdom; suitors must present them to the parents of women before asking for their hands. These certificates would require only minimum skill to forge, but forging a document involving clan-based kingdom matters is considered too immoral even for conmen to contemplate.

To what use, then, can the clans, which have proven so resilient in the past, be put in the 21st century? The most obvious would be the fight against climate change and for building climate resilience. This was a key role of the clan system hundreds of years before environmental studies were formalised in European and American universities. Now that the kingdom has become a melting pot of cultures and economic activities, environmental preservation is more difficult than ever to guarantee. But each of the 52 clans still has a base that usually includes a forest, a hill and some other environmentally important features. The Republic of Uganda, the Kingdom of Buganda and bodies like UNESCO would do well to designate these places for official protection, since they have millions of people ready to protect and conserve them with more than religious zeal.

Clans also could mobilise development finance. Pooling of resources remains a big weakness for many Ugandans after six decades of independence. Corruption is widespread; even churches have not been spared. Clan funds can be safer than most, and in this digital era, they could and should be collected, invested and protected globally.

Buganda's clans may have to invent new survival strategies, though. The almost mystical attachment Baganda feel for the land from which they sprung has endured for centuries, but our unsettled times and uncertain future represent unprecedented challenges. Virtually all land in Buganda is now on the open market, and even if some survives the land-grabbing epidemic, it eventually will go to the highest bidder.

Under these circumstances, the 52 clans may need to claim new homes. Cyberspace may be the answer. With attachment to land becoming transitory, the digital world may offer the best opportunities to find new bases (obutaka) and burial grounds (ebiggya). Many Baganda who have moved to faraway places like Europe and America, and some non-Ugandans might jump at the opportunity to connect with their clans online. For instance, some Indians, who were exiled during Idi Amin's 1972 mass expulsion of non-indigenous communities are lobbying to join the clans of Buganda, possibly because of their attachment to the kingdom that their grandparents long described to them in glorious terms; several Golden Jubilee festivities were held in different towns around the world to mark the August 1972 Exodus anniversary from Uganda. Similarly, many Banyarwanda, a people who were driven from their homes in Uganda in the early 1980s and live mostly in Rwanda, are maintaining old ties by joining Buganda clans, as are some Sudanic Nubians.

Can Buganda's clans survive a time when genetics and parental ancestry are becoming less important? Maintaining cohesion in cyberspace could be their biggest test yet, but I wouldn't count the clans out.

Mountain, Ostrich and Giraffe: A Journey through the Ateker land of Karamoja

By A. K. Kaiza

THE TWIN PEAKS CAN be seen from hundreds of kilometres away, rising above the horizon of northern Uganda like the jaws of a vice clamp closing in on the U-shaped gap between them. The companions stay in view but seem to shift positions as you drive north. Past Soroti town, when you have gained elevation and are properly in the plains, they emerge with clarity, playing an enchanting game of expectation in a sweeping, twisting dance of road and mountain.

This description may seem an overly dramatic gateway to Karamoja, like the beginning of a medieval tale. Yet the deeper you get into the land, Uganda's most isolated and misunderstood region, the less the place tries to dispute this.

I was born not 200 miles to the southwest, in Lango. But I did not see Karamoja first-hand until I was well into my 30s. By then, I had visited nearly every continent on the planet. But things said darkly and wearily kept me away from Karamoja. The land of warriors. A backward people. A society that did not want to "develop." A place where the least provocation got you dead. For years, I had been led to believe there was nothing for me in Karamoja, that paths to fortune and knowledge led elsewhere.

As I grew older, government bureaucrats and international organisations shaped my views. I learned about poverty indices, mortality rates and development indicators – concepts that experts use to define the place. I tried to employ social science categories like tribe, ceremonies, modern, traditional rituals and culture to explain it. These are the streets that you must walk when you are in postcolonial Africa. Without them, the land is bereft of features. You see nothing. But what do you see *with* them? The more I learned, the less I seemed to know.

Finally, I decided to go look for myself. Now I come to Karamoja every chance I get. A dozen trips in eight years have taught me many things about these ostracised and abused people, about post-colonial Africa and even about myself. I have learned to avoid talking too much about things that obsess outsiders – like cattle rustling, civil war and such matters as "the impact of these indices on that factor which leads to an overall conclusion about the status of the girl-child." The NGO lingo that had been my calling card years ago seems as capable as a sailboat in the age of ramjets. I am ashamed that I used to read United Nations reports to draw conclusions. Outsiders are often dubious interlopers who assume their own wisdom and superiority. I may be guilty of those sins too. But I now see Karamoja's supposed refusal to develop as the reverse side of something else: Much more than other parts of Uganda, Karamoja emerged from colonial rule with its culture nearly unscathed. Because of that, the British said it was backward. When the British were gone, new rulers mocked and mistreated it. Karamoja suffered, but it still did not let go.

This perspective makes it easy to romanticise Karamoja. But when you go on a journey like this, you need to find out what markers the locals use to describe themselves, even though that makes things complex – and in this case of Karamoja, terribly sad.

When you finally pass through the twin peaks, which are known as Mount Napak, you almost immediately see a town. Most towns and cities possess an outer penumbra of smaller towns, farmland and factories to herald their presence, but Iriri appears unannounced as if lying in ambush where the road starts to make its final climb into the high valley beyond. Brief and compact, it consists of a handful of drab houses sitting in the shadow of the mountain. But in addition to people garbed in the familiar Ugandan get-up of untucked shirts and tattered trousers, something else stands out: Fierce red, green, black, blue and scarlet blankets – nakatukok – slung over the shoulders of older men or worn by herdsmen as kilt-like skirts. Colours define the headgear too – stove-pipe Dr. Seuss hats tilted at a rakish angle on the young men, who also sport vests and sometimes t-shirts in zebra stripes. Thick, car-tire sandals on males young and old. This get-up is not complete without another definer of Karamoja: Small, carved wood headrests – ekichelong – which also double as easily portable stools. Young women wear pleated wool and goat-skin skirts made to sway like sheep tails. Yards and yards of bead-work jewellery rescue the wearers from what would otherwise be drab attire.

You know at once these people have not come out dressed for office work or shopping. Indeed, the town is an invader here, an echo of the cheek-by-jowl life in walled, sedentary, urban quarters elsewhere. But there is no time to unpack that. You drive past the small town in less than a minute. Again, there is no gradual ebbing away of the town. A new landscape takes over. These are pastoralist lands, home of the people of the outer ranges. In these higher elevations, the wide marshes and tended farms of the Teso region you left to get here are gone. Now you see vast grasslands and new mountains – handsome

Mount Kadam to the far right and directly ahead, the massive Mount Moroto.

Along with the vast, sweeping vistas of mountains and flat plains come enchanting paradoxes. The biggest of these is that throughout your long drive, you may fail to see what makes this place what it is. The Karamojong keep their cattle very secretively. The sight of large herds of cattle is less common than you would expect. In fact, when a herd comes into sight, it can be oddly discomfiting; you quickly learn that whenever you see cattle in Karamoja, there are also guns close by, so you approach herds with dread. Cattle are gold here. They are national secrets. They are guarded.

Even though you may not see them, cattle sculpt the landscape. Unlike the lush green plots of Teso or the monotonous fields of grass you passed on the way to Napak, you now see only vegetation that cattle do not eat. There is mostly one kind of tree, acacia, whose sharp, poisonous thorns are unattractive to cattle.

The human population that lies past Napak has dimensions I had never imagined. The Karamojong do not accept the designation "Karamojong," which they say was given to them by uncharitable neighbours, but it has stuck. In Napak, people call themselves the Bokora. In Nakapiripirit, to the west of Iriri, they are Pian. In Moroto, to the northeast, the Matheniko. In Kotido, a town about 120 kilometres north of Iriri, one finds the Jie. Farther north still, in Kaabong, are the Dodoth. Researchers variously call these groupings "tribes," "clans" or "ethnic groups," or lump them all together as "Nilotic Peoples" – people of the Nile Valley. When I first started coming here, I wondered, do they have a distinct culture as a people? But what is culture? And are the things they do – their "rituals" and "ceremonies" – "traditional," in contrast to "modern"? Who gets to say?

My search for answers once took me past Mount Moroto, which stands about 65 kilometres from Iriri like a sentinel overlooking Uganda's border with Kenya. It was the height of the rainy season, and vehicles looked as weary as I felt after making the journey as a passenger on a motorcycle. I was told it would take three more hours to reach Lodwar, in the Turkana region of northern Kenya. Perhaps this was said so I would not lose heart. After one hour on the road, we had just made it past the mountain and started to descend into Kenya. Three hours later, with Mount Moroto still in sight behind us, we ran into sand dunes. Then I learned about what they called laga – rivers that come and go with the rains. They did not have water when we arrived, but there was evidence they had been full less than a day earlier. Obviously, rivers and sand make bad companions. Twice, we fell off the motorbike. By the time I reached Lodwar, six hours had passed.

I made two discoveries during a quick stopover there. First, the people speak the same language as the Karamojong. But more intriguing than that, I heard a shapely, bright-coloured word: "Asapan." A pleasant, erudite young man, Simon Lokoremi, explained it: "When you have gone through Asapan, you can slaughter a bull. Asapan makes you become a big man. You can marry. It is like baptism." In halting English, he went on to say that before receiving Asapan, a man must gather sheets, beads, posho, sugar and shoes for a distinguished elder, who then instructs him for a week in the people's culture. When that is finished, a ceremony is held, and the initiate is empowered to slaughter a bull.

I had to tuck that treasure away for later because a bigger, more uncertain leg of my journey still lay ahead. From Lodwar, I squeezed into a Land Cruiser with eleven other people, part of a convoy headed north into the unremittingly arid and hostile Turkana Desert. Temperatures there regularly climb into the 40s (Celsius). Fortunately, it was a bit cooler when we were there. That may be why I saw – another paradox – a river of sand, a phenomenon that results when hail in the mountains hits the desert and collects sand, lubricating it until it literally flows downhill. As night fell, my companions talked of bandits – something I had not wanted to hear. But we safely crossed the border into South Sudan, and finally arrived in Kapoeta, the centre of a region that is home to a people known as the Toposa. My watch told me it was 2:30 am, the end of a journey that had started at noon the previous day.

It was worth the ordeal. I had thought I understood a few things about Turkana, but the Toposa were a mystery to me. Yet when we reached Kapoeta, I found perhaps the closest people to my own, the Langi. This discovery, ringing in my head through a mix of chants, words, sandal-throwing, and names of things and people, made me see Karamoja differently. I realised that it is misleading to talk of the Karamojong, the Turkana and the Toposa as separate nationalities. They are one people – the Ateker – not the separate tribes described in colonial accounts. This may not be evident at first. The British drew lines on the map that separated the people for more than a century. Dialects, accents, and even the bodies of the people diverged. The Kiswahili spoken in Kenya and the guttural Arabic of Sudan have coloured the language as spoken in Turkana, just as in Uganda, the flattened vowels of Ugandan English now make the Ateker spoken there distinct. But if you look past these superficial differences, you see a profound connection between all these people.

In the rush of new learning, I had to throw out old prejudices and the certainties built around them. But I found I was less and less able to understand the country where I had grown up. Among the many things that I did not know growing up was that my own ancestors had once been Karamojong. But now I knew. I had to remember the reasons why I had failed to make these journeys in the past – and what I hoped to learn now. There were things that happened to these lands, and they are still happening. The Karamojong, condemned by neighbours and nation for keeping their ways, have suffered traumas that have been almost completely unacknowledged.

What did it matter to an illiterate, put-upon, and half-starving pastoralist family that they are descended from a grand past, an empire of sorts? Most likely a lot, but how is the connection to be sorted out when you have become tenants of a postcolonial state, the kind of small, cramped and airless warehouse where billions of unhappy people now find themselves?

Mzee John Napua

I arrived back in Moroto utterly beaten from sitting so long on a motorbike while carrying a heavy rucksack stuffed with Ateker stools and bead-work art. But my most precious souvenir was lighter than air – a word. Asapan. I had crossed a mountain, a desert and two international borders to find it, but after I did, I began to hear it everywhere. Once I learned to look beyond superficial differences that obscure the reality of Ateker, I realised it had been all around me in Uganda. In Moroto, it once seemed there was no Asapan. But I finally realised that the Matheniko, the group of Karamojong who live in the foothills of Mount Moroto, lisp. In Moroto, they have "Athapan." My untrained ears failed to perceive they were hearing the same word with just a slightly different pronunciation.

Only when I came back to Karamoja did I come to understand that Asapan embodied much greater significance and depth of feeling than I appreciated from the slightly bleached version that Simon Lokoremi gave me. It was the missing key to the safe that held clues to an entire people. My discovery came with considerable irony. In Africa, the most told stories are stories of migration. But my travels to far-flung Ateker lands led back home to Karamoja, for it is said that before the migrations that flung the Ateker to distant places, they all once lived in Karamoja.

I owe my breakthrough to John Napua, an elderly man I met in Nayitakwai, a little hamlet below the western slope of Mount Moroto not far from Moroto town. He had spent his youth working for the Ugandan government. Educated and well-respected, he had gone without Asapan all his life until he reached the age of 76. Only then was this grandfather considered a man in his community.

I spoke to him through a translator, and as he spoke, I affirmed once more that spoken Ateker is one of the more beautiful languages I have come across – the poetry of a very poetic people with a predilection for the single-cast, the minimalist and the very exact. Their language is their art; its beauty is the singular stroke, the line not belaboured, the space left bare, the tongue not tasked too much.

Before we got to Asapan, we discussed how Karamojong society is organised. The atomic unit of the Ateker society, he explained, is Ngikalia. The "Ngi" is not really part of the word. The Ateker assiduously articulate their nouns, proper or otherwise, so that milk (akile) is not just "milk," it is "the milk" (Ngakile), and people (Tunga) are "the people" (Ngitunga). The use of articles gives a language some measure of lofty high-mindedness. "Ngikalia" is "the Kalia." Kalia sounds like a diminutive of Ekal. But it is not just that. As with most languages mindful of articles, there are gendered articles. "Milk" is "Ngakile" because milk is masculine; "people" is Ngitunga, the "Ngi" denoting that it is a feminine noun.

Ngikalia is a single household headed by one of a man's wives. So, women are the basis of the organisation of the society, a point often misunderstood. Together, a group of Ngikalia headed by wives of the same man form one Ekal. The Ekal together form Ngireria, the village. From here, it gets complex, for leadership of a village requires a process for selection. The stakes get higher as you go above the village to the Ngikudenyeta, or division.

"And how is a leader chosen?" I asked.

"First of all, we look at the age of someone," Mzee Napua told me. "If he is 40 or 45 and he has a sound mind, maybe he can chair (meetings)." Beyond that, he said, the way a person speaks can show whether he would say "something reasonable" in a gathering. Who is the judge of that? This isn't laid out in formal rules, but the elders size up the candidates and a consensus develops.

I pushed the conversation further. "Are some rituals carried out?"

"Oh, this is something," Mzee Napua exclaimed. "Akiriket." He did not have the appearance of an easily excitable man, but I caught a rising tone in his voice as he spoke this word. I looked up from my notebook. "It is so, so very important. They call for a gathering. They get one or two bulls. They kill them. It can take two days while they are looking for the right person to be a leader."

The Akiriket is a spectacle without equal in all of Ateker. People come trimmed and fettled with bright colours, billowing capes, and jauntily angled headgear of flouncy ostrich feathers. The men turn up in their nakatukok and striped and checked kilts gathered in knots at the small of the back like a cock's plumage; the young women wear skirts of wool and goat skin that sway as they move. After the bulls are slaughtered and their intestines are removed, candidates for leadership begin smearing the people with the bulls' blood. The elders inspect the intestines to learn whom Akuj, the supreme God, wills to be leader. "When someone looks into the intestines and says who should be a leader, I am sure it is God who gives him power," Mzee Napua told me. "After choosing a leader, who is called Ekatukon, there is always dancing and eating and what is called Ekomomor, which means praying to God, saying thank you for choosing this leader, thank you for rain."

From John Napua's description of the Akiriket I finally grasped the full significance of Asapan. Men who receive Asapan based on their proven ability to care for cattle and their education in culture play a crucial role in the elevation of leaders, whose selection is ordained by God. Asapan is both a political and a spiritual investiture. It ties people together as a society and links them to God.

The old man then introduced a surprise: The people do not choose a single leader; they choose two. One is responsible for the animals from the kraals; his job is to make sure water is available and the cattle are healthy. The other is responsible for people; his work is to take care of the homesteads, the Ngireria, and maybe to stay with the elders.

Most of our conversation focused on the Ekatukon, who is responsible for cattle. The idea of assigning cattle the same level of importance in governance as humans was no misplaced priority. For centuries, cattle have been the lifeblood of Karamojong society. Without them, survival is impossible. Without cattle, there is no Asapan, and the link to Akuj is cut.

John Napua explained that if there is no food or the cows need medicine, the Ekatukon calls a few people to go to the village to look for help or to buy drugs for the cattle. If there is no water or grass, he calls a gathering so people can choose some youths to look for a more suitable place to keep them; when they find one, the whole village moves, though an effort is made to explain to people already there why the newcomers have arrived. "Can you please take us in?" they will ask. "Let us stay peacefully, we have come from far and we are your brothers."

I asked John Napua about his personal life and was surprised to learn that he was born right there in Nayitakwai where we sat. I surmised that people were perhaps more settled in these parts at the foot of Mount Moroto than elsewhere in Karamoja. For pastoralist people, staying in one place is testimony to its capacity to provide. The mountain looming over us orchestrates the rhythm of life in all of Ateker, from Uganda to Kenya to South Sudan and even to Ethiopia. If you live close to it, where it sheds much rain, I wagered there was no call to move too far away.

John Napua's father had two wives who bore ten girls and two sons. They were well-off, with more than 200 cows, about 150 goats, and assorted donkeys. John Napua's childhood started typically. In Karamoja, shepherding is a boy's lot. Watching over sheep is the herdsman's kindergarten. Goats are elementary school. I have seen this in my travels up and down Ateker lands – stick-thin boys controlling goat herds that blanket roadsides. When a boy reaches his late teens, he graduates to cattle. But in 1956, when John Napua was still a boy, the family lost everything in a devastating cattle raid. In pastoralist terms, he did not make it past elementary school.

Stock rustling is so common it almost seems casual, but the consequences are devastating. Most often, elderly men hang themselves when all their cattle have been taken. Sometimes, the old men do not even have to reach for the rope; in Amudat, amongst the Pokot, a pastoralist people sharing culture but not ethnicity with the Karamojong, the story is told of an old man who lost all his animals in one day. He just died. No prelude, nothing needed to be said. It was as if his life simply stopped. Not so the young men with families. When their animals are gone, the women and the children stare at them. There is no milk. No blood. No meat. What do you tell them? You pick weapons and go in search of animals to raid. You do not return empty-handed.

The Napua family did not have that option. With just two young boys, the family did not have enough manpower. The ten sisters, whose likely dowries could have attracted enough cattle to replace the lost livestock, all died before they were nubile. The family became destitute. John Napua eventually ran away from home. The aunt at whose Ekal he took refuge decided he should go to school. The news pleased his mother, but his father was not so happy. The truth of the matter, he said, is that he did not go to school for education. Schools in pastoralist lands offer food as an enticement for young people who lack much to eat at home. The meals at school sustain children and keep mothers less weary. The fathers often see school as an indictment; the fact that his son had to go someplace else to eat was, to the father, a sign of failed manhood. But school brought John Napua life-long benefits. With his education, he came to be in constant demand from NGOs, researchers, governments, and peace committees. Able to read and write English, he became an interpreter – of language and of cultural nuance. He was at every peace talk, it seemed, to take notes, to send letters. He served in local government until he retired.

But his Ateker account was empty. The loss of animals in the 1950s haunted John Napua for six decades. Without cattle, there can be no Asapan. Without Asapan, a man has no voice. From afar, the lack of Asapan may sound peculiar, but it is the equivalent in other cultures of becoming a grownup who cannot read, failing to graduate from college, or, for Christians, not being baptised or for followers of Islam or Judaism of being uncircumcised.

John Napua might have had a chance for Asapan before he reached middle age, but in 1980, the centuries-old rhythm of Ateker life ended. A combination of factors led to a severe shortage of cattle throughout Karamoja. This froze the normal passing of power from one generation to the next. Ateker generations bear names; when the regime of the mountain generation (Ngimoru) comes to an end, they will pass power on to their sons, who might be called ostriches (Nguwana), who will pass it on to their sons, say the giraffe generation. But without cattle, this lineage system became strained. Not until the early 2010s did some cattle return. Only then was calm restored. John Napua finally could receive Asapan. At 76, he became a man.

I returned to Moroto town charged with all that Mzee Napua told me. To have no cattle – to lose "stock" – is devastating; the 1980 disaster was Karamoja's version of the market collapse in 1929 that triggered the Great Depression. It was not the first time the Ateker had suffered such a blow. Centuries ago, drought and lack of cattle broke the people, forcing the Turkana, the Toposa, the Teso and the ancestors of the Langi to migrate from Karamoja. The separation was not amicable. The Karamojong refused to pass on Asapan to the emigres, a punishment that disabled those societies; to this day, these "runaway" tribes still have no recognised leadership the people respect. Deprived of structure and social philosophy, the Teso, Langi, and Kumam were and continue to be absorbed into the culture, language and philosophy of the Luo people, who live primarily in what is Uganda, South Sudan, Kenya, Ethiopia, Congo and Tanzania today.

Tolim Lomer

With such notable exceptions, the Karamojong kept their animals – and their people – alive for centuries. But the story that is told does not fully explain how. Someone has been left out. My next set of questions were for one such person – a potent but complex, elusive, and misunderstood figure whose kind is found in all of Africa. In Ateker language, the man I was due to meet is Emuron – one who gathers and processes medicine, diagnoses illness and then applies medicaments. The word denotes an esteemed office, but it is clouded. Before colonisation, he was known simply as a "doctor." But missionaries, declaring African ways heathen and satanic, started to call his ilk "witches" and "wizards." The colonialists put him into a criminal crowd along with murderers, child abductors and grave robbers. The issue wasn't spiritual. Witchcraft laws banning "fetishes" came at a time when symbols of culture united opposition toward British rule. Banning them helped to defeat rebellions.

In the decades since the end of colonialism, the Emuron's successors have come to be known as "traditional healers." But the term is dismissive. Why the adjectival caveat? The colonial era in Uganda is over, but the animus remains. Post-colonial times are characterised by settled sclerosis. The power that once punished people for following their ways is no longer there, but the shame and the fear are now self-administered. The resulting confusion leaves one an outsider to his own society – a society that is outside of itself. Thus, in my childhood, the homes of the . . . them . . . were never directly connected to habitual pathways because feet naturally learned to move away from those who combine power and spirituality. If you did not turn up at church, you were labelled "one of them." If you had a wrist band, a neckpiece made neither in Europe nor China or wore clothes of leather and bark cloth; you would be dogged by a persistent question: "Just what are you up to?"

Outside of this charged history, I wanted to see an Emuron because I wanted to know how traditional veterinarians kept animals alive. Considering the fine form of animals in Ateker lands, even though there are hardly any "modern" veterinary clinics, the question asks itself. How do they do it?

In search of answers, I set off to drive up Mount Moroto to meet Mr. Tolim Lomer. He treats animals. He never went to a "modern" school. His father treated animals. His grandfather treated animals. His great grandfather treated animals. And so the line continues back into the dim mists of memory and time. It makes sense that Lomer lives on a mountain; in all these mountains, I am told, are many Emuron – probably because herds of cattle and goats have stripped the plains of all but the hardiest and thorniest of plant life. Medicinal plants can mostly be found in the hills.

Finding Tolim Lomer demanded some work. In Karamoja, you need to go through someone who knows such a man – or someone who knows someone who knows someone who knows him. It does not matter if he carries a phone; it is word-of-mouth business. My companion for this leg of the trip was a translator – not of words, but of meaning. Like me, he was a recovering post-colonial, a man with western education now seeking his cultural roots.

We set off under an atypically low sky. The higher we went, the lower the sky got. In the distance to our right were the twin peaks of Mount Napak. Directly ahead of us, Mount Kadam. We could see Mount Toror to our rear; I do not know why they call Toror a mountain; it looks more like an exalted hill. As we gained elevation, the wisps of rain clouds felt like cold smoke. We kept a wary eye for what they might portend. April and May are heavy rain months in these parts. In Turkana, I was told that the rains can stay away for up to ten years. But when hard rains come, flooding follows. The dry riverbeds bear millions of cubic litres of raging water. Trees, shrubs, houses, and even humans and their waste are washed away. Cholera ensues.

When we reached our destination, I twice waited in the silence as my interpreter ventured into the shrubbery. But each time, he came back alone. Finally, we started back down towards some wattle and iron-sheet structures we had passed on the way up. But before we got there, the interpreter stepped out of the car once more. This time, he returned with a man whose air of calm solemnity, simplicity and unforced authority immediately told me he was the person I had come to see.

Tolim Lomer had no bone in his nose. He was not wearing a leopard skin. He did not come with rattles to shake. I was struck by his immense dignity. He is a busy man, but he listened patiently, dispassionately, and impersonally. Judging by the limber, spritely manner of his walk, he was not elderly, but his office, the secretiveness of it, its haloed air of seriousness, granted him elder status. He clearly was a man apart, not to be commanded, subjected or questioned. But nor did he command or assert. He was simply aware of the moment.

I was completely unnerved. I brought out a tobacco roll – the requisite greeting gift you bring to a man of exalted position in Ateker. It had been pounded and densely compressed. The leaves were crushed into a paste while still green, and then rolled into a dense cylinder slightly wider than a man's palm and some 20 centimetres long, with the top tapering into a pointed end like a bullet shell. It weighed about a kilo. It could be stuffed into a pipe and smoked or picked and crushed in the hand as snuff. This is the Ateker way of translating tobacco.

I asked about his name. "When I was young," he replied, "my mother brewed beer, and there were always people in our compound who were drunk." The Luo word for a drunk, is "amero." In Acholi, they front it with the definite article, "la"; hence, it became "Lamero," which was simplified to Lomer. Another paradox: A man with the most sanctified air I had encountered in all of Ateker bears a name that means "the drunkard" – another example of the wry sense of humour I have come across many times here.

One more matter remained to be settled. Tolim Lomer rarely talks to people about his work. I understood the concern; charlatans take advantage of stray knowledge, so he has to guard what he knows lest the unscrupulous misuse it. "We are not going to misuse this information," I assured him. "We are not going to pass it to anyone we don't trust." Thus assured, Tolim Lomer set about calmly. He had a calm, deliberate, unhurried way of talking. We were an audience, not interlocutors.

I decided to ask first about morbidity and pharmacology. He listed a range of diseases that afflict animals in Karamoja, explained how he diagnoses them, and told me what medicines treat them. I asked how he practices. He told me that he goes alone into the mountain area and gathers plants – shoots mostly, but bark and roots as well. He neither lifted nor lowered his voice. He gathered his legs neatly about him and placed his hands gently about his knees, making few movements as he talked. I realised that to learn the mystical aspects of his trade, I would have to speak to third parties.

The Emuron's core goal is to keep cattle alive – and thereby to secure milk production. Milk is the most central of all pastoralist food, the cornerstone of pastoralist existence. Goat or mutton are eaten regularly, but cattle are rarely slaughtered; cows are kept for exchange and storage value – and for important occasions.

People lose cattle to rustling, but loss of cattle to disease is more devastating. A rustled cow is not exactly lost. The Pokot may take it away from the Matheniko, but then find it stolen by the Pian, who might lose it to the Bokora, who will in turn lose it to the Matheniko, taking it back to where it started. Losses are counterbalanced by gains all around, so an overall stability is maintained; I was told in Moroto that cattle are so liberally stolen and re-stolen that it is quite possible that all Karamojong women were married with the same cattle for their dowries. Epidemics break these cycles of loss and gain. You cannot counter-raid a dreaded disease to recover the animals it has taken. When disease strikes, the entire Ateker ecosystem suffers. The death of a rival group's cattle does not bring good news; when their animals die of disease, yours become targets for replenishment.

Years ago, I was told that cattle rustling occurs during the rainy season. This may seem counterintuitive, but it makes sense. Dry season comes with relentless heat; running cattle too hard at such a time is a risk to the herd, so people resist the urge to strike out. Friendships are formed during jaunts to watering points, where people invariably speak gently to one another. You must cooperate with others to share the little food and water there is. But this is overlaid by another pragmatic purpose: They give herders a chance to see who has the best-looking animals. With that piece of intelligence squirreled away, they await the rainy season to conduct raids.

The rainy season is the worst time for animals' health. Cattle are at their healthiest during the dry season. Yes, there is less water and pasture, but the grass and the water are clear and clean. During the rainy season, vectors that cause disease multiply. The wet grass supports insects. I felt slightly ajar absorbing this logic only to realise that I had an agrarian view of seasons; my unexamined assumption was that rain equals abundance. But the paradox of the seasons makes much sense; mosquitoes, the bane of Ugandans' existence, come out during the rainy season. Even where I come from, we are sickest in the rainy season.

I asked Tolim Lomer about his fees. He told me that he does not charge for his work. Medicine, he said, becomes ineffective if you ask clients to pay. I sensed he was talking not just in a simple, anti-capitalist way; his deeply communitarian selflessness put greater weight to his words than that. He explained that drug resistance, which is more or less the translation of his comment that medicine becomes ineffective, occurs when drugs are over-prescribed, and that happens when profiteers jam them unnecessarily down patients' throats. Years ago, I visited Brazil and was told that it only managed to control malaria by taking its drugs out of the market and making them free.

In the last moments of the interview, Tolim Lomer told me that he had developed a working relationship with "modern" medicine. Many times, he said, when he is unable to find the medicine the animals need, he sends herders into town with prescriptions to buy western medicine. Prescriptions, I have also been told, come the other way too; university-trained vets sometimes send herders to Tolim Lomer.

In the end, we never discussed spirituality. The topic just did not seem to fit in this down-to-earth conversation. Christianity has made such deep inroads into these parts over the past century that people are afraid or reluctant to discuss their non-Christian beliefs. They have been reticent for so long that it is rare to find someone who even knows what those beliefs are anymore. I did not know where to begin, and Tolim Lomer opened no door. It is a sensitive matter, for another kind of journey.

The "Sweep"

Going down the mountain, we found that the sky had darkened considerably. Barely a kilometre from Tolim Lomer's home, it opened up. In a violent, lashing wind, white and grey sheets of water blocked the views of the plains I had been looking forward to seeing. Ahead of us, we saw the road starting to wash away. We felt no sense of panic yet. Maybe we did not want to think about it, being high up, with sheer drops on one side of us and embankments of earth that could easily slide on the other. We drove on, dropping in altitude. Then, it was suddenly over. It had been mountain rain, mostly. This frightening interlude was not one of the big rains that can wreak havoc in the valley, plain and desert below.

Down in the foothills, my thoughts stayed with Tolim Lomer. Without cattle, the culture of the Karamojong does not exist, so it depends for its survival in part on men like him. But something broke down in 1980. First there was the gun. When President Idi Amin's government fell the year before, the government armoury in Moroto was left open. That nearly destroyed the social equilibrium. Just about anyone could get a gun. Soon, raids and killings increased. News reports of 1980 bear the urgency of the moment. Nick Morral, a journalist stringing for Agence France-Presse, reported in May 1980 that people were dying at the rate of 100 a day. Central government was no help; indeed, there was no central government in the aftermath of Amin's overthrow in 1979. A tentative authority stuttered into half-life in 1980, but it was relatively ineffectual for years.

That was not the first time that guns upset the delicate balance of pastoral life in Ateker. It is said that in 1911, the emperor of Ethiopia, Menelik, sent guns into Turkana to keep the British busy on their northern frontier of Kenya and thus stop the northward expansion of the British empire in this region. A desperate move for Menelik, it doomed Ateker. That is when borders were drawn. Of course, ethnic groups spilled across these new dividing lines, but the "spill" was cleaned up by the invention of Ateker sub-tribes, so that in Uganda, they came to be called Karamojong; in Kenya, they became the Turkana.

Seventy years later came the second introduction of guns. Horrendous in its own right, it was followed by three years of drought and famine. The United Nations struggled to supply relief food, but its vehicles were beset by ambushes. Then came cholera. Then cattle were hit with an epidemic of Lopid, which Tolim Lomer told me is the most serious of cattle illnesses he has witnessed. The fever changes animals' skin. Their mouths and noses turn yellow. They vomit, pass watery stool and stop eating. This illness is spread by ticks.

The triple horror – guns, famine and disease – came to be known in scholarly circles as the "Karamoja Syndrome." The Karamojong, in their wry, humorous way, summed up the conflagration in a single word: Lopiar – "The Sweep." No family was left untouched. Some families never made it, not even one person. Paul Otyang, whom I was about to meet, fled the region, only to return to find his whole family in a feeding centre set up by what he called the Sisters of Charity. He slaughtered a bull in hopes of saving his grandmother, who was ill, but, he said with a sense of hopelessness creeping into his voice, she died anyway. Some 21 per cent of the population of Karamoja perished the same year.

Those who stayed struggled as best they knew how. One strategy was to stage massive cattle raids throughout northern Uganda. My family lost all the stock we had to Karamoja's desperate attempt to re-stock. It is hard to get the facts, but we heard that the cattle stolen from us were re-stolen by Turkana, who took them to Kenya, where many were lost to Toposa from South Sudan and Nyangatom from Ethiopia. Our cattle, which were unsuited for the harsh Ateker climate, died in large numbers along the way.

It was like grand opera – tragedy, passions, drive, failure. Instead of securing a livelihood, the Karamojong reaped the wrath of the non-Ateker who sat – and still sit – in power and who, when they look up here, see only troublesome, anti-modern people.

Paul Otyang

We arrived back in Moroto town, going past its residue of colonial bungalows and rotting 1950s gas stations. It is not a big town. Set up by the British as headquarters of their colonial holding in Karamoja, it has about a dozen roads, all of them walkable from end to end in less than ten minutes. You can take in the whole town with one broad sweep of the eye. A few of the town's roads are now paved, and paint has arrived on some of its structures. I hear that there is a stridently policed ban on removing your nakatukok and going starkers in town. It is a story repeated in varying ways all across Africa. Decades after independence, you are not allowed to be African in the former colonial towns. Why? Is it because powerful outsiders in these towns – international people, UN officials, diplomats, dignitaries and reconstructed Africans – would be offended by the uncovered backside? So it goes. Colonialists start to make rules for a people in their own lands. The subjugated obey. It becomes easier with each passing era to keep telling them what to do. Soon the Africans start to make those rules themselves against their own interests.

Entering Moroto, the transition away from the old Karamoja is evident almost instantly. The big hotels are manned by non-Ateker chefs and waiters. The big shops and the vehicles from large towns to the south are commanded by non-Ateker. We outsiders must stir a mix of shame and resentment when we come to the town. Where are the clean hotels, we ask? What is the food going to be like? Where can we stay where it is not too hot and where the warriors cannot enter? There is an edgy undercurrent because everybody knows that gold, marble, limestone – some say even oil, to say nothing of the cattle –

are in the crosshairs of big and powerful outsiders, many of them not even Ugandans. Some are Chinese. These interlopers are asking the Ateker to make more room, to move from their perches to make way. There is much wealth underneath the soil. The outsiders want it. The government has been disarming the population, but some voices question the motives behind disarmament. The brand-new roads making their way this far north for the first-time breed fear as much as hope – yes, they will make transportation easier, but they also will make it easier to carry Ateker wealth away. Visitors may consider the town an oasis, but these matters wreath the place in tensions.

As I sat in this post-colonial milieu, I wondered what Paul Otyang, my next interviewee would say about that. It is hard to pinpoint Otyang's age. He looks young; like most Ateker men, he is in remarkable trim, nary a wrinkle in sight. You could mistake him for being in his late 40s. But he recollects the last years of British rule; that puts him closer to 70. It is like that in these lands. If one is not lacking for means and, like Paul Otyang, does not drink and keeps to the straight and narrow, old age is kept a long way away.

Paul Oytang is the leader of the Ngilukumong, one of Karamoja's 19 clans. This makes him one of Karamoja's highest-ranking indigenous leaders. Karamoja sends representatives to the Ugandan Parliament in Kampala, and it has officials who serve in the country's ministries. But clan heads have a different kind of power – one grounded in long-standing tradition. To understand the dynamics of power in Africa fully, you must understand clans. Their roles are not captured in the constitutions of the post-colonial state, just as the work done by people like Tolim Lomer is not taught in western universities. But their authority is immense. Somali communities, cast out of their country in the last of the Cold War era's conflicts pitting proxies for the Americans and Soviets, thrive around the world today partly because their clan mechanism remains intact. The African clan decides all aspects of life and its word is final, no matter which part of the world you are in.

I started with a very basic question: What role do clans play in Karamoja?

Paul Oytang first discussed how clans oversee branding of cattle. Each clan has its own recognisable marking to indicate the cows it owns. The same markings also appear on people – yet another indication of Ateker comity with animals. He described another form of branding; men from different clans tie cuttings of particular trees around the necks of women they want to marry, thus announcing that the women belong to their clan. Clans also have rules for what animal skins their women wear so that people can readily see the clans to which they belong. And they have rules about what foods people can eat and how it must be prepared, though not surprisingly for a society where food can be scarce, Paul Oytang said the Karamojong are very flexible in applying these rules.

I moved to a more personal question. How did he become clan leader?

His reply, like John Napua's, was lively understatement. He already had the power. He would not be voted out. "What helped me so much is that I am a very simple person. I do not fight, and up to now, I have never taken any alcohol. I think the community chose me for that. I have been living in the village and not having any problem, not disturbing any people. What made me famous was when I said to the community, to the clan, 'Let us go and look for greener pastures and water for our cattle.' The community did not accept (this proposal). So I went by myself. Later I returned and called them, 'You people, let us go; there is enough water.' They followed me. They started praising me everywhere. Also, during the gatherings, I always came and advised them to soothe their hearts, not to worry. Our cattle will continue producing, we shall have more and more."

Paul Otyang said he manages five homesteads, but he actually "takes care" of about 50 clusters of huts comprising about 370 members of his clan. He has a group of about 10 people who help him. Even members of the clan who have left Karamoja still obey him. But he says his job is getting more difficult.

"Life has changed in Karamoja. People have given up their customs. They have adapted to new lives. They want everyone to take their children to school – boys and girls. I am one of the pioneers of schools in my community. They chose me to be the chairperson of the school community in Rupa sub-county. I took all my children to school and advised others to take their children to school. But the problem now is the children themselves. We parents are doing our part. But you find that after taking your daughter to school, she has not finished senior four, she comes back with a child. Even the boys – most of them – have left school."

While sparing parents harsh judgement over the generational divide, the clan leader has some harsh criticism for adults too. Increasingly, he says, they are dissolving the laws that used to define the clan. "They feel they should adapt to western ways of living, the muzungu way of life – the way they dress, the way they behave, everything. They are abandoning their laws to adapt to the western culture. They have forgotten our culture. They dress differently. They eat differently. There are few who still hold on to the culture, but most of them have dropped the culture."

This sad comment brought to my mind a perplexing thing Mr. John Napua told me. He mentioned an office called Erwothit. I did not need head-scratching nor second opinions to know where that word came from; when you remove the 'E' fronting the word and the 'it' propping up the back end, you end up with a Luo word, Rwoth, which means "chief." But Karamoja has never had "chiefs." This is a concept imposed from outside. I have met this before. *Karamoja Politics*, a book by a British anthropologist, Neville Hudson-Dyson, who was busy in these parts in the 1950s, mentions that the British had created the office of Prime Minister in Karamoja. Prime Minister of what? They modelled it after the office of Buganda's prime minister in the former kingdom that includes the capital, Kampala. Here in Karamoja, it was called Katikiroit. Take away the suffix "it" and you end up with Katikiro, the official word for prime minister far to the south in Buganda.

This British attempt to introduce centralised government in Karamoja may reflect a failure to understand the Karamojong, who have no supreme authority akin to a chief or prime minister. The Karamojong are essentially a democratically governed society. The Ekatukon hold authority limited to management of particular groups of people and cattle, and the 19 clan leaders are responsible for people who share a common lineage, but nobody speaks for the Karamojong as a people. It would be a mistake to interpret this lack of any person at the top of the political hierarchy as a sign of anarchy, though. The Karamojong have long been united by their social structure and beliefs.

The sole purpose of the British attempt to introduce centralised government was to take away the will of the people. The British spent 50 years experimenting with different models before their rule eventually foundered. One model was to declare Karamoja a closed territory; they said that nothing good would come of investing time and effort in the place. But that was dishonest; the British came to take away Karamojong cattle in the name of taxes. They bullied the people. Perhaps their final idea before giving up was centralised Ugandan government rule. The idea was carried forward to the new nation they left behind – Uganda. Will its rule be the endgame for Karamoja, which has been kettled, its head twisted to a point where "culture" may now refer to little more than a display of costumes and staging of tourism-worthy dances?

I have long tried to keep a level, clear focus so I can learn facts and basics. But the truth is that a story of Karamoja is deeply sad. Here is a place that has been remarkably successful in maintaining cultural traits and mores from pre-colonial Africa. But in the past decades, these have been disappearing very fast. You cannot visit the place without feeling fear for the future. When I sat down with Paul Otyang, the feelings I had been keeping in check welled out.

The Uganda Era

After decades of contemptuous suspicion, the government of Uganda decided to work with the traditional systems of the independent nations that the British brought together to form the nation of Uganda. But it did more than that; it also invented offices. These new entities did not always go down well with the people. "Kings" and "queens" appeared where there used to be none. The idea of the Erwothit, the government-designated "chief" who some describe as an overall leader, fits uneasily with Karamoja's decidedly republican spirit. But over time, the lines between Karamojong governance and that of the Ugandan government appear to be melding into a unity of sorts. John Napua told me of the office of Ekethera, a kind of liaison who meets with big leaders like the clan heads, did not sit well with Karamoja, but the Local Council, a Uganda government-created office, seems to be less objectionable, perhaps because its members are elected locally rather than being appointed by outsiders. The government of Uganda, meanwhile, has created an entire ministry for Karamoja affairs, with a cabinet minister. Karamoja also sends several people's representatives to the national Parliament. Thus the state grows stronger. People and culture yield. Tolim Lomer said it, John Napua said it and finally, Paul Otyang said it.

The Uganda People's Defence Force – the army – is the nation's strongest presence in Karamoja today. It is still camped here even though it drove Joseph Kony and his Lord's Resistance Army (LRA) out of Uganda in 2006 and, the government says, it has succeeded in clearing the place of guns. It says the soldiers have brought order and peace. It is true there is a calmness about the place now. Distances between places are covered in a shorter time. You can move about, even in the dark, without fear of getting shot. People should be happy about that. But there is disquiet. People instinctively know that "peace" was achieved for many reasons, and not all those are for the benefit of Karamoja.

I once sat next to a soldier in a cramped matatu, a minibus "taxi," driving south out of Moroto. He and I found out we were both from Lango. That made us talk freely. He described to me the difficulty of military training. We drove past children returning from school. "Those return home for the holidays, and you have to start being ready for the rustling to start," he told me. "They come back to steal animals." They still have guns, he said, almost shouting. They move into Kenya, into Sudan, to steal. They even steal among themselves.

The soldier told me he had spent more than ten years in Karamoja. He had been served a transfer a number of times but managed to stay. The key thing, he said, is to have an understanding with the commanding officer. I did not ask for more. I understood. But he explained anyway. If you are savvy enough, Karamoja is a good place, he said. Later, he picked up the conversation in Luo, obviously assuming we had no audience beyond ourselves (a reckless assumption). He said that keeping the Karamojong from stealing animals is a lot of work, and the army at one point had to change its strategy. Rustlers found to have gone over to, say, Acholi or Teso, to steal animals were taken back to where they had stolen the animals, and were tried and jailed there. That put fear into their hearts, he said. He also said that a kraal found to have even one stolen animal was forced to give up all its animals.

But the government's main tool for control is its military might. In Karamoja – in all of Ateker – animals belong to those with guns. The Karamojong had their guns taken away. The army now carries big guns. And as if to underline the lingering colonial mind-set, the soldier told me: "When you bring an AK-47 against these people, they feel nothing. It is the machine gun that can manage them. Bring a helicopter gunship."

I will always remember that soldier and his idea of pacification. It was nothing new. Sitting with Paul Otyang, I recalled that during the times of Idi Amin, people in Karamoja were forced to wear clothes. Some people who did not comply were killed. I asked if he remembered things that were being done to Karamojong people.

He began to answer with a smirk. He almost laughed. "The [army] even used to take spears away from us. It is only God who helped me. I was one of them." We laughed as though we had all participated in outwitting Amin. We say "Amin," "Obote," or "Museveni," as if these heads of state came personally rather than dispatching the soldiers who did the dirty work.

"This man (Idi Amin) came with his soldiers one time. He grabbed all the elders – those of Apaloris, all those big names, the Adokes, the big warriors from Karamoja. He grabbed them, brought them to the offices of the army here in Moroto, and he tortured them. Since these big men used to have too much hair, he took their walking sticks, shoved them into the hair and then twisted the sticks. It was terrible."

I asked him how he felt when people show they despise Karamoja.

"To me, the one who says the Karamojong are bad is the one who is bad. The Karamojong allow all tribes to enter into Karamoja, and nothing happens to them."

The worst of the crisis triggered almost 40 years ago has subsided, but threats remain. I suspect that the story of disarmament in Karamoja is not at an end. The government of Uganda and the Ugandan army have been accused of gross human-rights violations. There are disquieting news reports about land grabbing. News of oil and mineral deposits in the area brings fears that foreigners with money and power will want the Karamojong to give way.

But there is worse, and it comes as yet another paradox. I first started to hear it in Kaabong, a district north of Moroto, in 2012. I was told that the army now supervises routine cattle keeping, including telling the people when and where to keep the animals in kraals. The enclosures clog up. Cattle get stuck. They get diseases. "We need to keep moving the animals," I was told. But that is not the paradox. It is that peace, while a welcome thing, has also meant not having the means to defend ownership of your animals and land; it is peace as pacification, as "pax," a terrifying flattening of local interests by aggressive imperial means to make it easier to rule the people. In the past, the cycles of animal ownership were maintained by having mostly equal abilities to defend herds. But now, the Karamojong have nothing to throw back at their neighbours who come raiding. They cannot recover lost animals. New means to do so have not been established; the Karamojong do not trust the army.

I asked Paul Otyang what he thinks the future will bring for Karamoja. "I would tell my community to start digging for cattle underground," he said, in a voice downbeat and oracular. "The cattle are now in the ground." In case I missed his metaphor, he explained it. "They should start farming because there is now no way we can recover what has been lost. The only way is to start farming. That is what I would tell my community." He spoke with a forlorn look in his eyes, with a sadness he had not shown before. "My only hope is this rain. My hope is that people grow more crops this year. I hope we get lots of food this year. Otherwise, I am not hopeful for Karamoja. Maybe after some five, ten years, we may get some animals back. I used to have my cattle, but when disarmament came, these people came and lied to us, they deceived us that they were going to take care of our animals, that we only had to give them the guns. But they took the cattle too."

And so the decline of Ateker continues. Paul Otyang, speaking from the very heartland of Ateker in the foothills of Mt. Moroto, told me that his people would be better off turning to agriculture. The cattle are no more. In Turkana, they say camels are more viable and that Asapan is now a private, family matter, no longer the backbone of a durable hierarchy. In Toposa, I hear, the elders no longer have any authority. My mind goes to the Langi, the Kumam, the Iteso – people who, without the singular adherence to pastoralism, lost their names, theology and language when they branched out to become farmers following the disintegration of Ateker in centuries past. If I came in search of my true ancestral home, I arrived too late. Like Mount Napak, the high points and pride of Karamoja are being relentlessly eroded away.

With some trepidation, I asked Paul Otyang, "Are you not afraid the Karamojong are going to lose their culture like the rest of the people in Uganda?" His answer was filtered, but it hit the emotional jugular: "I would not want to say so much about my culture. It pains me. Everybody is changing."

And Money Made Men Mad

By Joachim Buwembo

THE KINGDOM OF BUGANDA, around which the state of Uganda was built, conquered a brutal, older dynasty and thrived for six centuries under an unbroken lineage. When the British colonialists took over in 1894, the second Buganda dynasty was on its thirty-third king. By contrast, the Kingdom of Saudi Arabia was only 150 years old, and the United Arab Emirates would wait another 77 years to be founded. A dynasty could not have survived for 600 years if it was weak; it must have had attributes strong enough to overcome hostile forces, to expand and to prosper.

Colonialism undermined this remarkable history of stability and unity in many ways. One of its most harmful long-term effects was its introduction of money. When Britain established its dominance over Uganda, some forms of commodity money were already in use. Obusonko – beautiful snail shells that symbolised security – were one medium of exchange. The more internationally valuable obusanga and amasanga – ivory cuttings and tusks – also were used in international trade with other kingdoms as far away as present-day Tanzania, as well as with Arab traders from North Africa and Asia. Kabaka Mutesa

I, who reigned in the second half of the 19th century, used ivory to purchase more than 10,000 rifles for his army and to police Nalubaale, which the colonisers renamed Lake Victoria. However, use of commodity money was still limited, and much exchange was through barter. Within communities, people freely gave essentials like food to neighbours and strangers according to the recipients' need, not their ability to pay.

Transactions for profit began during the founding of the modern state, when colonial empire-builders paid senior noblemen of the kingdom in land and money to betray their king, Mwanga II. The first of these "sale agreements" were recorded in 1900. In essence, they were bribes. It's little wonder that money has messed up many things in Uganda ever since.

The modern state introduced the idea of salaried work. In addition to the treacherous officials who received money as compensation, the first people to earn salaries in Uganda were mercenaries from Sudan and their local collaborators, who were paid to help the colonialists crush popular resistance to colonialism. The mercenaries became the Uganda Armed Constabulary at the close of the 19th century before finally being absorbed into the modern Uganda Police Force in 1906.

For a long time after the British colonialists introduced currency – first the Indian Rupee and then the East African shilling pegged to the British pound sterling – most exchange continued to be based on humane considerations. Basic necessities like food and land were not exchanged for profit. It was said that a young man who wanted to establish himself would leave his parents' homestead and "eat land" (okulya ekibanja). First, he would introduce himself to the residents of a new village. The elders would allocate him land, and he would be given food for about four months until he made his first harvest. When the new resident was ready to marry, he would pay bride price in the form of farm produce to the girl's parents. Neighbours would contribute food and drink for the marriage feast. Local drumming and dancing troupes provided entertainment. No money changed hands.

With the introduction of the new order based on western capitalism, things began to change. Education ceased being a community-led process designed to impart needed skills. Newly introduced formal school education was neither free nor universal. It had to be bought with hard cash. To get children educated, one had to sell something; thus food, which had been a right, became a commodity. The transformation accelerated with the growth of cities and towns; people who moved to towns had nowhere to grow their food and thus needed to earn money to buy food.

Because education was expensive, it became a preserve of the elite – a self-perpetuating class since only children who finished schooling were given jobs in colonial administration. Members of this new elite saw no need to work the land; once they acquired the white man's knowledge, they probably considered farming too dirty for them. Instead, they joined the ranks of people like soldiers and chiefs, who already had aligned themselves with the ruling power. That explains the origin of a sad anomaly: Although agriculture is the mainstay of Uganda's economy, Ugandan youth dismiss farming once they attain school education. To this day, many people who study agriculture in public universities do not work anywhere near the farming sector, preferring to look for clerical jobs upon graduation.

After the end of World War I in 1918, money came to be glorified. Many folk songs were composed in praise of money, and when Ugandans started recording modern music in the 1950s, money competed with love as the favourite themes of popular songs. It still is a big music theme. In 2017, one of the biggest pop hit songs in Uganda urged people to take loans and buy cars so they won't die before driving. So pervasive is the pursuit of money that industries based solely on money – like gambling – are growing faster than sectors engaged in production of tangible products. The obsession affects all age groups. Today, even youngsters under ten in the most rural areas of Uganda expect "consideration" – a quid pro quo – before doing anything for somebody else. "Nfunira wa" – What is in it for me? – has become a common refrain. An American ambassador who was completing his three-year tour of duty in Kampala around 2010 joked at his farewell party that he had learnt enough Luganda to survive in Uganda since he could say, "Nfunira wa?"

Today, people operate under a monetary system without significantly adjusting their traditional attitudes. Yet the two systems are irreconcilable. Perhaps that's why most Ugandans fail to manage their personal finances effectively. Financial illiteracy abounds. The country's crème de la crème, elected national legislators, are the epitome of personal economic mismanagement. Once elected, many go on spending sprees. Members of parliament earn about ten thousand dollars per month tax-free, but most end up hopelessly in debt within a year of taking office. After signing away most of their earnings to money lenders, some end up pocketing as little as five hundred dollars a month. Press reports have described some who, after just two years in office, find themselves living in hiding from court bailiffs hunting them on behalf of angry money lenders.

Problems with money play out on a national scale too. Economic mismanagement after independence led to high inflation. As money failed to hold its value, salaries lost significance. The relationship between workers and employers deteriorated. This was especially evident in the public sector, which has been gripped in a vicious circle ever since. As salaries fail to keep up with living costs, civil servants find it difficult to sustain lifestyles that require everything from paying school fees to taking their families to popular holiday destinations, which many people now see as a social imperative. Discouraged, some public employees have responded by refusing to work hard, giving their bosses little reason to increase wages. A popular saying cynically holds that in Uganda, the government pretends to pay its civil servants, who in turn pretend to work. Worse than that, many public servants resort to making claims for non-existent expenses – for instance, by colluding with private contractors to inflate bills. Such theft is now rampant, though the word "theft" is carefully avoided. Instead, it is described with fancy terms like "abuse of office," "diversion of funds," "misappropriation," or at the worst, "corruption" or "embezzlement." Whatever it is called, failure to manage money at the national and personal levels has led to the normalization of theft in the country.

People today greatly misunderstand the role of credit in modern society. Until the government launched a privatisation drive in the mid-1990s, many people behaved as if money borrowed from banks was free; the largest banking chains belonged to government, and defaulters were rarely held accountable since they could bribe banking staff to approve their loans. When banks were privatised, they suffered massive defaults by borrowers. That helps explain today's astronomical bank lending rates; the few who don't default have to pay for the many who refuse to pay. So while inflation has been contained to be around six percent per year, most loans carry interest rates of about 30%.

Failure to understand money has led to another ill: the absence of a culture of saving. Ugandans commonly claim that their income is so low they cannot afford to save. Forced saving through the National Social Security Fund (NSSF) enables many workers to find some money awaiting them upon retirement. But alas, the funds usually end up being wasted. NSSF officials estimate that, on average, people who claim their savings at age 55 after thirty years or so of work blow their nest eggs in as little as two months. It is that sad. Savings accumulated over thirty years vanish in two months. That does not happen just in isolated cases; it happens in the majority of cases.

Most corrosive of all, money has turned land into a commodity. Peasants – at least two-thirds of the population – are the biggest losers. As legislation to prevent money laundering (part of the war against global terrorism) has shut down safe havens for stolen public funds in Europe, criminals have resorted to hiding their ill-gotten gains in real estate, buying up land anywhere they can get it.

The resulting surge in property values has led many Ugandans to see land as a better investment than bank accounts and other financial assets. Many young people are lured into getting titles for family or clan land and selling it to big people or their agents in cities. In many such cases, the boys then buy boda boda motorcycles in hopes of supporting themselves by offering taxi services to people in town. Girls get passports and air tickets to seek domestic employment in places like the Middle East, where many are sold by migrant labour agents into modern slavery. All too often, remaining family members only learn that they no longer own their land when demolition crews arrive to raze their homes to make way for "development" ordered by the new owners.

Unlike kings in much of Africa, Ugandan kings protected their people from slave traders. In the 17th century, for instance, Kabaka Ssuuna sent Arabs packing when they suggested that he sell them some slaves. But today, money enables slavers to operate more covertly and insidiously. Many of our youth who dispose of family assets to transport themselves abroad in search of better lives end up committing suicide after finding themselves forced into sex-slavery.

Today, the distortion money has wreaked on social values is complete and self-perpetuating. Much of the political instability in Uganda today can be traced to money. Politicians bribe voters to get elected. But once in office, they aren't accountable to the voters because they bought their positions, so they start trading their offices and legislative votes to the highest bidders. Voters have become so hardened that they want only money from political leaders instead of service or good policies, which they know won't be coming anyway. Now political leaders literally carry bags of money to throw at the people to buy their votes.

When the COVID-19 pandemic hit in 2019, it brought out the worst qualities that money has generated in Ugandan leaders. A nasty fight burst out between members of Parliament and the Executive (President) over money. MPs allocated themselves about six thousand dollars each, supposedly to administer relief work. President Museveni called the action "morally reprehensible." Noting that the lawmakers were not accounting for how they spent public money, he ordered that they hand the funds over to the accounting officers of the districts where their constituencies are located. MPs reacted swiftly by passing a motion of displeasure against the president. They also passed another motion against the Deputy Speaker, who they said had "betrayed" them by following the president's guidance.

And that is how, in Uganda, money made men mad.

If It Takes a Village, What Happens When the Village Dies?

By Caroline Ariba

They came and took
They said they would bring
They came again and just took
They didn't bring
They took it all
So we sat down and agreed
When they came again
We went with them

WHEN I WAS GROWING up, every dress I owned – even my Sunday best – had stains. Call them badges of honour – child-play honour. My brothers would climb fruit trees and shake branches heavy with ripening fruit while I spread my light blue dress to catch whatever fell. Soon, the dress would turn purple with splotches from jambula (java plum) and yellow from juicy mangoes. But that was no bother. It was so exciting!

Those stains remind me of a time when joy was free, laughter was plentiful, and sharing was a given. I can still hear my brothers counting to three before vigorously shaking the high branches. I can still hear the splutter of fruit hitting the ground as I ran to collect the harvest.

My village was in Kacumabala in the Bukedea District of eastern Uganda. Officially, I lived and went to school in Kampala and Mbale, rapidly growing urban areas. But school breaks invariably found me in the village. When my brothers came down from the fruit trees and my chase for falling fruit ended, we made our way to a giant tree that was in many ways the heart of the village. The sun was not as ferocious as it often is these days, but on days when it did beat down on us, the huge tree's shade provided all the air conditioning we needed.

We shared meals in the giant's shade. Food came from a different kind of tree – a family tree. Homesteads belonging to each of my uncles were arrayed like branches linked to the shade tree. Everyone with a kitchen brought their day's meal there, creating a buffet of sorts. A mound of atap (millet bread) was placed in the centre, and little plates of soup were given to everyone. We each took a pinch from the mound and scooped the flavourful soup. There was joy in sharing. As a rule, no food was left on any plate. No wonder children walked around with bellies like shiny balls and remained docile under the tree for hours after the meal was over.

Plenty of fruit. Bountiful harvest. Tree shade. We needed nothing more.

In those days, everybody looked out for and disciplined the children; a child belonged to no one in particular. When fights arose, elders settled them quickly. "Do you want to be like white people who only live with their cats?" they would admonish anyone who didn't want to share. "Or do you want to be like those people in Kampala who close their gates and only open them wide when someone dies?"

Every school holiday brought a harvest season (or was it the other way around?). First term was the maize season, second term the time for groundnuts and mangos, and third term was all about potatoes. Harvest season also was the time for drying and preserving. No matter how much we ate, an ample supply of produce remained to be preserved for the future or for planting. We woke early to help spread out the maize, ground nuts or peeled potatoes, and when it threatened to rain, we rushed to help take it back in, laughing all the way. When children left for school, older adults normally sat in the compound, ensuring that birds and goats wouldn't steal the drying produce. Once dried, the food was stored in granaries to last until the next harvest.

Roles were never assigned; they just happened. My tata (grandmother) spent most of her days under the shade tree. If there was a new baby, it was always in her arms. Little ones would snuggle close to her as she sang folk songs mimicking the sound of birds. When they finally found voices, they sang with her. "Kuku . . . Kariete . . . Kuku . . . Kariete," Tata and a toddler would sing, exposing their mostly toothless gums. My tata entertained the babies while their parents were away. Or was it the babies who entertained her? There's no saying. She loved it.

The parents made sure Tata had three warm meals and clean clothes every day. No one had to be told to do this; it just happened.

Evenings were magic. It didn't matter that we had no electricity. The moon took charge. We would lie on a mat in its pale light and make wishes to the shooting stars for the smallest of things. Nothing complicated – a well-ironed Christmas dress, a pair of shoes, maybe an Adidas ball. Life was simple, but the village brought more joy than I can describe.

Then something changed. No, *everything* changed. Today, the compounds that once were filled with children are grim, peopled mostly by neglected old women. Mango seasons come and go fast, as most of the fruit are now put on trucks and taken to nearby townships. Gardens are tilled by strangers because the owners would rather hire the land out for quick money. Harvest is no longer a social event; people harvest their produce for consumers in townships.

And the townships? They are unrecognizable. When I was young, adults went to Odukai, the village trading centre, only to buy specialty items like sugar, soap and kerosene for lamps. For children, market days were mainly about clothes, music, snacks and fun. Laughter coated the air. But out of nowhere, Kacumbala Trading Centre has grown from the few shops I remember into a little town. People who once lived in spacious compounds now crowd into its little rentals and gather around cinema halls to catch premiership games and bet away the day's income. Motorcycle taxi stages, peopled by young men who have abandoned agriculture, grow busier every day. It doesn't help that Mbale City, less than 20 kilometres away, is sending land buyers closer each day. Chunks of land that used to be gardens are being bought up by outsiders, who replace the gardens with concrete houses.

"This place was all trees," says my auntie, recalling the old days. "It was green and so quiet. There were plantations of maize, millet, sorghum and bananas. It was so hopeful. But look at it now. All the big trees are gone, and the land is quickly being sold to strangers. Look at that place," she says, gesturing toward a distant spot to drive her point home. "It was a swamp, and in the night, the freshest of air emerged from there. Now, someone has put up a structure."

Worse than the physical changes are social ones. "Everything is headed for the market these days, where people buy all of their food," says my Mum. Sharing is a forgotten habit. "If you pick a maize cob from someone's garden, you'll get slapped. If a hen wanders out of your compound, it will not be seen again." The thieves are not even strangers. They could be neighbours. "I blame the markets, radios and beer," Mum says. "Now there is a ready market for everything – even stolen chicken."

My auntie puts special blame on how money has come to define daily activities and interaction. "Maize. How can I *buy* maize? We never bought maize. You just picked some from the garden, roasted or boiled it, and ate it . . . There was so much to go around."

"The old days of abundance have given way to scarcity," she continues. "All my life, I never heard of people stealing food from the garden, but then again, everything is for sale these days; people sell food to buy food! What happened? Making matters even worse, some people roam around the trading centre gambling, leaving nothing for the children at home.

"It is no wonder that communal eating is no more; nowadays, couples stick to their own yards, and children are rarely seen playing except in their fathers' compounds. When it's harvesting time, a fee is charged before any work is done – yes, even by relatives. Money is everything now. Mothers line the roadside selling everything – even mangoes and boiled maize that used to come for free. Never could I have imagined buying mangoes and maize in the village."

All this leaves me feeling empty. Is the kind of society and love I remember disappearing forever? To try to understand what has happened, I turned to a man who left his village and settled in the sprawling Kampala region more than 20 years ago. He not only agreed to talk, but even offered to take me back to his original home to meet his two brothers – one who stayed behind and one who is struggling to fulfill hopes of moving to the city and building a new life there. And so I found myself riding with him over rain-soaked roads bound for Iraapa, a village 150 kilometres northeast of Kampala in what is now a sugarcane-growing region.

My companion, Suleiman Kairugala Etembeya, is a pioneer of sorts, part of an early wave of people who left their villages for the thriving city. The seven acres of land he shared with his brothers were not enough to support their families. He had dreams of becoming rich but saw no way to achieve that with so few acres. So he and his young wife bundled up their baby and moved into a tiny room in Iraapa trading center, where he used his meager savings to start a charcoal business. He wasn't yet 30 years old.

That turned out to be just a first step. Suleiman had completed the first stages of secondary school – more education than many in the village had – but he failed to achieve a better life in the small town. The even bigger city to the south, Kampala, beckoned him every time he turned on the radio. At the time, he recalls, radios were playing a popular hit by a singer named Rasta Rob. "If you want good things, come to Kampala," it said. "If you want to look good, come to Kampala."

After visiting a relative in the city, Suleiman's wife agreed that friends who had moved there looked healthy and happy. So he gathered seven sacks of charcoal – a nest egg worth about 100,000 shillings at the time – to start a new life, and they set out.

The city quickly taught him a painful lesson: Don't readily trust people. Still staying with a relative after spending less than two weeks in town, he met a man who told him he could find a market for the charcoal. The friendly fellow also offered to find the newly arrived family a home and a job. Suleiman, accustomed to generosity from his years in the village, accepted the man's help, handing over the charcoal and renting a house the fellow showed him. In a flash, the charcoal and money it was supposed to bring were gone, and Suleiman could find nobody who had heard of the company where a job supposedly awaited him.

A Key to City Life: Be Versatile.

Fortunately, Suleiman got a second chance. Another, better friend helped him get a job at a construction site, and he sought and received training to become a builder. That led to a job with the National Housing Corporation. He had his toehold in the city. For Suleiman it turned out to be just another step in a long journey full of pivots, changes and transitions. Even though he had training and a job in construction, he took odd jobs, amassing skills along the way. Eventually, the glamour of politics beckoned, which led him to what he calls better friends – including one who introduced him to a six-month training course in business skills. Soon, he was bidding on government jobs.

That was nice when it worked, but he learned that he couldn't always count on getting government jobs. So in 2012, he became a boda-boda man, joining the hordes of young men whose motorcycles swarm the city. He made some progress, and now could afford to take his children to schools in Namugongo and Kireka, suburbs of Kampala. He was still restless, though. "I decided to talk to my fellow youth," he says. "I told them we can't keep riding bodas without a culture of saving." He started a sacco (savings and credit cooperative) and persuaded his friends to pool their savings in it to raise funds to start businesses. As his share grew, he eventually had enough money to start making bricks from a piece of land a friend had asked him to watch. He also started a dry-cleaning business and opened a shop to sell chicken feed. He even tried to rear chickens himself; that didn't work, but the shop thrived, enabling him to build a modest house.

To this day, it is hard to tell what Suleiman does, not because he won't tell you but because he can morph into whatever the city needs him to be. In Kampala, a man like him has to be a jack of all trades. In recent years, he has become a land and house broker on top of everything else. Tomorrow, there's no saying what he will do. Whatever brings in the money, he says. As proof of his success, he boasts that he now has two wives.

"Turn here," Suleiman says, pulling me out of my thoughts about his successful transition from rural to urban living two decades ago. The car approaches a yard that leads to an unplastered house that can't have more than two rooms. We have reached our destination. The house's bare bricks have been there a while; there is no sign of new construction. Two smaller houses sandwich the structure, which is the main house in the compound. Smoke escapes from one – obviously the family's kitchen. A little boy drags a goat into the other; it could be a storage facility or a pen for animals.

Children scamper away from the vehicle. Soon, each toddler or small child is clinging to a slightly older child and shyly peeping at us in pure innocence. There is an older child for every little one. There are children everywhere; this looks like a little school.

"Tusangaire," a woman's voice calls out in greeting. She bundles her oversized skirt and drops to her knees in greeting. Soon another woman emerges, a baby clinging to her back and a bright cloth wrapped around her head. With a smile spread across her face, she too drops to her knees. All the little ones echo the women's salutations. Before Suleiman can make any introductions, a man in an unkempt, oversized jacket and a face creased with lines emerges from the main building and adds his voice to the greetings.

The biggest tree in the tiny compound defines the day's meeting place. Chairs are brought. The two women are co-wives. The children are theirs. The man is their husband, Juma Kafafa, Suleiman's big brother.

The difference between the two brothers is stark. Suleiman's skin glows, while his brother looks haggard. Despite being just a few years older, Juma stoops and walks slowly, as if he has thrown in the towel. During the introductions, one of the women runs off into the tiny smoke-filled structure, where the day's lunch – roasted corn – awaits. There is no village buffet; we soon learn that is a luxury that has long been abandoned.

As the conversation unfolds, their 71-year-old relative, Wilson Kategere Ngobi, arrives. Like most of the village's people, he wondered what a car, not a sugarcane truck, was doing in the compound. When he learns we have come to talk about how life in the village has changed, he jumps in without hesitation.

"Life was easy," he begins, recalling the old days. "We used to make juice from ripe bananas. When the British left and Uganda became independent, the Indians arrived and picked up where the colonisers had left off. They wanted cotton, so our grandparents planted it. In return, they brought us rice and sugar. We had not known these things."

The new goods were a mixed blessing. For everything that was introduced, he says, a new need arose. For example, before the Indians brought sugar, there were no cups, at least not the kind deemed modern. "We were using small pots for taking tea, but then the Indians kept teaching us these things," he says with hands mid-air.

Soon, a community that had no use for machines, let alone processed foods, changed. "When rice was introduced, the older people would not eat it. They thought the [outsiders] had brought rice to kill them," Ngobi says. "Even factory-made clothes – they taught us about them."

People began getting rid of bark cloth, the reddish material made from the abundant Mutuba tree that for centuries was the material that comprised the standard garb of Ugandans. Missionaries had denounced it as "satanic." In Ngobi's telling, merchants were more influential than priests in changing clothing styles. The village market was growing, and some of the items on sale were imported clothes. The society embraced them.

The 71-year old's description of how the modern era crept up on the community that could have cared less was interesting, but the younger people steered the conversation to a more immediate concern: education. Ugandans have an almost religious belief in it, but not just for enlightenment. Since the days of British colonialism, when academic performance was the key to getting a job with the colonial administrators, many have seen it as the ticket to a better life.

But the best schools are in a few major districts, mostly in the city and surrounding areas. If distance isn't a barrier, cost is. School fees in the best, urban schools are higher than in the more scattered rural schools. Many children who don't have the option of moving in with relatives residing near a secondary school give up on education altogether. Juma is one such person. "The reason I stayed here is that I did not go very far with education," he says. "When I did not get a job in government, I had nowhere to go except to stay here in the village."

Which would he prefer – living in town or the village? He'd rather live in the village, he says, but adds an important caveat: "If I had got a job here." In case I missed his point, he explains, "Here in the village we have a problem making money." Everyone bursts out laughing at this understatement, but with his next comment their mirth turns to silence. Many can't comfortably afford even a kilogram of meat, he says, because it costs 10,000 shillings (about $3).

Agriculture is not an option for many these days. Weather patterns have become unpredictable, and people who used to harvest 10 bags of produce per growing season can only take home three bags these days. For a family like Juma's, which has a few acres, the garden can't be an adequate source of income. At best, it provides the family's daily bread and maybe something extra to store for hard times. But he still needs money because village life is nothing like it used to be.

"Back in the early days, life was different. Today, everything is about money," he says regretfully. "You need to have money. Back in the days, we didn't struggle that much. Now, everything here is scarce." The scarcest item is money, which used to be needed for just a few items but now is required for everything, including food and a host of new items – mobile phones, for instance – that have come to be seen as necessities.

People have tried to adjust. Communities that used to grow food crops now mostly grow cash crops like sugarcane. But still they struggle. "People go and cut or dig in the sugar cane gardens and they get, say 3,000 (shillings) each day, which they use to buy necessities like soap and medicine," Juma notes. One might boost his daily income to 6,000 shillings by taking on odd jobs in the sugarcane plantations, but that's not guaranteed.

Many people, young and old, have resorted to selling their land. The elderly sell for cash to survive and maybe offset some bills like school fees. Young men sell or use the land as security for loans they hope will enable them to find a life far removed from agriculture; a favourite strategy is to buy a motorcycle and start offering taxi services. The would-be entrepreneurs often fail, but not before their land is taken over by debt collectors. They end up with no motorcycles, no land, and few prospects.

As I cast about for a villain to blame, money seems a strong candidate. After all, St. Paul himself said that "the love of money is the root of all evil." But Juma, as if he is reading my mind, points to another, more complicated reality. Even in the old times, he says, "we needed money, but when we got it, it was able to help." Land was available, protein was available, we had oranges, even milk," he notes, "But now you can't easily see a kraal for cows; people have occupied everywhere."

"Our grandfather had a lot a lot of land; you couldn't even tell how much, maybe more than 100 acres," he continues, his lack of precision demonstrating that land used to be so abundant that people never officially marked or policed property lines. The old man had 19 children, but he was able to give all his male children enough land to support their families the same way their ancestors had. Juma has even more children than his grandfather did – maybe 20. But there no longer is enough land for all of his heirs. Land fragmentation has gone about as far as it can go. Today, people live on plots that are a tiny fraction of an acre and have just three or four acres for agriculture. Their property lines are carefully marked. Every piece of land either has a building on it or is already being cultivated. Many youths are driven into urban centres in search of cash because they have no choice.

As for his own children, ten are still in school. Some girls are married and live in villages in Kamuli. Some boys who are not in school live in towns. And some have moved to Kireka, a township just outside of Kampala. "Those who have tried to study but get stuck run to Kireka to figure out life," he says. "So, they study a bit. Some are boda-boda drivers."

I ask him how he thinks their lives would be turning out if they had stayed in the village. His answer is blunt: "It would have been very bad."

Suleiman's younger brother, Ibrahim Khaima, joins the conversation. His message: A young man without much education faces more difficulty supporting himself in the city now than when Suleiman made the move two decades ago. Ibrahim has tried. With Suleiman's help, he found a man in the city who would help him get started as a boda-boda driver. The man offered him use of his motorcycle if he would pay 3 million shillings, due in a year and a half. That was a steep price, but Ibrahim gave it a go. Then the man took the bike back. Next, Suleiman found a corporation that was offering bikes to young men on the terms Isma had described – a 1,500,000 shillings down payment plus 70,000 shillings a week for two years. Ibrahim declined and kept looking, finally taking another deal; he pays a man 10,000 shillings a day to use a bike, but the bike is only available part of the time because the man uses it himself on some days and lends it to a cousin on others.

To supplement his meagre income, Ibrahim has tried some of his older brother's strategies. He tried making chapatis and selling them from a small stand, but the heat from the charcoal stoves made him sick. He looks for construction work but can't find much. He dreams of finding a regular job for a private company, but his hopes are unfulfilled. He contemplates joining the army. In the meantime, he scrapes by. He can make about 25,000 shillings a week, barely enough to cover rent and his daily diet of two kikomandos (a bean stew and unleavened bread dish). He skips breakfasts. Sometimes, he has to ask the restaurant to give him credit. His eatery is a shade tree by a dusty road. He can't afford utilities, so he lights his home by candlelight. His wife left him, taking their young child with her back to her village.

He is desperately short of options. "I reached a point that I thought maybe I could return to the village, but the truth is I cannot return to the village. I would become helpless," he says. Reminding me of old Ngobi's comment about how the modern economy creates new needs people never had imagined, he explains, "I would have no phone even."

While Kampala and other urban areas increasingly shape Uganda's culture and perception of itself, we are still primarily a rural society: About three quarters of our people still live in rural areas, and on weekends and holidays the roads are jammed with city people returning to visit friends and family in their villages. Unfortunately, when they reach their destinations, they often find places that are being left behind.

In the language of economists, who use money to measure our lives, the three quarters of Ugandans who work in agriculture account for just one quarter of our Gross Domestic Product. Agricultural output per capita is low partly because many farmers still live for subsistence, an "output" that isn't tabulated. But this can't hide a harsh reality: Many farmers who find themselves on ever-shrinking landholdings can't support their families. Again, it's a matter of money. President Museveni has said that a farmer can earn more than 20 million shillings a year from an acre of land, but to earn that much, a farmer would have to invest 10 million and somehow survive for a year before he can collect his profits, according to Charles Dikan, a relatively successful farmer in my village. Dikan says he is making ends meet only because his two brothers have left the village for jobs in the city, leaving him with 15 acres to farm on his own. When they return, he predicts they will have to divide the land. When that happens, his farming days will be over. Not surprisingly, he doesn't foresee a future on the land for his children. "Once they are educated," he says, "They will know what to do. So I am not scared." Whether for emphasis or to convince himself, he repeats his conclusion, "I am not scared."

Experts believe that the many village people who are leaving the land have the right idea. "People don't have enough land in the villages to do meaningful agriculture," argues Gemma Ahaibwe, a research fellow at the Economic Policy Research Center (EPRC) at Makerere University. "And if people have not gone to school, they can't buy their own assets. The parents have to distribute the little they have, but in the end, they can't do much."

As people flood into the city, they often bring a touch of the village with them. Some raise, slaughter, cook and deliver chickens ready-to-eat to busy working families. Unofficial "aunties" tend to young children of working parents. City slums all have jack-of-all-trade fixers who help newcomers find accommodation and go on to provide them a wide range of services, including help dealing with bureaucracies that bewilder immigrants. Women roast maize by the roadsides for sale to commuters too tired to make dinner after busy days. Hawkers sell newspapers and household goods to the people stuck in traffic jams at busy intersections. And, of course, hordes of boda boda drivers ferry passengers through and around ever-worsening tie-ups; it is not unusual for a boda driver to work long days and spend nights sleeping on his motorcycle. Then there are "Mama Nights," women who serve drinks and light meals in their homes to small groups of friends – an urban replica of the rural "drinking circles" of old, in which farmers gathered for drinks, camaraderie and information-sharing after long days working in their fields (the moniker "Night" is an apparent extension of the term used in the 1980s and 1990s for children who were born at night).

But these are just small reminders of village life transplanted to an urban setting, not the answer for most of the migrants from the countryside. If other societies are any guide, many of these functions eventually will be professionalised and become part of the formal economy. Most formal-sector city jobs are in services, which now account for 21% of employment in Uganda but 43% of GDP. The strong per capita output figure explains the relatively high incomes associated with work in the sector, but the sad fact is that service-sector growth is likely to be limited – and most of the jobs will continue to go to people with good educations. Many immigrants from rural areas can't land coveted service jobs.

Aside from service jobs, the other major option is manufacturing. This is understandably appealing, given Ugandans' economic dilemma. Manufacturing already has edged ahead of agriculture as a contributor to the country's overall economy, accounting for 26% of GDP. That's a remarkably high figure considering that manufacturing businesses employ just 6.5 percent of the workforce – greater payoff per worker than even services. But how can we build this sector? Paul Lakuma, another EPRC economist, says "agro-industry" – large-scale production, processing and packaging of goods – would make the most sense since it would build on Ugandans' familiarity with farming. But he says growth has been slow in that sector so far. "Government has built very nice processing plants, but people don't use them," he says. He remains hopeful, though; as people interact more in cities, Uganda may see a new wave of entrepreneurship, he says.

In the meantime, today's struggles may get worse. The World Bank estimates that Uganda's labour force is growing by about 700,000 people a year, while the economy is generating just 75,000 jobs. Lakuma says that modern economic institutions like insurance and pensions could provide a cushion, but these programmes have a long way to go before they can protect everybody. Out of an official labour force of 20 million people, only 2.8 million are saving in the 68 existing private pension plans.

Another set of policies seek to slow the birth rate – mainly by discouraging early marriages and encouraging more women's empowerment and spacing between births. These all make sense, but again, progress has been slow. In recent years, western aid organisations have touted the "demographic dividend" – the idea that slower population growth will reduce the number of dependents that working people must support, thus leading to increased economic growth and higher incomes. But I have trouble imagining village people reorganising their lives around the idea of reaping a "demographic dividend."

The road to the future seems full of blind curves, potholes and, I fear, many dead ends. And even success could turn out to be a mixed blessing. If we achieve the economists' dreams, will old-fashioned rural values – community, the sense of joy I remember, and a feeling of being connected to each other and the land – survive? And what of our grandparents, our parents, our brothers and sisters who still live in villages or are crowding into cities where their prospects are clouded? They defined who we are, and they are in trouble.

There are still glimmers of the old spirit I remember, though. They come from those who have the most to lose if the situation does not improve: Children.

As I start the return trip from Iraapa, I catch a glimpse of a trace of the village life I remember. Children are playing by the roadside. Their spirits seem undimmed by the gloomy sky, rains and ferocious roar of thunder. They sing. Their clothes, adorned with mud painted in play, remind me of the fruit stains that once decorated my childhood dresses. They try to outrun the wind with the same abandon I once felt trying to catch the fruit my brothers had sent raining down from trees.

On the road, overloaded sugarcane trucks can be seen slowly snaking along the slippery murram roads. One gets stuck. Children whose faces are stained with sugarcane run gleefully towards it to gather the tiny canes that fall off. It's a game. When the engine starts and the truck resumes its slog, the children cheer while nibbling on their rescued cane. Food crops are a luxury. The children will chew until they are called for the day's meal, if there is one. Maybe it will be sweet potatoes this time; their diet, like the rain, is not predictable anymore. But at least for now, they cheer for the truck that has started moving again. At least one farmer will be paid cash today.

Of Healers, Quacks . . . and Confusion

By Joseph Elunya, Sr.

NOT VERY LONG AGO – within memory for many people who are still alive today – nightfall often brought the sound of singing and drumming in the shrouded farmland of Teso, a region in eastern Uganda that is my ancestral home. The sound is not heard anymore, but it echoes in my mind – a remnant of a culture that, I am sad to say, is disappearing.

The sound came from traditional healers summoning ancestors to help people who were ill or troubled. The rites marked a moment of anxiety and worry for those who participated, but they also expressed common beliefs that held society together. Healers were pillars of the community who offered hope in the face of distress and embodied a shared understanding of the nature of existence beyond what the eye can see.

Much has changed in the past 40 years. Today, traditional healers are no longer leaders in Teso. Many are gone, and those who remain find themselves at the centre of a cultural war. Doctors trained in western medicine dismiss them as agents of superstition. Pentecostal revivalists denounce their practices as satanic. Quacks invade their turf, cluttering the airwaves with bogus claims that they have the healers' powers and can cure anything from infertility to cancer and HIV/AIDS. Government authorities try periodically to regulate the fakes, but often to no avail.

People live through the clamour in a kind of suspended animation, neither fully believing nor completely dismissing traditional healers. More often than they care to admit, some people – even well-educated ones – still seek healers' help, especially when medical science lets them down. They often make their visits these days furtively, almost shamefully, though.

As a journalist, I believe in science and modern ways, but I have turned to traditional healers myself on some occasions. They may not always be right, but I am convinced they know much that so far has eluded modern science. I believe their knowledge should be preserved. But in today's confused and contentious climate, preservation of such indigenous knowledge is far from assured.

The battles swirling around traditional healing are symptoms of a larger social breakdown. When I was a child and spiritual healers thrived in Oderai, my village, Teso was different from what it has become. I cherish the days gone by. I remember going on hunting expeditions with other children, armed with catapults (some westerners call them slingshots) to fling stones at birds, squirrels and fish. We felt pure joy when our stones hit their targets. The hunt and the trophies we brought home made us feel like men, not just because we killed our prey but because our trophies helped feed our families.

At the age of ten or twelve, we ventured out of our parents' houses and built our own huts (though we stayed safely in our family compounds). We learned how to make clay bricks and assemble them into structures held together by mud, and how then to look for reeds to weave into roofs for them. Our parents were pleased with our construction skills. The huts were cool during dry seasons, and the thatch roofs kept us dry and turned downpours into gentle lullabies that coaxed us to sleep.

Young girls contributed to household affairs in many ways, from fetching water to grinding millet or sorghum. They stored drinking water in clay pots that kept it cool and gave it a delightful taste that I miss to this day. They used small grinding stones to make flour for food for their families. Our parents told us that if any of us sat on the family grinding stones, our mothers would die, but that was just a ploy to keep us away; children hardly wore any clothes in those days, so sitting where food was made would be unsanitary.

We were as resourceful at play as we were at work. Children made balls from banana fibre and fashioned dolls from clay and leaves. Meanwhile, men toiled in the fields by day and cooled off in the evenings by sharing malwa brew. This was an important event – a chance to compare notes on issues affecting everybody's well-being. We called after-work drinking circles acowa iteso – the source of knowledge.

And then there were the special days. When a child was born, all clan members would have a big party. Elders would put a small drop of malwa, a local brew, into the newborn's mouth to welcome him or her into the clan. Then the rest of the drink would be passed among clan members. The child would be given a clan name during this ceremony. The first harvest of millet also was an occasion for making merry. A goat or chicken would be slaughtered, and people would paste bits of food on their faces in a giddy celebration before eating.

One of the most special days was Christmas. It was the only day in a year that we put on "new" clothes; of course, the clothes were second-hand, but they did not carry the smell of freshly washed clothes like everything else we wore. Ironically, we took pride in wearing unwashed shirts or dresses because that signalled to everyone that they were new. The whole clan would join the feast. Merrymaking would last from Christmas until early February.

In the Teso of my childhood people regularly consulted traditional healers, herbalists and diviners about health and spiritual issues. Healers' power rested on a belief that they could mediate between the living and the ancestral world. Sickness was often assumed to arise because the ancestors were angry, and healing occurred when they were appeased.

Healers were not a homogeneous group. Some conducted rites to heal people. In sessions I attended, the healers sacrificed animals, beat drums, sang and danced the whole night until the sick person became possessed and told people what they had to do to appease the ancestors. The healers then gave the sick person herbs to drink. After such sessions, the ancestors' demands would be met, and the patients would get well. I cannot explain how it all worked, but I saw it happen.

Other healers administered concoctions of herbs without evoking spirits. They were a distinct group who said they inherited knowledge of the healing power of various herbs from their ancestors. They zealously guarded this knowledge, passing it on only to a carefully selected few. This is the indigenous knowledge I dearly hope we can preserve.

People also use the term "witchdoctor" to describe healers; the term often carries negative connotations, as it often is used to describe people believed to use mystical powers to harm others.

Spiritual and herbal healers gained credibility because people were convinced their methods worked. But people did not take that just on faith. Word quickly spread through villages about which healers were effective at treating which afflictions. This smoothly-functioning marketplace was upheld by clan elders, who would refer sick people to healers, in effect certifying which ones were reliable.

Today's Teso is almost unrecognizable. Among the most notable changes, it is awash with fake healers. Many of them not part of the community. They are unknown to elders, whose scrutiny they avoid by flooding the airwaves with wild claims about having "miracle" cures for just about everything. If you take a bus ride to eastern Uganda, you are sure to encounter some of them in person, handing out flyers filled with wild and unprovable promises. The old checks and balances have been weakened or ceased to exist.

Between 2000 and 2005, when I worked with Voice of Teso, a local radio station in Soroti, I came in touch with several herbalists, both genuine and fake. A young man who called himself Yahaya used to come to the station periodically, paying us to announce on radio that he had travelled from Uganda to Dar es Salaam, Tanzania, to get better herbs and more healing powers from the ancestral world. He told us privately that he was just going to his home in nearby Mbale and had never been to Dar es Salaam. But we needed the advertising revenue, so we crafted radio announcements to help the deception. "Dr. Yahaya from Zanzibar has returned to Soroti town with better herbs and more spiritual power from the ancestral world to solve all your problems," said one. "Visit him, and you will never be the same."

Quacks often substitute fancy names for their real names. Another herbalist pretender we promoted called himself Dr. Dumba wa Dumba. "Are you sick and have you tried to visit all hospitals, and yet you are not realizing any change?" asked one of his typical advertisements. "Dr. Dumba wa Dumba has the answer. He treats all kinds of diseases that have failed to be treated in hospitals and by other herbalists."

I once visited a traditional herbalist who had advertised her services on radio stations, saying she could heal all kinds of sicknesses in return for just two eggs. When I arrived, I joined a queue waiting to see her. Her "assistant" asked me why I had come, and I explained that I was a journalist seeking an interview. The assistant went back inside. A few minutes later, I saw the herbalist flee through the back door and disappear into the nearby bush. I later learned she suspected that I was a government official.

The only surprise in that story may be that she feared the government. It has little, if any, clout. Traditional healers are supposed to register with their village chiefs or chairpersons of local councils, specifying their original homes and what services they perform. If a healer is not born in the area, he is supposed to present a letter of recommendation from the leaders of his previous village to prove he is truly a healer and person of good repute. But in practice, council officials rarely vet new healers who come to their area. Most are interested mainly in the fees they can get in return for their stamps of approval. Many herbalists have told me they only see government officials when law enforcers want to extort bribes from them.

The medical code of ethics prohibits health practitioners from advertising their services. The National Drug Authority periodically tries to enforce that rule, but it has no power to act against any radio station that ignores its directives. And while the Uganda Communications Commission officially has power to enforce the law on advertising, it has only one official in all of eastern Uganda – a 40,000-square kilometre region that is home to more than nine million people and has 50 radio stations. The commission occasionally warns a radio station to desist from hosting or advertising traditional herbalists, but only if it receives a complaint.

Voice of Teso stopped running advertisements by traditional herbalists after receiving a warning from the National Drug Authority. But the station acted mostly because it feared losing listeners in the devoutly Christian area, where churches denounce traditional medicine as satanic, according to station Manager Simon Ochen. Teso Broadcasting Services, another station, also stopped running advertisements for traditional herbalists. Julius Esegu, the manager, said the herbalists kept "backstabbing" each other with accusations of fakery, and the station could not determine which ones were genuine.

Despite this, you can still turn on the radio and hear outlandish, unproven claims. And in a sad footnote to this story of government failure, the only herbal medicines that are legally allowed to be advertised in agriculturally rich Teso, which has a long history of herbal medicine, are processed natural-healing products from China.

It is hard to pinpoint any single major cause for the disappearance of the old ways. No doubt there are several factors. In the late 1980s, cattle rustlers from Karamoja took away most of the region's cows, effectively ending the practice of sacrificing animals to appease ancestors. Around that time, a group called the Uganda People's Army launched a five-year rebellion against the central government. In response, the government ordered civilians to leave their villages and stay in camps. Those who stayed back risked being killed by the rebels or government soldiers. Traditional healers were especially vulnerable because the rebels targeted them on the belief they were witches. Most healers responded by going underground. Their drums went silent; beating drums at night, a common feature of traditional healing, became too risky because it would signal people's whereabouts to government or rebel soldiers. On top of all that, the region suffered severe famine.

During these unsettled times, Pentecostal revival churches began converting new members en masse. Missionaries successfully urged people to burn the traditional shrines built for ancestral spirits and to follow Jesus Christ instead. I have always wondered if people put their faith in God because they had grown tired of trying to appease the ancestors, whose dissatisfaction and demands for appeasement appeared to be insatiable.

At the same time this was happening, elders started to lose their influence. In the old days, they safeguarded family and clan assets – and thus solidified social bonds – by deciding what land and cows young clansmen would inherit and whom they could marry. Youths were compelled to uphold cultural customs to ensure their chances of inheriting good land and winning good brides. But as the population grew in the late 1990s, the elders ran short of land and cows to bestow to all their children. As hopes to inherit land faded, more and more youths sought opportunities in cities. Unlike their elders, they came to view land not as a sacred trust belonging to the clan but as a private asset that they could sell to finance businesses like motorcycle or taxi operations, chapati kiosks, salons and more in urban centres. Others just wanted cash so they could pursue urban lifestyles – a short-term, but nevertheless very tempting, escape.

Eventually, young men convinced people to end the system of leadership based on age and seniority; henceforth, it was decided, leaders should be chosen through elections. As more and more young men unattached to clan traditions got elected, they sanctioned the sale of clan property, hastening the conversion of land into a commodity to be sold to the highest bidder. The buyers often were outsiders. The changes have been profound. In the past, people knew and shared family and religious bonds with their neighbours, but today when I walk through my old village I don't know most of the people who live there.

When I see how my own relatives are selling land, I sometimes wonder what would happen if our grandfather came back to life and found out that all the land he bequeathed to us had been sold. I also wonder what future children will face since many of them are not going to school and the land that was once a sure source of livelihood has now slipped from their hands.

Today, Teso is but a shadow of what it was when I was growing up. Children no longer hunt for birds or build their own huts. Expanding population has eaten up much of the grassland that provided bird habitats and grass for thatched roofs; ten years from now, our children will only be able to see a grass-thatched house in photographs. Living in the kind of modern, tin-roofed houses that have become increasingly common, they will not know the joy of sleeping under a grass roof they built themselves.

Today, extended families have shrunk or even disappeared. While children used to call their uncles "Daddy" in recognition of the strong role they played in their lives, they now use the more formal title "Uncle." Christmas is no longer an extended, community-wide celebration. Now, it is just celebrated within nuclear families, and it lasts only a day or two before everybody scatters.

As elders have lost their power and community solidarity has vanished, authentic traditional healers have also become few. Because people no longer know their neighbours, the old check on charlatans – grassroots community information – is weak. Government is supposed to fill the gap, but it so far has proven to be, at best, an imperfect protector of public well-being.

Today, people usually are referred to hospitals for health ailments and to evangelical pastors for spiritual cleansing, but institutional roles often get mixed up. While hospitals are valued for their treatment of so-called modern diseases like diabetes and high blood pressure, people still turn to traditional healers to treat afflictions like snake bites and ailments that elude medical science and are attributed to witchcraft. And while the Christian pastors connect people to God and Jesus Christ instead of ancestors, they still play a role akin to traditional healers, singing and drumming in ways that whip their congregations into cathartic frenzies to drive away demons.

Some authentic healers are adapting to changing times. A new breed is staking its credibility not so much on spiritual claims as on empirical methods akin to science – actual observation of how herbs work in practice. They have allies among young people interested in "natural healing." Participants in a Ugandan Facebook group called Healing Naturally Together share notes on possible remedies for rashes, ulcers, bad breath, recurring uterine infections, motion sickness, tonsillitis, haemorrhoids, blocked fallopian tubes and arteries and more. The group has almost 50,000 participants and is still growing.

Will herbalism prove to be effective as it is removed from its traditional, spiritual context? Africans are practical and likely will try whatever they think will work. As western diseases become more common, it stands to reason that treatments proven to be effective in the West are gaining more Ugandan adherents. But some old African ailments still defy modern medical treatment. People in Teso periodically complain about intense leg pain, for instance. Tradition holds that the pains result when people with hostile intent spread a poisonous substance in their enemies' footsteps. When such pains strike, most people in Teso know that only a spiritual healer can help.

There also is a kind of excruciating headache that seems to baffle modern doctors. Local people say it results when people who wish other people ill somehow throw stones or bones that end up inside their victims' skulls. I once had such a headache. When it hit me, the pain was unbearable. I couldn't work or even eat. I went to a clinic, where doctors told me I had malaria and treated me accordingly. It didn't work. In desperation, I turned to a traditional healer, who told me I had stones in my head. She brewed a concoction of herbs and gently put them on my forehead in a warm compress. The next day, I could eat for the first time in days, and the day after that, the headache was completely gone.

I am a modern man, and I believe in science. But modern medicine couldn't heal me. Traditional medicine did. Many people have had the same experience. The only explanation I know is that there really were stones in my head although I did not see them. Someday, maybe modern science will offer a different explanation for the affliction and for why traditional treatment worked. But for now, in the absence of such knowledge, we believe what we already know.

A Cultural Melange

Charles Ekimu is a survivor – a member of the shrinking band of traditional healers in eastern Uganda. In his five decades as a healer, he has been deemed a pillar of society in some quarters and condemned from pulpits as satanic. For a time, he had to go into hiding from a rebel army that was bent on killing him and his brethren. He is now safe but keeps a low profile. I visited him at his shrine in Orwadai village on the outskirts of Soroti town in eastern Uganda.

Outwardly, Ekimu conveys no evidence of the tumult he has experienced. He dresses just like other men in the village, and there are no shrines around his home (there are no visible shrines anywhere in Teso anymore). I learned after we spoke that his shrine is now simply a converted room in his house; instead of the animal skins, gourds and beads one would expect to find in a traditional shrine, his shrine has just some baskets filled with cowry shells and several bottles of herbs. His comments – and the reactions of current spiritual leaders to things he told me – demonstrate that the spiritual lives and health strategies of people in Teso remain in flux, with some traditional healers posing as priests and some priests who practice something that looks a lot like witchcraft.

Here is Ekimu's story and two responses to it:

> *My name is Charles Ekimu. I am originally from Ajonyi village, Katine sub-county, Soroti district. I have been a traditional herbalist since 3 May 1967. I mostly treat mental ailments, syphilis, elephantiasis, blindness, poisoning, and swellings in the stomach and legs. All this I do with the help of the supernatural powers, which granted me this knowledge through my ancestors.*

> *When I was 12 years, I fell sick and became mad. I was taken to my grandfather, who was an herbalist. He told me that the spirits of the ancestors wanted me to become an herbalist. He then performed some rituals, and I became healthy again. Then I was taken home to set up a shrine for treating people. At first, it was hard for me, but as time went on, I got used to it. I have managed to build two permanent houses using proceeds from treating patients with traditional medicine.*

> *To become an herbalist, a person traditionally would undergo training on the use of herbs for treatment, and then be given herbs to drink that enable ancestors to come to him in dreams with revelations about which herbs treat various diseases. That used to be the way to become an herbalist. But today, some people just wake up and declare that they are herbalists without undergoing the right procedure. They advertise their services on radio, but they do not have papers of accreditation. Those of us*

who underwent training do – from the village, sub-county and even up to district level. Also, genuine healers do not advertise their services over the radio. We get our clients through referrals. If I give you medicine and it works, then you will tell another person, "Ekimu is a good man – he knows his work." I don't have to advertise my services over the radio.

The government should deal with such fake people. It should make all of us prove that the herbs we have really can cure people of ailments. Any person purporting to be an herbalist who fails such a test should be struck from the list of genuine ones.

We also are facing a challenge from religious groups that duplicate our services. For example, some religious leaders claim that they can remove charms from homes. They use our ancestral spiritual powers to chase away the evil spirits, but they claim that they are getting their power from God. They are just blindfolding their followers. Some so-called pastors are our fellow herbalists who failed in the business because of competition and then ran to the church to perform what they claim are miracles from God.

There is no way a born-again man can come to a home and say, "Dig here and there," and then pick charms that were buried years back in a pot unless that person is using the spiritual powers that have been our work from time immemorial. They have messed up our work because they keep condemning our practices while hiding behind religion. Some of them burn our shrines. That can cause problems. We inherit two types of spirits from our ancestors – those that get into you personally and those that dwell in the whole clan. When you burn their dwelling places, they can become dangerous and cause pestilence for a whole family or clan. That's why we now have very complicated diseases that are hard for us to treat. The ancestors are angry.

There have been a lot of changes in traditional medicine, and treating some diseases is a challenge. In the past, people mostly ate wild greens, but now people are eating all kinds of foods. Because they have abandoned traditional foods, we are now having challenging diseases like cancer, diabetes, and high blood pressure. In the past, we treated few diseases – like syphilis – that we could easily diagnose and treat using roots from certain trees.

Also, in the past, we performed rituals to drive away evil spirits. Nowadays, people have embraced Christianity, and they ignore us. As a result, the spirits are now wandering and causing more complicated diseases. Some of them appear as women who dupe unsuspecting people into making love with them. This has resulted in complicated diseases that are hard to treat.

There is another big difference between past traditional healers and the ones of today. In the past, we would toss coins in front of patients to learn from the spirits of our ancestors what kind of sickness patients had. But today, most traditional healers use evil spirits (ifaru) to help them diagnose ailments. And you can't tell whether the voices you hear during sessions are the herbalists or spirits speaking because the herbalists work behind curtains.

The future looks bleak because most people have embraced Christianity. Even when they have been bewitched, they opt to go to the hospital. It's still common here for someone to bewitch another person's legs. Traditional herbalists can treat the problem, but at the hospital, people are told that the problem is caused by diabetes. Then they are given the wrong prescription and end up dying. Also, only we can effectively treat poison; in case of poison, we give patients a concoction that can make people vomit the toxins.

Government has been trying to regulate our activities by making us form groups and pay 150,000 Uganda shillings for membership. It promised it would give us licenses and machines that can process our herbs into modern medicines. We need this support because the current generation is shunning herbs in preference for drugs. But the government is not helping us. It abandons us after collecting the money.

I discussed Ekimu's observations with two respected members of the clergy.

Retired Bishop Justine Edweu, the overseer of the National Fellowship of Born-Again Christians in the Teso region, acknowledged that some witchdoctors pose as pastors. *"These people have lost customers, so they hide behind religion to continue their trade,"* she says. *"They claim to be prophets, but they are purely witchdoctors. They should not deceive people."*

The bishop opposes the use of traditional medicine.

Personally, I wouldn't recommend that anybody go to a traditional healer for anything. I don't see the point. We have hospitals where people get the best treatment. These people (herbalists) don't know the quantity of medicines that one should take. They just give their medicines wholesale. It can be a danger to your life. So my advice to people who are suffering from diseases such as syphilis is that it's useless to go to a traditional healer. Just seek better management from the hospital. And for those who are having problems with demons, seek spiritual help from church leaders who can cast them away.

Pastor James Prince Eparu of Elim Pentecostal Church, on the other hand, believes there is nothing wrong with using traditional medicine – provided the practice isn't linked to traditional spiritual beliefs.

I have no problem with anyone taking herbs. My problem is the source. If someone has an idea of an herb that can heal an ailment and he can pick, prepare, take it and get well, there is no problem. Herbs don't belong to the devil. Some herbs have very high food values. The modern medicines that we take come from herbs. It's people who work for the devil who have made herbs bad. Witchdoctors work with evil spirits. Everything they give as medicine is, first of all, dedicated to evil spirits, so herbs that come from them come with evil spiritual powers behind them that have double effects. They might heal you, but your life might not remain the same. If you get herbal medicine from a witchdoctor, it's wrong.

Witchdoctors who join the church are doing much harm, according to Pastor Eparu.

I can tell you a story that happened in our village. There was a guy who came to our village [and stayed with a certain family]. He would go around praying for people, but when he left that family, everybody started running mad – even the girls who were married far away developed mental problems.

Just as Pastor Eparu decries some traditional healers who masquerade as priests, he expresses concern about priests who perform spiritual healing sessions that once were a preserve of traditional healers. He cites efforts by some priests to expel demons. In early Teso, demons were considered the lowest ranking of other-worldly beings. Originally, elders bought them from witchdoctors to protect cattle; they would appear at night, either in human or animal form, and then vanish. Today, many homes in Teso are thought to be haunted by these demons, and people commonly turn to religious sect leaders – especially Pentecostals – to chase them away. Pastor Eparu does not question the existence of demons, but he is troubled that some priests seem to accept a perception that demons have the power to create spirits, a higher level of otherworldly being that can shape day-to-day events and even people's destinies. Moreover, he says, some pastors practice witchcraft by "chasing" demons away.

> *This business of telling people that spirits have produced demons and then praying and dancing around to chase the demons away is wrong. Demons don't produce spirits. I have witnessed these people (pastors) come in the name of praying, and they will come and pray and fast for three days. The third day they say they remove demons. But can we chase a demon? The word 'chasing' is not in the Bible. 'Casting out demons' is, but these people run after demons. These people are very violent; they uproot trees and burn things. Did Jesus uproot trees the way these people are doing? Did Jesus run after demons?*

> *Christians should not involve themselves in things of witchcraft.*

Such is life in Teso today, where people live in two worlds. The confluence of traditional and contemporary beliefs creates a confusing mix.

Dance of Death

By Regina Asinde

I WILL NEVER FORGET the day I saw my father dancing at his brother's funeral. That may sound odd, but among my people, the Jopadhola tribe who live in Tororo District in eastern Uganda, it is a standard part of funeral rites. Growing up, I used to think that we celebrate, rather than mourn, death. But the truth is much darker, as I learned through a harrowing struggle that began in childhood and grew to shake the very foundations of my being in my adult years. This is the story of my spiritual odyssey.

You must understand at the outset that the Jopadhola, like many Africans, believe people do not cease to exist when they die, but become spirits that live on – most of the time in a different world, but sometimes in ours. The living are expected to cater to their ancestors' needs. If they do not, the deceased become vengeful. There is a saying that dead people are not friends; when they feel slighted, they retaliate without mercy.

My first close encounter with death was when my father's only brother died in March 2001. I joined my father and the rest of my family to send him off. My father was a very reserved person, rarely given to displays of emotion. But when the distinctive funeral music known as fumbo started to play and he began dancing as custom dictates, he was quickly transformed. Tears coursed down his cheeks, and his t-shirt became damp with a mix of rain and sweat. Barefoot, he danced the night away, finally falling exhausted on the bare, muddy ground in the early hours of the next morning. I could not imagine what had driven him to such a frenzy. People later said it was good he had danced for his brother; maybe then the pain of his loss would not be so sharp. But I did not understand.

Five months later, my father died. My siblings and I joined other close relatives in dancing for him. We danced out our grief through the cold, dark night and early morning. By the time my father's corpse was lowered into the grave, I had no strength left. The dance had drained me physically and emotionally. It seemed to unleash forces more powerful than I could bear.

I had a close but complicated relationship with my father. It was no secret that I was his favourite child. I cannot really say why. Perhaps because I was named after his mother, or maybe because he was my favourite family member too. In 1987, when I was five years old, he separated from my mother and started a new family. My three sisters and I had to join my step-siblings and stepmother. I felt like a stranger in this new family. A year later, I was sent to live with my grandmother in the village. I spent more than three years there before re-joining the family in 1991. Father visited me often. For a long time, he and grandmother were the two people with whom I felt most comfortable. He was a quiet man, calm and collected. We related mostly in deeds and silence. I often would sit quietly watching as he worked on his laptop or listened to music while consuming cup after cup of coffee. Sometimes I would enter data into the computer for him. When I needed to communicate something, I would write him long letters. Most were rebukes or complaints about ways he had offended me or the family and how he could rectify the wrongs he committed. The only indication that he read them would be an uncomfortable silence between us. After a day or two, the silence no longer felt uncomfortable. I knew then that everything was forgiven, and my gripes were under consideration.

Silence was also my language of love with grandmother. She spoke to me through stories. She taught every lesson through one tale or another, often about plants and animals that talked and displayed human characteristics. It seemed she always had a story ready to feed my curious mind. But there also were moments of silence when we just sat and listened to nature, which was full of life around us.

Both my father and grandmother ignited in me a longing for the knowledge and wisdom I sensed they both held. The family followed the Catholic faith, but my father became a Mormon during a period he lived in Scotland. The new wife he brought home also had converted, so we practiced Mormonism. I no longer understood the world in which I lived – why my father had left only to come home with a new family, why my mother was no longer a part of our lives, why I had to be sent to live with my grandparents, why I then had to be taken from my grandparents and sent to a boarding school, and why I had to go for holidays to a home where the language spoken was totally foreign (my stepmother was of a different tribe, so we spoke English, which I did not know).

I chose to hide in stories – to escape to worlds where children were loved, people sought truths and found them, where there was a spiritual power controlling and determining their future, where battles were fought and won or lost, where heroes failed and cried and got broken but there was always hope, a promise of better things to come. The amazing stories of the Bible and Book of Mormon fed my yearning mind, though I was frightened by the notion that we were in the last days – the end times – and that if Christ found me unworthy, I would be damned forever.

Grandmother was a devout Catholic who recited the rosary and knew all the novenas that had to be said at various times. She always paid her tithe on time, went to church on Sundays and was the first to commit to anything that needed to be done at church. But she was also the very embodiment of a traditional person. Maybe she adopted Catholicism easily because the entire way of life of the Jopadhola, from conception to death, was wrapped up in customs that had to be followed to the last letter; for them, Catholicism was just another set of rituals people had to practice without question, even if they did not quite understand them.

As a child, I delighted in performing and participating in Jopadhola rituals. No one explained to me why a newborn baby had to sleep on fresh banana leaves that had been sprinkled with fresh cow milk to be recognised as a child of the clan. Or why and how a child might reject a given name at birth and cry unceasingly until the name was changed. The only similarity between Christianity and traditional beliefs was their belief that disobedience had dire consequences. If one did not obey and follow the rules, the deities would punish her severely, possibly even with death or its spiritual equivalent – eternal damnation.

Jopadhola beliefs, like Christianity, had a frightening side. Once, when it rained heavily, I watched my grandfather thrust his spear into the ground to command the heavens to stop – and they did. Grandfather was a mystical being. If he predicted something, it usually came to pass. I was ordered to watch my words and actions when around him because he had a "bad tongue." When I was older, I learned that meant he had the power to curse or bless.

In the years after my parents' separation, grandmother fell ill with a mysterious sickness. After several visits to the hospital, where the medical personnel failed to diagnose the problem, the priest of our clan's shrine said she was suffering from a spiritual sickness caused by witchcraft. Her co-wife was accused of buying some powerful spirits from the coast, commonly known as djinns, to torment and kill her. I remember her shouting that these spirits had come to take her away. In those moments when she was in torment, she would grip my hands, begging me not to let her be taken by the djinns. My mind is blank on how exactly she was healed. All I know is that one night she was screaming, imploring me not to let the djinns take her, and then passing out. I must have passed out too, for the next thing I knew, she was cured. I tried to question grandmother about it later, but she kept silent and then changed the topic.

My uncle's funeral taught me much about the Jopadhola way of dealing with death. During his funeral, we slept in the compound on dry banana leaves and participated in various traditional rituals. As is the custom among the Jopadhola, he was bathed and dressed in his best clothes. A fire was kept burning for him and friends, in-laws and relatives who came to keep vigil. After a few days, the fire was allowed to burn out, the ashes were collected and poured at the foot of a banana plant. A cock or chicken was slaughtered as a sacrifice, and a meal was prepared for the mourners. Millet beer was also offered to the deceased.

According to custom, my uncle's body was wrapped in white sheets and blankets brought by his children, sisters, brothers, and parents. The number of sheets and blankets shows how much a deceased person was loved or valued. Each clan has a specific compass direction that the head of the deceased should face when buried. Men are buried in front of their homes to signify that they are the heads of the homes and still watch over them. Wives are buried next to their husbands so they can keep each other company, while children are buried near their grandparents so they can provide company to each other. Twin children used to be buried under the verandas of their parents' houses, just outside where their parents slept, but this practice ceased with the construction of permanent houses, often with cement verandas. Twins are believed not to die, though, so it is taboo to mourn them with loud wails or even tears, especially if one of a set of twins is still living. It is taboo even to say that a twin has died. Instead, they are said to have just taken a walk to the spiritual realm.

Such funeral rituals and norms are found, with minimal variations, in most tribes within Uganda. But the funeral dance I saw my father perform is unique to the Jopadhola. Women punctuate the beat of the long fumbo drum with shrill, anguished wails, interspersed with recitations of their relationships with the deceased and blow-by-blow narration of how he died. At my uncle's funeral, the dancers, mostly women and children, occupied a makeshift arena in front of the house where the corpse lay; periodically, a group of the women danced to the doorway of the house and called out my uncle's name, begging him to get up and speak to them. Some women danced away from the house, all the time narrating his life's story and asking who would be doing the things he used to do. Most of these mourners carried items that belonged to him, while others tied different garments of his around their waists. My late uncle had been the headteacher of a nearby primary school. A cousin of mine carried his briefcase and played the role of him walking home after a long day at school. Some kept telling him to send their regards to other deceased relatives, giving him different messages to deliver to the spiritual realm.

My father made no sound as he danced. The only testaments to his anguish were the silent tears running down his face and the frenzied movements of his big body trying to keep pace with the throbbing drums. He was not schooled in the art of dance, and his movements were not coordinated. Apparently, his body was just responding instinctively to commands from the drums, wails and his emotions.

I saw my father again about five months later. I had gone home from the boarding school where I was studying for my Uganda Advanced

Certificate in Education. He wasn't feeling well, battling a persistent cough that he said had been diagnosed as pneumonia. One morning while he picked maize from the small garden in front of the house, I saw something that left me shaken and confused. He called out to me, telling me to light the charcoal stove on which we would roast the maize. When I looked up to where he stood, all I could see was a skeleton, bare bones with no flesh, speaking to me. I was frightened, and I looked away fast. When I looked back, the skeleton was gone and all I saw was my big father.

He died a few weeks later. I travelled home to our village, Mulanda, with my two sisters. Our arrival triggered wails and dirges. As I stood before my father's corpse lying on the bed in the sitting room, I saw grandmother seated silently at the head of the bed. I moved to her and stared down at her in silence. After a few seconds, she said, "Your son is gone. He is no more." Referring to me as herself may sound strange, but even my father called me "mother." Perhaps the family's attitude bespoke a deeper reality: From early in my life, I had a soul tie with my grandmother. It would be a source of much pain later.

I don't really remember much about the rest of the day except that later that night, my siblings, close relatives, and I danced through the night for my father. By the time his body was lowered into the grave the next day, all I felt was an overpowering sense of connectedness to him. Though I didn't see him, I knew he was watching over me.

In the West, people sometimes talk about "coming to closure" — the process of putting sad or upsetting thoughts behind them. That never happened after my father's funeral. For years after his death, I saw him repeatedly in my dreams. His presence, which I had felt when I danced to the beat of the fumbo, was so palpable that I expected to see him in the physical realm too. I wasn't the only one who felt this. Some people told stories about him keeping watch over the family house. A number of relatives testified that they had seen him standing under the big mango tree at the edge of the compound. Others saw him walking around the compound or into the house. Soon people in our village feared our home. No one dared go there unless one of us was around or there were people in the house. I never saw these physical manifestations of him, but he was with me every moment. Sometimes, he visited me in my dreams and sat on my bed, talking. I would wake up when he walked away, certain that I hadn't been dreaming. I still wrote him letters in my journals, telling him about the challenges that I was going through, ranting and rebuking him for betraying me. Most nights, I slept hugging my journal with tears washing my face. On such nights, he would come to offer solace and tell me what I needed to do to overcome my challenges.

As the days became weeks and months, the dreams changed. I saw myself searching for him – walking through graveyards in the dark, trying to get to where he was standing waiting for me. Sometimes, I would be crossing huge bodies of rushing water, nearly paralysed by fear. He was always on the other side of the water, telling me it was okay, that I could make it. All I needed to do was take one step at a time, and I would reach him and be with him forever. I often woke up drenched in sweat and fear. Later, as the dreams continued, other deceased relatives started visiting me too. Sometimes my dreams were prophetic. I would dream about something, usually tragic, and not know how to respond to it. Later, my vision would be borne out. The burden of guilt was staggering. I wondered whether it would have made a difference if I shared such dreams with someone – perhaps my mother. Sometimes I did, but I stopped when I realised that she, like most people, believed the dreams were of no consequence.

Through this all, I was in a kind of spiritual limbo. Questions of which was the true church often swirled through my mind. I considered myself a Christian, but I had many questions that never seemed to be answered by the church services I attended. I felt a yearning that never seemed to be quenched. I withdrew into the world of books, reading novels through the night, spending my days depressed and deprived of sleep. On nights when I did fall asleep, I wandered the land of the dead, roaming strange lands and fighting bizarre creatures or doing other crazy things.

In the meantime, my first child was born. But a troublesome pattern emerged. Whenever I dreamt I was with my father, my child or I would fall sick. When I dreamt of my grandfather, I would fall into a depression that forced me to travel home and spend some days there. When the torment was too much, I shared my dreams with my mother and grandmother. My mother said my father loved me so much when he was alive that he wanted me to go be with him. My grandmother said nothing. When I kept complaining, she advised we hold a symbolic ritual of "burying" my father again. Since my father had died when I was a young girl, I had not done all the funeral rituals tradition demanded of daughters. Now, along with two of my sisters, I spread white burial sheets over his tombstone, slaughtered some cocks and he-goats, and cooked them for relatives (as daughters who were "burying" our father, we were not allowed to taste or eat the meal).

After this ceremony, I had dreams in which my father complained of rain hitting him. A few months later, we decided to rebuild his tombstone. A ram and a cock were slaughtered at the head of the tombstone before the old tombstone was dismantled. Lo and behold, we discovered that a portion of the grave had not been covered with cement during its construction. Aggregates had been poured over the steel bars that were used as a base in building the tombstone, allowing rainwater to drain directly into the grave. Shrubs planted around the tomb had prevented anyone from noticing this.

Though we fixed that problem, dreams of my ancestors kept bringing misfortune. I joined the Mormon faith again and asked for special prayers from the missionaries, but their prayers did not keep the tormenting dreams away. Eventually, I turned to traditional religion for help. I visited a diviner, who assured me that if I purchased some items, he would help take away the curse of bad luck and misfortune following me. I purchased some milk with which to bathe, and he added some herbs, including coffee seeds, to it. Later, he gave me some ground herbs that I had to mix with petroleum jelly and rub into my skin. I followed all the instructions, but his treatment did not help.

I tried another diviner whom I had heard mentioned on a radio station. She told me to buy certain items for a different bathing ritual. I was given a basin with a mixture of water and other herbs. This time, local beer brewed from bananas was added to the water instead of milk. I had to step on some paper money notes while bathing. After bathing, I wasn't supposed to pick up the money or look behind when getting out of the bathroom. I was given more herbs to burn every morning after bathing with water in which coffee seeds were placed. But all this, and a number of follow-up visits to the diviner, had no positive results.

Soon after that, my husband and I decided to formalise our marriage. In 2010, we started planning for the wedding. Our parents and relatives had the initial dowry negotiations and settled everything. My husband's grandmother offered him almost all the cattle he needed, and his paternal aunts offered the goats. But once again, a voice from the grave intervened. A few weeks after the dates were set, my mother sent word that my late grandfather was demanding that his last funeral rites be held before the dowry payment ceremony. This would cost more money than we had.

My grandfather had been a tribal warrior – a status he attained years earlier. At the time, young men from two nearby hills would meet in the valley between their ridges and ritualistically "fight" each other (basically whipping each other with sticks on the buttocks) in what was known as the akisili dance. Women from the two ridges would watch and cheer their young men. Whichever team won – by enduring the beating better – was considered heroic. It is believed that warriors return after death to the place they were initiated. But before a man can return, his family must hold a special ceremony, the okelo (its literal meaning is "the drums that bring the warrior to the decision-making circle"). That meant we would have to organise not only the regular funeral rites (chowo lumbe), but the okelo ceremony too. To organise both ceremonies, we would need a minimum of two bulls to sacrifice – one for each of the ceremonies – as well as a number of goats and chickens for those who would officiate.

I suggested we hold the last funeral rites after the dowry ceremony since the first event would bring us enough cattle for the second. But at this, grandfather's spirit went on a rampage. Speaking through a younger cousin, who walked miles from her marital home when the spirit of grandfather possessed her, he threatened to destroy the entire family if his demands were not met. Daily sacrifices of cocks had to be offered to pacify the spirit. Then a new demand came – this time through my mother: All relatives and grandchildren were to go worship at the clan shrine in a nearby village.

My two encounters with diviners had left me sceptical about all this, but some members of the family did go. After lots of pressure from the spirits, including mysterious deaths of the cattle and poultry of family members and strange sicknesses that attacked children, we acceded to my grandfather's demand; the dowry payment ceremony would be held after the funeral rites. Most of my family members remained reluctant about holding the funeral rites, though.

The okelo typically runs from a Saturday evening through Sunday afternoon. But when we were ready to start, the okelo drums refused to produce sound however much they were hit. The trumpet also went silent. Next, a sudden thunderstorm lifted the tent that had been set up for visitors, throwing it over my grandfather's tombstone some metres away. Then grandfather apparently possessed one of our uncles; he seemed to want to spear our brother, who is named after grandfather, for failing to do what was necessary to bring him honour. After this, our reluctance vanished. By the next day, when we had to go dance the okelo in the bush, we were more than willing to adhere to all the demands.

However, it seemed the spirit world was still intent on wreaking havoc on our plans to formalise my marriage. A few days after our return from grandfather's rites, my husband lost his job. Sales at the secretarial business, which was now our only source of income, suddenly disappeared. Friends and family who had promised to contribute to the dowry ceremony and wedding reneged. Two of the cattle supposed to be part of the dowry died suddenly. Another cow died on its way to the ceremony. The secretarial business was robbed twice. I started having dreams in which a friend stood at the head of an open grave, calling out my name and sending fire to burn me. I also had dreams about walking through graveyards, carrying corpses around and fighting strange creatures. Worst of all, I started feeling a strange presence attached to my back. It was cold and felt like a caterpillar holding tight onto a tree. When something bad would be about to happen to me, the cold would shoot up my back.

I believed that some supernatural force had to be behind all these unexplained misfortunes. In desperation, I went to yet another diviner. She had me hold beads close to my mouth and whisper my name over them. Then she threw them on the cowhide carpet in front of her. After a few minutes of staring intently at them, she gave the verdict: My misfortune arose from witchcraft practiced against me by a lady interested in snatching my husband. Furthermore, ancestral spirits from my father's house were tormenting me. She offered to dig up charms my nemesis had planted against me. When I asked how we would know where to look, she laughed at my naivety. The spirits would dig them up, of course!

I had to provide a cock, some local beer and cash as payment for the digging and cleansing rituals. I went through the cleansing process; this time, blood from the sacrificed chicken was added to the mixture of beer, herbs and water. Totally naked, I had to be covered with a bark cloth near an incense pot filled with a variety of herbs. Hours later, when my body was drenched until every pore was reeking, I was declared cleansed. Now the charms that had been planted against me had to be uprooted. The diviner placed a clean goat skin in front of me and asked me to cover it with a basket. I did. On the basket, I placed the cash demanded by the spirits for dealing with the charms. I placed bells the spirits inhabited on the money. Then I ordered the spirits to go dig up all charms ever planted against me. Minutes later, the diviner announced that the spirits had accomplished their duty. Using a cow-tail whisk, she upturned the basket, revealing some tiny bottles, knotted pieces of cloth and polythene bags. They all had signs of having been dug out of the wet earth. A charm to protect me from further attacks was planted through a cut in my head (the hair where this cut was made later turned grey). Then I was released to go home without looking back.

Still, nothing changed.

Several months and visits later – after I had spent more than five million Uganda shillings for consultations, sacrifices and payments to the spirits – I realised that whatever supernatural power was bent on tormenting me wasn't going to be defeated as easily as I had anticipated. I had short spans of relief from some of the torments, but the strange presence on my back got heavier than before, and in my dreams, my dead ancestors were filled with violence and fury. Every time I dreamt of my grandfather, we were having a furious quarrel. Opportunities continued to elude my husband and me, with most of them falling through at the last moment.

Finally, I decided to try Christianity once again. I went back to a nearby Anglican church. I had nothing to lose. Unlike trips to the diviners, there was no cost. One Sunday in church, I heard an announcement about a prayer retreat to be held the next day. When I woke up depressed the next morning, I decided to attend the retreat. It was the beginning of a whole new chapter of my life.

The meeting was held on a mountain outside of town. About fourteen people attended. When it began, a Reverend rose and started talking about indicators of being under demonic dominion. It was uncanny. Though her comments were not aimed at me in particular, she described a mental and physical state that was exactly mine – the tormenting dreams about dead ancestors, the trembling fear of finding myself in the middle of rushing storm waters that threatened to sweep me away, repeated failures that always seemed to come just when I was on the edge of breakthroughs, the dire poverty and even the constant quarrels I was having with my husband. For the first time, I realised I was not alone. Countless people suffer torments like mine. As the day progressed, I found new hope.

The day ended with the Reverend asking us to fast for seven days while attending prayer sessions. Our focus was to confess and repent our sins and those of our ancestors. It was during these seven days that I learned the group I had joined were intercessors. I had never really understood what intercessors were, though all the churches I know – Catholic, Protestant, Evangelical – have them. Some are members of the clergy, and some lay. Their basic mission is to pray for members of the congregation and others. I came to know that they had to have been purged, trained, bruised, and scourged in preparation for their work. They are very much in demand. Every day, hundreds of people flock to the Mutundwe Christian Fellowship in Kampala seeking deliverance. The same happens in countless ministries. Many people seek relief from the overpowering demands of ancestors' spirits and evil spirits. I am convinced that this is one of the major reasons Christianity took root in Uganda in a remarkably short time.

Intercessors became an important and regular presence in my life. Besides being always available, they understood my world and sought to rescue me from my demons. After the seven-day fast, I started attending Wednesday prayer meetings. Between 20 and 30 people squeezed into a small room with long hard wooden benches lined against the walls and a deep red mat carpeting the floor. The sessions always started with prayers. A big drum accompanied vibrant praise and worship. Then an intercessor would teach about some aspect of spirituality. I learned, for example, that people and events I saw in dreams weren't so much coming from another world as they were reflections of my own inner turmoil. I also learned about "generational sins" (evil habits and tendencies inherited from our ancestors that attract God's punishment on the offenders, their families, communities and even nations), "foundational bondages" (covenants with demons made by our ancestors but passed on to those who follow), and witchcraft. Such topics were leavened by prayer, repentance, and gifts of the Holy Spirit.

There also were sessions for people to work on their particular torments, have their dreams interpreted, receive personal counselling and have prayers said on their behalf. Nine out of ten times, evil spirits manifested themselves during these sessions, often with victims letting out hysterical laughter, screaming, crawling on the floor, or making animal or unnatural sounds. Sometimes, evil spirits spoke through the possessed, usually threatening the intercessors, sometimes begging not to be cast out. Sometimes the victims fell down and lay motionless. Other times, they twitched like epileptic patients having seizures. When evil spirits manifested, the lead intercessor would rebuke them and command them to get out of the afflicted ones, using as weapons the name of Jesus, biblical verses, the "fire of God," "thunder and lightning," and "prayer bullets" (quotations from scripture crafted as declarations or prayer points).

During the prayer meetings, I noticed that one of the intercessors, a young man, seemed to understand my torments particularly well.

Every time he prayed for me, I felt some relief and encouragement. I approached him one Sunday after a church service and asked him to pray for me. Thus began my individual deliverance sessions. Every Sunday afternoon, we would go into the prayer room, where I shared how I was doing, described dreams I had received since our last session, and explained challenges I was facing. He would encourage me using the scriptures, rebuke me sometimes, interpret dreams for me and give prayer directions. Then we would have exorcism prayer sessions, which usually culminated with different evil spirits manifesting. I rarely remembered what transpired during these intense times; one moment I would be praying in earnest, and the next moment I would find myself sprawled on the floor with my clothes and hair in disarray, my face stained by tears, and my voice so hoarse I could barely recognise it as my own. This would sometimes be more than two hours from the time I last remembered. After about four Sundays of such sessions, my spiritual guide told me I was getting more and more violent during these sessions. He said I usually flew into a rage and tried scratching and hitting him. One time, I sank my teeth hard, scarring him. He invited another intercessor to join us during the sessions. Since I barely had enough energy to walk back home after the sessions, my husband was invited to join the sessions so he could help me.

During my counselling sessions, it was revealed that I had been chosen to serve as priestess of the family shrine. With this revelation, my treatment reached a climactic moment: The team of intercessors said we had to travel back to my ancestral home and destroy some of the evil altars standing where the covenants of dedication had been made. My whole family would become part of the healing process.

The first step was for me to fast for twenty-one days and travel to the village to do "spiritual mapping" to identify the evil altars that needed to be destroyed. I also was to use this occasion to gather more information from my grandmother and other relatives. And, of course, I had to seek my family's consent for a visit by the intercessors.

When I got home, I learned new things about my family – why, for instance, we always had fewer males than females (most of the men in our family never lived past their youth). Grandmother revealed that this resulted from a curse that had passed down when our great grandfather found his brother committing adultery with his eldest wife. In a fury, he speared his brother, who in turn cursed him as he died so that all his male descendants would die young.

I initially was worried that my family, especially grandmother, would not allow me to take the intercessors home to pray and destroy the family shrines. I was surprised to find everyone open to the idea, with most saying they were tired of customs that required them to make enormous sacrifices but never brought the relief they expected or needed. My grandmother surprised me greatly. When I told her I was born again and wanted to bring intercessors home for prayers, she kept silent for a while and then said, "You can't get saved. But if you want to bring people to pray for you here at home, it is okay."

I travelled back to Kampala and met the intercessors to give them feedback and share the information that I had gathered. The intercessors, some of my sisters and I then made the long trip to the family home together. It was 10 pm when we arrived. We were surprised to find most of the family, including extended family members who lived nearby, waiting for us. We launched into a teaching and prayer session that lasted until 4 am, when the team finally dispersed so the people could get some sleep. But just two hours later, the team woke up, and we went to meet grandmother, who had been asleep when we arrived. From her panicked expression, it was clear that she hadn't really expected me to come with a team of people to pray and destroy the family altars. She tried to deny any knowledge of what the team was asking. But she reluctantly allowed us to pray and destroy an altar that had been built beneath huge fig and bark cloth trees. The rest of the family hesitantly followed us. As we approached the trees, we heard the constant hissing of snakes. We began by doing a Jericho walk around each tree – circling it seven times while chanting prayers of repentance for worshipping the snakes that live in them. After saying the prayers, the team rebuked the evil spirits that had received homage there, nullified the covenants made between them and the family, and spiritually destroyed the altar. At some point during the prayers, a dead green snake fell out of the fig tree. The incessant snake sound stopped abruptly. This showed the group that the prayers had been effective. The trees were huge, so it was not possible to cut them down at that moment. But symbolic cuts were made, and it was agreed that I would come back later and cut them down completely. The place was then sanctified by the sprinkling of salted water.

After prayers, almost every family member brought different fetishes and charms and handed them over to the intercessors. Some family members identified personal altars where they worshipped different gods and asked the intercessors to destroy those too. My grandmother was told to break the soul tie she had with me and cancel the dedication covenant she had made on my behalf while I was a child. Reluctantly, she laid her hand on my navel and said a few words denouncing the dedication covenant that installed me as the family shrine priestess. She handed over a number of symbolic items, which the intercessors set on fire. I guess she felt overwhelmed and resolved to go along with us since all the family members were eager to denounce the old ways and start afresh. A number of aunties, cousins, sisters and even my mother converted and were born again. Later that evening, the team broke the fast, and we returned to Kampala.

A month later, I returned to cut down the fig tree and bark cloth tree. Family members said the snake sounds had ceased, and dead snakes occasionally would fall out of the tree branches. But the silences between grandmother and me were slithering with new tensions. I could sense her hurt, confusion and anger. Her face joined the furious faces of dead ancestors who yelled and threatened me in my dreams. My father rarely appeared in my dreams anymore, but my late grandfather was a dominating presence. He was always furious, threatening to kill me for destroying the core of the family. Grandmother always appeared too, sometimes laughing at me in scorn, telling me that my Jesus would not save me. I always stood firm in my faith, declaring that I was no longer a part of them. Physical and verbal fights with strange women, snakes, cattle, leopards and all sorts of creatures were a common sight in my dreams. I usually won these fights, though.

I remained strong in prayer, fasting and studying the word of God. But sometimes, I still would fall into depression, usually after dreams in which I fought my grandmother. I would wake up feeling drained, both emotionally and physically. It seemed that a part of me was destroyed every time I defeated her in the dream world.

A few months after my trip to the village with the intercessors, the family willingly joined a group of Charismatic Catholics for further prayers. They felt there were things that still needed to be done and so invited the charismatic Catholics home for further "uprooting of the foundational curses" prayers.

Losing my relationship with my grandmother was one of my deepest regrets to come out of all this. Every time I went home, I hoped she would be willing to open up and accept the changes just as everyone else had. But now we were not on the same side. The accusatory silences hurt more than the spiritual battles we fought in my dreams. She died a few years later, but the battles continued in my dreams. For a while, I was even afraid to go home because every time I went, I could feel her belligerent presence haunting me. Eventually, after a number of fasts and prayers, the soul tie between us was broken, and she stopped appearing in my dreams. But it remains my eternal regret that she died without renouncing the old ways.

Even after all this, my spiritual rebirth hasn't been an easy walk. There have been moments when I have fallen into the ditches of despair, thinking that what I have had to go through was not worthwhile. However, I am no longer confused or afraid because I know that there are always people willing to stand with me and support me. With just a phone call or message, I will receive an outpouring of love, understanding and emotional support that I was not able to get before.

Meanwhile, my thoughts about family have changed greatly. My father, mother and grandmother had been my major influences, the first points of reference in life. Rarely do I think about my father and grandmother now. While they once were central pillars in my life and great sources of comfort, they now are just fading memories. When they appear in my dreams, I denounce them and chase them away. I have come to understand that family can be someone with whom you are not blood related.

My biggest fear has always been that I might fall back to the old ways. People always backslide. The mere thought of reliving those dark days chills me. Though I sometimes miss my father and grandmother, I shudder at the thought of walking the path they had traced for me. I understand the spiritual world and powers that fight constantly to control man. I realise that it is naïve to believe that one can live in this world without choosing a kingdom in which to belong. The kingdom of darkness and the kingdom of light will always struggle to have dominion over man.

Awori Evelyn

My struggles are not unique. Others have suffered much as I did – and have found similar paths to salvation. Here is an account by one woman whose experiences closely paralleled my own.

I am Awori Evelyne from Mulanda, Tororo district. I was born in a Muslim family. My name then was Awori Hawa. I married into a Catholic family in 1978. My husband and I never had a stable marriage. Many times, he left me for other women. My mother-in-law did not like me. I practiced witchcraft to keep my marriage and fight my co-wife. After the death of my husband, I converted to Catholicism and decided to settle down in my marital home and look after my children. That is when I changed my name to Evelyne.

Growing up, I believed in following the traditional ways of doing things. There were many rituals one had to observe, and when you did not practice them and misfortune befell the family, the entire community blamed you.

For example, when someone died, one had to observe many funeral rites. As a married woman, when my husband died, I was told by my sister-in-law to pad myself with the cloth my husband and I had used after having sex. After his burial, I had to bury that cloth in the banana plantation and say that his wife was buried there. This was to ensure his spirit did not return to demand sex from me.

I had no happiness even though I was practicing witchcraft and adhering to traditional rituals. With time, I realised these were not helpful. My wealth always got wasted. Whenever I tried rearing goats or cows or poultry, they would die. One time, two of my goats were knocked and died by the roadside. Another tethered goat tightened the rope around its neck at night and strangled. Another time, I found one of my cows dead in the field where I had taken it to graze. On another random day, about five of my goats got stolen. Frightening things were happening in my homestead. Many times, I would hear mysterious sounds of chicks, stones hitting the roof, and knocks on the doors. But when I would open the door, no one would be there. My children would fall sick, yet when I would go to a hospital, no sickness would be seen or diagnosed.

When I heard that clan members were carrying out the Charismatics' renunciation prayers in a nearby village, I decided to join them.

The process of the renunciation prayers lasts fifty-four days and involves several steps. It starts with listing one's genealogy at least four generations back, including all wives, children, brothers, and sisters, to ensure that their souls are included in the prayers of repentance and renunciation. You must mention what they used to do, whether they committed abortions or murder or were robbers, died in war, committed suicide, were idol worshippers or sorcerers and so on. The genealogy is written in two books; one is taken to the parish priest who intercedes for the families throughout the period of prayers, and the other is kept at the altar where the prayers are held.

The next step includes saying the rosaries and prayers dealing with forgiveness, repentance, the divine mercy chaplet, mysteries of glory, misery (which talks about the passion and suffering of Christ on his way to Calvary), pleading on the blood of Jesus Christ, and calling on the army of the Archangel Michael. Teachers and intercessors guide us in what is supposed to be done.

In our village, a map was drawn of the different places where the family used to hold traditional practices that are considered evil. Then we did a Jericho walk around the homestead, just as the children of Israel walked around Jericho for seven days when they overthrew it. The walk represents surrounding all the evil altars and covenants within the area and overthrowing them. The walk usually includes neighbouring villages. We had to walk around six villages, starting from our home and going through bushes and gardens and valleys and hills. During the walk, we confessed, repented and broke the covenants we made at the different places. The entire family joined in the Jericho walk, with different groups saying different prayers. Someone carrying the cross of Jesus was at the front of the line, followed by the one carrying the statue of the Virgin Mary, then one holding the burning incense pot, then one who had Holy water and sprinkled it on the path and surrounding area, followed by the person carrying and sprinkling the Holy Salt. Other members of the family followed in a queue, saying the different prayers. The intercessors and teachers within the procession helped members who got tired and collapsed. The incense chased away demons. Holy water and salt further cleansed and purified the area. The Jericho walk is done once every day for seven days.

After the seven days of the Jericho walks, we prayed for the souls of the deceased. We had to walk around every tombstone seven times. The teachers leading the prayers would ask for the history of the deceased. Everything known about the deceased was mentioned, including any evil practices they used to do while alive. Souls of the deceased would then be prayed for and forgiven. Soul ties between the deceased and the living were broken during these times. Spirits still roaming the world disturbing the living were commanded to go back to their creator.

Praying for the souls of the dead is the hardest part. It takes a lot of time. Some spirits of the dead are not willing to rest in peace; they fight the prayers and cause weird things to manifest. My father-in-law was a rainmaker, and one of the ancestors worshipped at the clan shrine. When we were praying for his soul at his tombstone, a huge storm suddenly started. We tried to continue, but the more we prayed, the stronger the wind and rain became. Almost all the grandchildren were possessed by his spirit, fighting the intercessors and teachers, screaming and howling and cursing and doing all sorts of things. Some were crawling in the mud. Others were barking like dogs. It was a frightening sight. We left his graveside when huge hailstones started hitting us. Every time we attempted to pray for his soul, the same thing happened.

After praying for the deceased, we said prayers for individual homesteads around the village to break the evil altars and covenants. This was similar to the Jericho walk process.

At the beginning of the prayers, an altar with the cross of Jesus Christ was erected at the periphery of the family homestead. All charms, symbols and articles used in ancestral worship and other rituals were brought and placed at this altar once the owner confessed, repented and renounced the practice. Sometimes the Holy Spirit reveals charms within the compounds and in houses. These are fished out and brought to the altar to be destroyed. For example, when we were praying, we suddenly saw the wife of one of my nephews lifted in the air to the top part of the roof of their house, where she frantically dug into the grass thatch. She then fell to the ground, ran and threw a charm at the foot of the cross of Jesus. She had put the charm inside the thatch.

Individual, family and clan altars were identified and subjected to Jericho walks. People had to mention what each altar was used for, what sacrifices were offered on them, and what covenants were made there. Then they would repent of these practices and renounce and break any covenants that had been made at these altars. All charms were dug up and taken to the cross.

I had planted a charm to protect my home. During the prayers around my homestead, I tried to dig it up but did not find it. The Holy Spirit revealed to one of the intercessors that the charm I had planted was actually two demons who now lived on a tree in the compound and were claiming my second daughter as their wife. That is why she had failed twice in marriage. She was constantly attacked by the two demons, who threatened to kill her if they were not allowed to have her. She had a number of sessions to exorcise the demons, and we had to cut down the tree and dig up its roots.

In between these group and family activities, there were individual counselling sessions during which people could meet teachers or intercessors and speak to them one-on-one about things they did not want to share publicly. Also, people who are constantly possessed by evil spirits had special exorcism prayer sessions.

Every night during the fifty-four days, we had teaching and prayer sessions. We were taught from the Bible and then had sessions of praise, worship and prayers. During prayers, spirits of lust, adultery, bestiality, abortion, murder, witchcraft, idolatry, lying, anger, bitterness and hatred would be commanded one by one to leave and set their hosts free. As they left, they usually manifested by making their hosts scream, cry, vomit, belch, fight, crawl on the ground like snakes, run, or laugh hysterically. There would be chaos all around. Holy water and salt would be sprinkled on the people constantly, and incense would be burned constantly to chase away evil spirits. Intercessors would keep commanding the evil spirits to leave the people. They also followed whoever ran away from the group and brought them back.

After prayers, we had sessions of forgiveness and reconciliation among the family members. I made many friends during this time. Now we eat and pray together. I discovered that if you have a friend who is in trouble, it is important to help them.

On the last day of the prayers, the parish priest came and led mass. Friends and people from other clans and families joined the mass in my compound. It was a time for the entire family to confess their and their ancestors' sins, renounce all the evil practices, and declare that they were setting a new covenant with the God of Israel. The priest witnessed this new covenant. He then blessed the people, served Holy Communion and burned the things earlier thrown at the foot of Jesus' cross. During the prayers, we also renounced some cultural practices that we learned were not good according to the Christian faith, like funeral dances and last funeral rites like chowo lumbe and okelo. These practices are not godly.

Since we held those prayers, my life has greatly changed. Those mysterious things that used to happen have stopped. All my children know that God is the protector, provider and the one who blesses. I am no longer worried about life. Even though someone wants to bewitch me, I no longer care because I know God is with me.

Our Justice or Their Justice?

By Aliker P'Ocitti

IN 2008, MY BROTHER Akena and I joined the largest crowd to gather on Kaunda parade grounds in Gulu since Pope John Paul II visited in 1993. But this gathering was different from the earlier ones. We were waiting to hear from delegates who were representing the internationally notorious warlord, Joseph Kony, at peace talks aimed at ending a war that had killed 100,000 northern Ugandans and uprooted as many as 2 million more over two decades.

The crowd was packed so tightly we could hardly move. As we waited, I wondered what the people around me were thinking. Some no doubt thought about the innocent victims who died or the tens of thousands of children who had been kidnapped to serve as soldiers, porters and sex slaves for Kony's band of soldiers, known as the Lord's Resistance Army (LRA). Many had experienced or knew victims of terrorism and brutal torture. Even more – 1.5 million people – had memories of being compelled to crowd into squalid camps to escape rebel raids that had routinely shattered the peace for years.

Suddenly, I was roused from my thoughts. Akena grabbed my hand in a grip so tight my fingers quickly became numb. He was staring intensely toward a pavilion that had been erected at the centre of the parade grounds. I followed his gaze, and there, to my amazement, stood our brother, Opoka, among representatives of the feared rebel army. He was smartly dressed like an African American Marine in full combat fatigues and desert-trooper boots. Dark shades were clipped to his chest, and his military cap was pulled low, blocking a clear view of his eyes. At his waist, he carried a big Revolvo pistol in its holster. He stood with open legs and a straight, inscrutable face, scanning the tightly packed horde around him as if on the lookout for a sniper attack. I was speechless. I had not seen him in a decade – ten years of worry and uncertainty about what had become of him.

Though he looked out on a sea of faces, our eyes somehow met. He smiled for a moment, but then he tensed. Then I saw a sight I will never forget. Tears began to run down his face. I could feel my own squinting eyes start to flood too. There was a murmur among people around us who witnessed but did not understand this intensely private moment between two men surrounded by a throng of strangers.

The spell was broken after a few seconds. Opoka nodded to us and turned away. I was so dazed I remember little else about the event, except that when it ended, Opoka and the other rebels immediately drove away in six green Land Cruisers with military number plates and tinted windscreens. We had no chance to speak.

The brief encounter sent a wave of thoughts and emotions flooding over Akena and me. Akena recalled a night two decades earlier when our cousin, Oruka, had come to our home to talk with our dad, the closest person he had to a father since his own parents had died years earlier. Oruka was a senior officer in the Uganda National Liberation Army (UNLA), which had rebelled when Yoweri Museveni claimed to represent the new government of Uganda after President Tito Okello fell in 1986. The rebellion quickly collapsed, and Oruka returned to Gulu as part of a team of rebels granted safe passage to negotiate a peace agreement. After his visit with my father, he left to re-join his fellow rebels, who were staying in military barracks during the talks. A little while later, gunshots rang out in the night. In the morning, our worst fears were realised. Oruka's body was found a metre away from the fence of the barracks. His head was facing the fence, and his arms and legs were stretched as if he was running for his dear life. His back was riddled with bullets and soaked in blood. The news broke our hearts. It felt as if our lost brother had come the previous night to bid my father goodbye. The murder was never solved, but Akena was convinced Oruka had been shot by government soldiers.

As we walked away from the parade grounds, he asked me whether I thought history would repeat itself. "Oruka trusted the government during the peace process, but his body was reportedly found around the fence of the barracks," he said. "Now, Opoka is a member of another military peace delegation, and he has to trust the same people his brother trusted."

My mind wandered even farther back – to our childhood. Though Opoka technically was my cousin, we bonded in childhood as if we were from the same womb. He often held me by the shoulder as we walked to school. One of my greatest joys was seeing him play at a karate club when he was only six years old. I used to tell him stories I had learned from Mexican films about Zorro, the legendary swordsman who used his prowess to fight injustice. Opoka was always thrilled to learn how Zorro outsmarted his opponents.

But his life took a sad turn. He lost his parents when he was just eleven, and Oruka, who was his older brother, became his guardian. By then in his early 20s, Oruka had enlisted in the UNLA. Perhaps overwhelmed by the thought that the two would have to fend for themselves, the young soldier taught his ward self-defense. Opoka used the martial arts skills he acquired in a passionate pursuit to set wrongs right. He always protected my siblings and me from bullies. One day, after an older boy had stomped on my leg at a football match, Opoka ran to the pitch and started a fight in my defence. I begged him to stop, but he continued giving the boy a thrashing until older players intervened. When he saw my swollen leg, he cried.

As we grew older, our lives diverged. I went on to secondary school in Kampala, but Opoka dropped out without completing his schooling. Our paths never met for the rest of our teenage years and early adulthood, but one day after I had completed my education at Makerere University and got a job teaching economics, a cousin breathlessly called me and told me to look at that day's newspaper. There I saw a picture of a group of rebel leaders who had been assigned to monitor violations of a cease-fire agreement to end the LRA rebellion, which had picked up the fight against the government after the UNLA collapsed in 1988. Opoka was among them. Evidently, he was still using the skills he developed in childhood – fighting, I was sure, for justice as he saw it.

The search for justice also brought Opoka to the parade grounds the day I finally saw him again in person. The rebels had won the government's permission to address the public on an issue that might determine the success of peace talks. The government had presented war crimes charges against the LRA's top five leaders to the International Criminal Court (ICC), but the rebels wanted the cases to be addressed through Mato Oput, the traditional Acholi system of justice. It was an audacious proposal. In addition to the government of Uganda, much of the global community agreed that the ICC was the appropriate forum. Although Acholi justice had survived colonialism and still had adherents in Uganda, it never had been tested outside of the Acholi clans (except among the Madi in West Nile, Uganda), let alone in a forum that would put it under the glare of global media. Could a clan-based system that was rooted in oral culture handle cases involving crimes that had taken place over large areas and affected thousands of people? Could it offer an alternative to a system endorsed by 120 or more nations around the world – one that had well-established procedures, science-based standards of evidence, and record-keeping systems to ensure accountability? To many, the idea of invoking traditional justice seemed a stretch. But for a moment, at least, it raised fundamental questions: What is justice, after all? And how can it best be achieved?

It is hard to imagine approaches to justice that could be more different than the Acholi system and the western-based one embodied by the ICC. The latter is what scholars call a "retributive" system. Its fundamental objective is to punish those who have done wrong. Whether that somehow offsets the harm done, comforts the afflicted by causing their tormenters to suffer, deters others from transgressing in the future, or somehow satisfies an abstract need for moral balance, I do not know.

Acholi justice is based on completely different principles. At its root lies a belief in a moral order defined by Jok – defined variously as Gods or divine spirits. When a crime is committed, Acholi believe their ancestors will send CEN – spirits of the dead – to bring misfortune, illness or death until an offender steps forward and accepts responsibility for his actions. Elders guide the process. They help learn the facts and encourage dialogue among those involved until the wrongdoer confesses and offers compensation to those who have been wronged. This sets the stage for forgiveness, reconciliation, and healing. Scholars describe this as a "restorative" system of justice since its overriding purpose is not to punish wrongdoers but rather to repair social bonds that have been torn by crime.

I observed Acholi justice at work in 2009. An LRA rebel combatant named Ambrose had killed a member of a family he knew well. The government had given him and many others amnesty in return for laying down their guns. But when he returned to his village, he was haunted by the memory of what he had done. With members of the victim's family suffering because of their loss and Ambrose's family ostracised in the community, Ambrose's family decided to seek justice through Mato Oput.

During the proceedings, Ambrose and his family voluntarily accepted responsibility for the killing and sought forgiveness from the victim's clan (for the Acholi, repairing the damage done by crime is a collective responsibility of clans). A council of elders had been established to mediate between Ambrose's and the victim's clans to restore their broken relationship. At the gathering I observed, the elders asked Ambrose to recount truthfully and in detail what had happened and why. Ambrose confessed that he hit the victim to death with an axe. He said the rebel leadership had forced him to kill, warning him he would be killed himself if he did not comply. This was a common LRA strategy; by forcing its "recruits," including kidnapped children, to assault their own people, rebel leaders sought to make it impossible for soldiers to abandon the rebellion and return home.

After admitting what he had done, Ambrose asked for forgiveness. An elder from Ambrose's family repeated the request for reconciliation with the victim's family so that they all could relate freely, share meals again and even allow their children to marry into each other's families, as was possible before the murder drove a wedge between them.

After hearing these pleas, the council of elders ordered Ambrose's clan to provide three cows and three goats to compensate the victim's clan for their loss. This may seem a small penalty for taking a man's life, but the elders said leniency was justified since Ambrose had been forced to act as he had. They thanked Ambrose for having the courage to seek forgiveness and present himself before them. And they asked the victim's clan to consider forgiving Ambrose and his clan so that healing could begin. Explaining that the penalty was not meant to inflict pain or hardship but to symbolise reconciliation, the elders noted that by tradition, the cows Ambrose's clan would give to his victim's family were not to be slaughtered or sold but should instead be used as dowry when one of their sons gets married. Moreover, by tradition, a male child resulting from the marriage would have to be given the name of the victim to uphold the dead man's legacy.

After the sentencing, participants engaged in a ritual that was rich with symbolism. Representatives of both clans drank a beverage that mixed oput (a bitter herb) and kwete (a local alcoholic drink made of fermented sorghum and cows' blood); this reflected the bitterness both clans felt. They ate raw liver spiked with thorns from a sacrificed animal. The thorns represented stored pain and revenge; the act of eating them indicated that the people were restoring their relationship.

Members of both clans next staged a mock fight in which they beat each other with sticks as if they were fighting with swords. They did not use just any sticks; their symbolic weapons were sticks normally used to open granaries, a reminder that the tension between them had kept them from sharing food. Eventually, an elder stepped in to separate the two clans, symbolizing an end to the conflict. Then each clan sacrificed a sheep. The two sheep were placed heads to feet. Each clan took half of the lamb it had slaughtered and half that the other clan had sacrificed. All parts were cooked and eaten to show that the clans had restored their friendship and were once again united.

I did not know what crimes, if any, Opoka might have committed as a rebel soldier, but I liked the idea of applying Mato Oput to resolve any suspicions that would keep him from rejoining our community. A retributive system would have made it difficult for him to tell the truth voluntarily and completely since the only way to get a trial would be to deny responsibility for whatever he might be accused of doing. Also, a clan elder told me that Mato Oput would be the only way the family who lost their loved one could receive reparations since the ICC has no authority to offer damages that can be paid directly to victims. The material value of reparations no doubt would fall short of the emotional and symbolic significance of what had happened, but my family figured Mato Oput would offer Opoka his best chance of becoming a full-fledged, respected member of the community. We also looked to Mato Oput, with its basis in voluntary confession by wrong-doers, as our best hope for ever learning who killed Oruka – and why.

Obviously, there would be obstacles to applying Mato Oput to crimes committed during the LRA war. As much as I yearned to see harmony restored to my community, I wondered how it could keep track of the countless number of cases arising from mass violence or how it could address the needs of thousands of victims who may not even have known those who harmed them. I also was impressed that retributive systems had developed rigorous, science-based standards of fact-finding. Putting elders in charge of fact-finding may work in small communities where elders know everybody well and have considerable moral authority, but that goal would seem more difficult to achieve in cases that were not confined to small communities where everybody knows everybody else. Also, Mato Oput is an oral process; clans had never established record-keeping systems to ensure the accountability that people affected by the LRA war were entitled to expect.

Still, after two decades of war, the Acholi desperately needed to mend broken social bonds so we could endure as a community. Retributive justice, reflecting the values of a highly individualistic society, assigns guilt just to the individual who actually commits a crime; it cannot meet the needs of a society where guilt and the consequences of crime are seen as collective responsibilities. Adding to all that, it was questionable that many Acholi would even be able to follow ICC proceedings, which would be held in a foreign language barely understood by victims or offenders.

I presented my arguments to those who would listen, but I failed to make much headway. An American friend suggested that western-style prosecutions would act as a deterrent to future crimes. I countered that even the risk of facing death sentences had not stopped people from committing murder. He pointed out, in response, that Uganda had signed the treaty that established the International Criminal Court, so it should abide by its commitment. I responded that America was helping to fund the ICC but did not sign the treaty and said it would not allow its citizens to be prosecuted under it. My arguments failed to sway him.

I also tried to explain Mato Oput to fellow students during a graduate course I took in San Diego, California. I presented my best arguments, but not a single student agreed with me. The students – especially those from Europe and America – could not conceive of a system of justice in anything but retributive terms. Maybe outsiders found the Acholi emphasis on voluntary confessions unworkable. Maybe societies built on individualism could not accept the notion of collective responsibility. Maybe the whole concept of putting reconciliation ahead of fault-finding and punishment was just too foreign.

The more I thought about it, the more I came to believe that the single, most important barrier to wider acceptance of Mato Oput was its foundation in traditional spiritual beliefs that are not shared by non-Acholi people. The belief in Cen – the conviction that crime triggers terrible after-effects that outlive its perpetrators and undermine the foundations of society – makes confession and reconciliation a moral imperative for the Acholi. Westerners sometimes translate Cen as being "guilty conscience," but that dilutes its significance. Guilt to the Acholi is more than a psychological state of mind for individuals; it is a tangible reality that affects all of society, including the innocent. If you take Cen out of the picture, Mato Oput loses an essential ingredient. That is why I could not persuade my western friends.

I was left with the realisation that we faced a bipolar choice: Would we follow *our* justice or *their* justice? And in that debate, the Acholi were powerless compared to the national and international forces who did not share our spiritual traditions.

And yet the question refused to go away. For one thing, the war never reached a conclusive ending. A peace treaty was negotiated, but Kony never showed up to sign it. Instead, he just vanished, probably into the vast jungles of the Democratic Republic of the Congo or the Central African Republic. While the ICC indicted five LRA leaders, only one has been detained. Some or all of the rest may be dead for all we know; there even have been rumours that Kony succumbed to the coronavirus pandemic that emerged in 2019 and 2020. Meanwhile, the government offered amnesty to most LRA rebels who voluntarily surrendered. Many took up the offer and laid down their arms. As much as I hoped to see a system that would seek to repair the damage done by war in a more fundamental way, I don't fault the government. It urgently had to restore peace, and amnesty seemed to accomplish more than years of fighting had. Thus, for all but the top-ranking LRA leaders and for the many victims who never received reparations, coming to terms with what happened has been largely a private matter.

Mato Oput remains an option to this day, of course. As the Mato Oput ceremony I observed demonstrates, it has been used in at least some cases, although nobody knows exactly how often. It is considered a private matter between clans, not part of the formal judicial system of Uganda. A consortium of nongovernment organisations, concerned about other conflicts, pressed the government to lend more support to traditional systems of justice. The government finally responded in 2019 by issuing a new post-conflict transitional justice policy. It created a legal and institutional framework for investigating and prosecuting allegations arising from internal military conflicts. It also committed the government to paying reparations to victims and outlined a role for "civil society," including "alternative justice" approaches such as Mato Oput. It set record-keeping standards for traditional justice systems, and in a significant bow to traditionalists, it provided that their proceedings could take place even in cases where an accused person agrees to plead guilty in a mainstream, retributive court.

This could transform Mato Oput from being an instrument of oral culture into a more systematic, rule-bound and documented part of Uganda's justice system. But it is too soon to say for certain how the hybrid, plural justice system will play out in practice. The answer may come only after some future conflict.

And what of Opoka? The little boy who loved Zorro and protected me from bullies when we were in primary school. The child who lost his parents when he was eleven and his brother when he was nineteen, and who grew up learning just one skill – fighting. The young man who had little chance to put that skill to work by joining Uganda's army since its ranks were filled with fighters from the south who saw northerners as their enemy. The idealist who found employment and a way to pursue justice the only way he knew – by joining another rebellion, even though he scarcely understood it except that it opposed the same government he believed had killed his brother.

Opoka's life is one of the many untold stories about the consequences, often hard to see, when a system of justice fails to achieve true reconciliation after society is torn apart by violence. Sometime after I saw him at the parade grounds, my brother accepted the government's offer of amnesty and quit the LRA. In addition to freedom, the government gave him a blanket, basin, jerrycan, saucepans and a small sum of cash (less than £100) to begin a new life. We finally reconnected and now stay in touch. He is trying to make a new start, but his life has not been easy. He is back in school. He has children, though he has not been able to sustain a relationship with a woman. He struggles with anger management, perhaps because of the stress of having to provide for a family with almost no means. He is the brunt of nasty comments when he ventures from his home, and he cannot return to our village for fear of retribution, so he stays mostly in town and keeps largely to himself. I believe he is wrestling with all that has happened, but he has never told anybody – not even me – about his experiences during the rebellion. He says he would be open to going through Mato Oput, but no one has accused him of anything, so there is no family to join ours in a proceeding. Nor could he identify any family he might have committed a crime against while he was in combat.

In short, my boyhood hero today is a man withdrawn from people. He lives in isolation. The tears that rolled down his cheeks that day more than 15 years ago on the Kaunda parade grounds are still rolling.

The Words Died in My Mouth

By Achelam D. Kinyera

I

WE CALLED IT OBARA. We came from Obara. We went back to Obara. Whichever region of it you came from, be it Casement, Amudat, Red Houses, Base or even Karatus, you were still from Obara. It squatted, unkempt below the trimmed hedges, pruned trees, mowed lawns and posh houses lined up as orderly as an English sentence on Naguru Hill. Then the government evicted many families, and the home we called Obara was bulldozed to create space for apartment buildings.

Obara was the first word that died in my mouth. My friends and I came from Casement. It was the northernmost part of Obara, cut away from Naguru Hill by Katalima Road. On our side were closely packed shanties, naked electric wires that crisscrossed each other a few feet above the ground, calls of children at play, and long lines of jerry cans at a single tap. The sound of activity was everywhere. Neighbours calling out to each other from their verandas. Woofers competing to be louder than any other. Hawkers singing their wares. Our fathers and friends recounting their brushes with criminals or discussing yet another cut or delay in salary.

The Hill was a mystery to us. My friends and I would cross Katalima Road, and by that mere act, Obara was peeled off us. We spoke in whispers, looking this way and that to avoid inhabitants and always ready to sprint when the German Shepherds barked. The beautiful houses with their balconies and glass windows stood quietly behind fences. The air smelled fresh, and we heard birds chirping and leaves clapping in the wind – sounds drowned out only occasionally by a car driving past. The fences bore beautiful patterns, and the grass was always trimmed. Everything was in order. We pointed to houses and made them ours in fantasies. We counted cars and imagined we owned them too. But we crossed back to Casement before nightfall, when security guards protecting houses on the Hill might mistake us for thieves.

We, the children, had our own language. We shouted, "Owit!" when we sensed trouble. "Alali" meant "the enemy" – be they parents at home, teachers at school, opponents on a soccer field, or the boys from Amudat. The latter were a menace – our main alali. They sometimes needed to be shown their place. At school, teachers would stop fights before rivalries could be settled, so we would adjourn to a later time and different location – usually the tap, because many of us had to fetch water when we got back from school. The time between encounters allowed us to gather allies and prepare squads to intimidate or fight the enemy. Squads were usually formed based on the region of Obara one came from. The number of times one shouted "owit!" determined how fast we fled. Without it, the mention of alali served to embolden us, but if coupled with alali, it meant something else entirely. "Owit! Owit! Alali – Owit!" meant, "Look out! Enemy spotted! Run for dear life!"

I do not remember how owit made its way into our vocabulary, but I can recall how alali got its meaning. Those days, my friends and I swapped VCR tapes of action movies. *The Last Stand at Lang Mei* and *War Bus* were among our favourites. Such foreign films came with a video jockey's translation and commentary in Luganda, the language of the Baganda, Uganda's largest ethnic group. Viet Cong soldiers were always the enemy in these movies. The VJs called them alali, which sounded like a word spoken in the film by a Vietnamese actor.

In lower primary school, we spoke our local language alongside the little English we were taught, but all through upper primary and secondary school, we were punished for speaking anything other than English, except in classes for languages such as Luganda and Swahili. English speakers were praised and rewarded, while we picked on any classmate who made a mistake in English. Okukuba embogo – "killing a buffalo" – it is called. Between convulsions of laughter, we would say, "you're killing buffaloes" or "you're poaching." Labelling miscreants "poachers" was funnier in Luganda because the hilarity comes from how one says it. We treaded carefully when we spoke English for fear of making a mistake and becoming laughingstock. Our parents measured the value of their school fees by the degree to which we spoke the Queen's language; they often complained to teachers if they found our English inadequate. "Where will you go if you can't speak English?" my father would ask after seeing my low scores. "In whose office? You will just go to the village."

When the bulldozers came, they took down Casement first. Many families were still packing their luggage. Some displaced families moved deeper into Obara – to Karatus, the southernmost part of what had been our childhood world, or to Amudat, the easternmost region. Others left the area altogether. My friends and I were separated and scattered. For a while after the forced eviction, we went to the same primary schools, but we spoke less of the Obara language, and our phrases and slang diverged. Those who moved closer to the Naguru Police barracks incorporated more Swahili-derived words into their speech since that was the dominant language of the barracks. Those from Amudat seemed to add an 'o' to every word they spoke; "my father came" became "ofathen okem."

English was everywhere – on TV, on radio, on signposts, at church, at school, and on my parents' tongues – while the Obara language died a slow death. Eventually, English became the language in which I think. Recently, a chance encounter with a childhood friend – one who always called out, "owit!" – made my tongue itch to speak the Obara language. But the words were dead in my mouth.

II

Linguistic diversity is a fact of life for Ugandans. According to our 2005 Constitution, 50 distinct languages are spoken in the country, which is remarkable given its small size (it ranks 33rd among Africa's 54 countries in land area). But estimates of the number of languages range from 35 to 63, depending on where one draws the line between languages and dialects. Adding to the confusion, the Uganda Bureau of Statistics assumes a one-to-one relationship between language and ethnicity – an approach that ignores the widespread reality of second language users. I, for instance, speak Luganda more fluently than my own mother tongue, Acholi.

There is a hierarchy of prestige among the country's many languages. At the bottom are the indigenous languages exclusively spoken by particular ethnic groups. Above them are languages that have come to be used for inter-ethnic communication; foremost among these is Luganda, which is spoken as a mother tongue or a second language by an estimated 15 million people – more than one third of the population. At the top of the hierarchy are the European languages that reign in official and professional domains. Many Ugandans prefer English to their local languages when it comes to political, economic or scientific discourse, a view fed by the belief that local languages cannot be used to present concepts clearly while English, as the language of instruction in the education system, is associated with intellectualism and success. In casual conversations and even in the media, powerful figures are criticised if they kill buffaloes.

The most common languages are English and Swahili (the official national languages), and Luganda. Parents push their children to become fluent in English, giving little or no attention to their mother tongues, which may only be spoken at home and to other fellow speakers. In secondary school, more students take up English literature than learn Luganda or Swahili, which don't even attract as many students as classes in German, French and Chinese. Students express admiration for classmates who study foreign languages while dismissing those who study indigenous languages as "chillers" – slang for people who are not serious.

Still, the government officially seeks to "develop" all indigenous languages, which means establishing standardised spelling rules and basic literacy and instructional materials so they can be taught in primary schools. Uganda's education policy calls for children to be taught in their mother tongues during their first three years of primary school, reflecting research that shows young students learn better if taught in languages in which they are already proficient. But in practice, only a few languages have been developed fully enough to be learned in school or used in official activities, and the government provides funds to incorporate only eight dominant regional languages into the curriculum – Lugbara, Acholi, Runyankore-Rukiga, Ateso, Luganda, Runyoro-Rutooro, Ng'akaramojong and Dhopadhola. Less widely used "minority" languages get no support.

Starting in later primary school years, all students are taught English tenses, grammar, sentence structure, idioms and more, so they speak less and less in their mother tongues. Their own languages are now termed "vernacular," and uttering a word of them is grounds for strokes on the buttocks or humiliation. In some secondary schools, students who lapse into their mother tongues are made to wear placards identifying them as vernacular speakers or to stand at the "vernacular tree," effectively making them outcasts to other students. Meanwhile, Chinese is now taught in 30 secondary schools, and the Ugandan National Examinations Board plans to include Chinese among the subjects examined nationally starting in 2023.

And so, students' tongues grow heavy as they find it difficult to form words in their original languages. Indigenous languages are not dying easily, though. The close connection between language and culture helps keep local languages in the struggle against displacement by English. Many Ugandans continue to speak their mother tongues or the local languages used where they grew up. Cultural ceremonies such as weddings, coronation anniversaries and funerals require the use of the local language, and some people even take a person's use of English as a sign he does not know his origins. Family elders, usually grandparents, take it upon themselves to train younger generations in their mother tongues whenever they visit their villages.

Language, in short, still functions as a means of identity. Though most Ugandans are multilingual, many still speak and understand their own local language best. Many casual conversations continue to be held in Luganda, Acholi or other local languages strewn with English phrases or words, and many conversations in English are laced with words or phrases from local languages. Some of the mixed-language phrases may be grammatically incorrect but function smoothly in conversation. The result is a hybrid approach to communication seen variably as a compromise that helps preserve cultural bonds or as resistance to the loss of identity and the heritage built into local languages.

III

This phenomenon is apparent in casual conversation, but it also happens in prose, poetry, music, movies, the media and even church.

I spoke to Mr. David Orach on a cool April evening at his home in Busabala, just south of Kampala. He is a presenter on several radio stations in Gulu and hosts Christian talk shows on Gulu FM and Choice FM every Sunday morning. He also is a civil servant, born-again Christian and translator for a Pentecostal church based in Kampala. One can easily tell from his accent that he is from northern Uganda, a Luo man. He speaks of himself as an original Acholi, and Acholi is his mother tongue. He also speaks English (which he calls the "uniting language" because it is used by civil servants), as well as Swahili, Luganda and some Runyakore, Rutooro, and Rukiga.

Living in a multilingual, multicultural society is not easy, he says. "As I'm talking to you, I may find myself mixing English, Acholi and even sometimes Swahili. Why? Because we live with very many different people of different tribes, different nationalities." His mastery of many languages is impressive, even by Ugandan standards. But ironically, his fluency in his mother tongue, Acholi, has suffered. "I'm now not so fluent in [any] one language. I can speak, but not so clearly in one language. I jump from English to Luo, Luo to Swahili just like that, depending on the people I am talking to. If I am talking to a young man, a youth, I find myself speaking Swahili, Luganda and English. When I am speaking to an old man in the village, I try very much to speak Acholi, but it is difficult. I'll be thinking first in English and then translating it to Acholi."

Because language and culture are closely knit, Mr. Orach must master more than language to communicate effectively. "When I'm in Buganda I try my level best to adapt to the culture and follow the culture of the Baganda. When I get back home, in Gulu, where I come from, I'm a very typical Acholi man and I stick to Acholi culture."

But that only gets him so far. Languages have different sounds and different vocabularies, making translation tricky. For example, Acholi has no word for an electric "switch." One solution might be for Acholi to adopt the English word, but Acholi has no letter "s." So Mr. Orach says cwic (pronounced "chwich"). Similar problems arise because Acholi has no letter "f" or "z." While such problems may seem manageable, an even bigger problem comes when similar words have wildly different meanings in different languages. If you translate the English word "ghost," as in "Holy Ghost," directly into Acholi, for instance, it means "devil." To circumnavigate this problem, one would translate it to "tibu maleng" in Acholi. Tibu means spirit. Maleng means clean, pure, or beautiful. Maleng here is used contextually when placed next to tibu to mean "holy"; in a sense, the translation is a description.

A common phrase in church – "Holy Ghost fire!" – compounds the challenge. Mr. Orach says he had trouble finding the right words to communicate the pastors' vehement meaning. "You know now, 'Holy ghost, fire!' means you're commanding the Holy Ghost to remove the evil spirit of a person. You will now say, 'tibu maleng tim ngo' – Holy Spirit, do what? . . . (hesitation here) . . . 'tibu maleng tim ngo . . . tibu maleng ryem ngo' – Holy Spirit chase away (further hesitation) . . . 'ryem jok mekumeni oko' – Cast out the demons possessing his/her body . . . 'jok mekumeni mac patibu maleng owange' – Demon possessing the body, the fire of the Holy Spirit, burn you. He settles on 'mac patibu maleng, wang jok ikum ngatini!' – The fire of the Holy Spirit, destroy the evil spirit in that person!"

Ugandans are talkative and somehow work their way through numerous communication challenges – words lost in translation, linguistic improvisation, people who must translate their own thoughts before speaking them, and conversations that mix languages or are laced with literal translations from other languages spoken to preserve the essence of phrases across tongues. The biggest losses in translation probably occur between natives and foreigners, for whom the pervasive nature of English masks important cultural issues. Consider the Acholi word "abila," which refers to certain things put in the centre of a compound – mainly items associated with Gods linked with homes. The standard translation is "shrine," but the English word is not the equivalent of Acholi's abila. "When you talk of 'shrine' in English, it is so vast, so big, it means a lot of things – including a place where witchdoctors hide and do evil things," Mr. Orach notes. "In Acholi, when you say abila, you are also talking about the home gods, which are not offensive."

How many people, I wonder, have been alienated from a benign and comforting part of their tradition because it was translated into a foreign term that linked it to darkness and evil?

Uganda's Constitution requires that a percentage of all radio programming be in local languages. But this is not the reality. Radio stations in Kampala broadcast mostly in English or Luganda. In 2010, after complaints, the government set up a community radio station for the local Luluuli-speaking community in central Uganda, about halfway between Kampala and Gulu. However, the station only broadcasts in that language four hours a week, with more hours dedicated to English, Luganda and Runyakitara. In fairness, there are so many languages it is difficult to satisfy everybody. In the West Nile region, the northwest corner of the country, for instance, there have been complaints of language discrimination from the Kakwa, a minority tribe, who complain that they are forced to listen to radio programs in Lugbara, the tongue named for the region's dominant tribe.

The goal of preserving local languages runs up against resource constraints and national interest in binding people together with a common language. Hence, the government has chosen to develop dominant area languages at the expense of less common minority languages. The New Vision Media Group – the government's media arm – publishes four local-language newspapers in different parts of the country: Rupiny (in Acholi/Lango language), Orumuri (in

Runyakitara), Etop (in Ateso-ng'akaramojong) and Bukedde (Luganda). These newspapers do not reach people who speak other languages, but they reinforce the government policy of developing and supporting dominant area languages. Thus, speakers of minority languages are forced to adopt regional languages as well as English. This is why most Ugandans are multilingual and why people belonging to minority groups often are less fluent in their mother tongues than in their second or third languages.

Many Ugandans believe their local languages eventually will be replaced completely by English, reflecting the overwhelming influence of the West. "The [local] culture in the years to come is going to be pressed to the edge – to research," says Mugoda Gordons Good, better known as Wake, a Mugwere poet, spoken-word artist and rapper from Pallisa in eastern Uganda. "It's going to be limited to research papers, documents, documentaries and stuff like that."

Wake believes everyone – artists, storytellers, filmmakers, policymakers and others – has a stake in averting the demise of languages. "It's really about the culture and who we are as a people. We can fight." But the decline in local languages, he says, is already upon us. In 2012, Makerere University, in partnership with Endangered Language Fund, a non-profit organisation based in the United States, embarked on research to document endangered languages and dialects in the country. Speaking to Uganda Radio Network, Mukasa Kiiza, the head of the department of African Languages at Makerere School of Languages, Literature and Communication, said its targets include languages such as Ik (a minority tongue in Kabong District dominated by Ng'akaramojong), Lebthur (dominated by Acholi and Lango) and languages in the central region such as Lunyala, Lusese and Luluuli (dominated by Luganda). According to Mr. Mukasa Kiiza, Lusese had about twenty speakers at the time; the youngest was 72 years old. Soon, the language may be found only in academic research papers.

IV

I first met Wake at Kelele@Makerere, a poetry open mic event that happens every fortnight at Makerere University. His style is a unique blend of his mother tongue, Lugwere, and English, with occasional touches of Swahili and Luganda. He speaks Lugwere, Luganda, Lusoga and English. He studied German, which he speaks less fluently. He studied English literature in secondary school and admitted to writing some poetry, but he says his journey as an artist began when he wrote rap lyrics in English for a friend who performed in Luganda. He took up the lyrics himself and has been going forward since.

"When I got into university, I got exposed to open-mic and poetry shows. I was amazed by the power of people's words, man. Like, I could hear the words clearly, and they would hit me. I started just speaking my rap lines instead of rapping over a beat, and this somehow became my style of poetry."

I asked Wake how he decided to use his mother tongue in his music and poetry. He said that he suffered for a time the same pretence that drives some young artists to mimic American accents in their music and poetry. But then he was introduced to the Milege Acoustic Project, which provides coaching and a platform for budding artists. It was set up in 2013 by Milege, an Afrojazz band that plays traditional folk songs using both traditional and modern instruments. Milege has made music in Luo, Karamajong, Lusoga and many other Ugandan local languages. Together with Uganda Heritage Roots, a charitable organisation working to promote cultural heritage through music and the performing arts, Milege mentors budding artists among traditional musicians in Uganda. Wake was one of their discoveries.

"Before I got exposed to Milege, I had never experienced music at that quality in indigenous languages," he said. "It was just amazing, man, like ecciisshh. . . Milege mentored me through the Acoustic Project." Then along came people like the Pearl Rhythm Foundation, who also are big on music based on African heritage. That organisation recorded Abantu Beira, one of Wake's earliest songs, which became one of his biggest hits. Other artists who grew out of Milege include the singers Afrie and Haka Mukiga, a singer-songwriter, poet and dancer who performs in multiple languages, including Rukiga, Rukonjo, and Rufumbira.

Working with these organisations "opened my eyes to who we are . . . we need to tell our stories," Wake says. "We are best placed to tell our stories. If we don't tell them, then who will? The onus is on us – we, the people. If [we do not] tell our stories, the languages will become extinct."

For Wake, music and language both start with the beat. "The Lugwere language – actually, most African languages – are very percussive. For example, in Lugwere there's a song where I say, 'Kikukakatakukakata okuzimb'eka.'" The rhythm pulses clearly as he speaks, achieving a unique beat, but it is completely lost in translation: "It's your responsibility to persevere and build home" (in other words, to make things better for your people where you come from). Wake may use a few English words to help people who do not understand Lugwere know what his songs are about, but Lugwere and his music are inseparable. He is not averse to playing a bit with the rhythm, though. "Kikukakata-ta-ta-ta-ta" might give a better vibe, he says, slightly altering the beat. "The beauty about being an artist is that you can break rules, you can create new things. You can break the language or change the language or manipulate the language to fit what you are trying to say."

Many Ugandan artists – especially those singing in Luganda – tend to adopt English words into their mother tongues and use the resulting new word forms in English sentences. For instance, "Nkufeelinga," which directly translates to "I feel you" and is used when wooing, is adopted from the English word "feeling." It's the title of a song by

HB Toxic, a female group of the early to mid-2000s. Other examples, also in the song, are "nkumissinga," which directly translates to "I miss you," and "nfreezinga." Such phrases appear in more recent songs by artists like Cindy, Sheebah, and the duo, Radio and Weasel, among others (Radio died in 2018). The practice of blending languages is not limited to artists. Ordinary Ugandans often break and splice English words with prefixes and suffixes from their local languages.

"Our culture has evolved. It has interacted with other cultures and people. Also, people in the ghetto have their own language – the ghetto language. That's who they are," says Wake. Words authentic to the ghetto show up in songs by Bobi Wine, a music star turned popular politician. "Kiwani," which means "ruse" or "con," is the title of one of Wine's songs.

Wake will not abide some changes when it comes to his mother tongue, though. "The Lugwere language has not been documented that much, and we have not yet evolved or grown to the level of achieving new slang. I'm sure there is some, but right now, what we need to do – or what I need to do – is to make sure I represent the language in its purest form. The language is still not well known. If I start to put in a few words here or change the words, it may confuse the younger Mugwere who don't know the language. I want them to know the language as it is without putting in [words like] 'nkumissinga' and 'nkufeelinga' because then that may become their language."

Wake pays a price for pursuing his artistic commitment to his language. There are only about 800,000 Lugwere speakers in the country. That makes them a very small market compared to the segment of the population that speaks Luganda. "I have had people tell me, 'Your music is great, but you won't sell,'" Wake says. "People are saying if you want to make it in Uganda, you need to think about singing in Luganda. In East Africa, you need to think about Swahili." The government's policy of promoting dominant area languages like

Luganda compounds the disadvantage; many Lugwere speakers grow up reading stories written in Luganda instead of their own language.

While music sung in less common languages like Lugwere rarely reaches beyond places where the languages are spoken, music in Luganda is promoted widely through concerts and other means. Bosmic Otim, who makes socially conscious songs in Acholi, is popular in the North, for instance, but barely registers elsewhere, while Luganda performers Vinka, Sheebah or Winnie Nwagi are well known throughout the country. The industry is shaped by sales and profits, not language, and the widely spoken Luganda is more profitable. In Kampala especially, people most likely will never hear music from their home districts via the channels where popular artists can be heard.

Wake and other minority-language artists have found support from organisations like Pearl Rhythm and Milege World Music Festival. Similarly, poetry groups such as Kitara Nation encourage and mentor poets who write in their mother tongues. They have published numerous anthologies and works of individual poets. Kitara Nation also is active in secondary schools, teaching and publishing poetry by students in their mother tongues. Another group is the Lantern Meet of Poets and the Lantern Meet Foundation.

The importance of such work cannot be underestimated. Mitch Isabirye, who writes and performs poetry in English and Luganda with Kitara Nation, put it succinctly: "Artists are the custodians of language."

V

When I was growing up, my family had a black and white television whose knob for switching stations was missing. Most of the time, all we could get was muchele – static. My friends had colour TV and

VCRs, so I often would spend time at their houses watching Chuck Norris in *Delta Force*, Jean-Claude Van Damme in *Hard Target*, and Arnold Schwarzenegger in *Commando*. All these films were "translated" – that is, they had voice-overs in Luganda by video jockeys (VJs) – which made them more fun to watch than the untranslated ones. The VJs always called Arnold Schwarzenegger "Swaz." Another popular action-movie actor, Wesley Snipes of the Blade superhero-horror movies, was forever referred to as "Billy Blanks Kayanja" or simply "Kadugala."

These movies, with their Luganda voice-overs, were vehicles for certain words my friends and I adopted into our language in Obara. Alali was one. Another was "mando," a reference to Swaz the *Commando*, which we adopted to mean anyone who beats up another person. After-school fights were the opportunity to be named Mando. Those days were the heyday of kung-fu movies, and the stereotypes were instilled in us. We assumed every Asian person could fight like Jet Li or Jackie Chan. A character of such descent was called a muching-chong. But VJs did more than give us ideas for neighbourhood slang; I owe much of the Luganda I speak to the VJs who translated films.

Video jockeys first appeared before Uganda had much of a film industry, when locals found it difficult to understand the language or what struck them as cultural oddities in foreign films. VJs gave Ugandan audiences an opportunity to hear their own language spoken in movies. But the translation went beyond language. VJs explained movies, offered commentary on them, and sometimes even removed passages they believed would offend Ugandans. They first appeared as live, jocular commentators in local cinema halls. With the rise of DVDs, the VJs started recording voice-overs and selling the enhanced discs to their fans. Today, film translating is a booming business in Uganda. Everywhere you turn in Kampala, there is a video outlet where one can find foreign films by a variety of VJs. People also can go online to choose films according to who translated them (http://munowatch.com/). There is even a VJ academy, which teaches the art of VJ-ing, run by one "VJ Mark" in Kabalagala, Kampala.

I spoke with one highly successful VJ, named VJ Mun, outside his house in Kampala. His real name is Kawaabi Bukenya Herbert. He grew up speaking Luganda, but also learned Lusoga and English. "A Video Jockey is a person who exaggerates," he told me, using the word agyubisa, which may also mean "to provide commentary." To differentiate that designation from "translator," he said, "Translating would have been the way you see those who made Jesus on film speak Luganda." One would never put invented words, slang or one's own opinions in the mouth of Jesus, he explained, so VJ's stick to strict, by-the-book Luganda renderings of anything the Lord is portrayed as saying. "That is translation," VJ Mun said. "We commentate, we exaggerate. You can also call us 'dubbing editors.'"

Though VJs often add levity to movie viewing, they are serious about their work. VJ Mun says he typically watches a movie more than four times and conducts his own research to understand it and its background. "We study very well," he says. "If [a movie] has scientific or medical terms, you have to find a scientist or doctor to explain them to you so that your commentating is true and not distracting to viewers. For historical films, you research the history – the settings, plot, characters, and other related information."

VJ Mun is idealistic about his work. "I believe no story is more entertaining than one narrated to you in your own language so that you understand very well," he says. But when the studying is finished and the time comes to sit in a studio and record the voice-over, VJs differ. This may explain why people have different preferences among VJs. Some people prefer VJs who explain plots and characters and translate dialogue strictly, while others like to hear funny comments and digressions in their voice-overs. In fact, some people watch translated movies even though they understand the English in which they are spoken. "They are looking to laugh," he explains. "They are looking for commentary to make it more entertaining."

Although VJ translations often do not correspond with actual movie dialogue, just hearing one's own language makes the stories more engaging. And part of the fun is that VJs, like many people in their audiences, have grown adept at inventing new words that enrich the experience. Sometimes they have to do this since some English words do not have exact equivalents in Luganda. Our ancestors never created a word for "apple," for instance, so we just call it "fruit" (ekibala). Other workarounds can be more amusing. A VJ came up with "mando maswi mando manga" to describe a hardened soldier, elaborating on the "mando" derived from the Swaz's *Commando*. The words maswi and manga have no translation or meaning without mando – they are used to emphasise the size, strength, and skill associated with a commando. Viewers often come away from movies with such words added to their conversational vocabulary. Growing up, my friends watched the same films, so these phrases became parts of our code, a way to speak amongst ourselves and exclude anyone who had not seen the films.

Another word adopted into everyday speech from translated films is "mangweno" – a crude, albeit euphemistic, reference to sex. Such words can get VJs into tricky territory. In the act of movie commentating, VJs have been compelled to become filters for their viewers. Words like "mangweno" are meant to be euphemisms designed to uphold morality, but when they make their way into everyday speech, they lose their euphemistic quality. VJs borrowed the phrase "eating sumbi" from a song, Sumbuusa, by local artists Eddy Kenzo and Barbi Jay, in which eating sumbuusa (short form sumbi) is a euphemism for having sex. But euphemisms can be serious business. Talking about sex and private parts outright is viewed as vulgar. "If I study a word and find it dirty, I'll mute it so people won't hear it. We take out a lot of scenes," VJ Mun said. "We call it kafufu (dust, dirt). Kafufu needs to be removed. It is not good for young children." He described this as defending Ugandan cultural norms. "We have decided as VJs to cut out some scenes that go against our culture."

Removing such scenes also is a form of resistance to western influence – an attempt to prevent moral corruption, according to VJ Mun. Apart from foul language and sex scenes, overly graphic portrayals of murder or torture are kafufu. But VJs also try to inject positive lessons through their commentary. "VJs are teachers," he said. In the translated version of *The Hate U Give,* a 2018 American crime drama, VJ Mun educated viewers, in Luganda, about racism in America by sharing certain facts obtained during his "studying" stage.

As movies have grown in popularity, the VJ fraternity has found itself caught in a battle with foreign and domestic filmmakers. Foreign filmmakers don't want them to remove portions of their films, such as scenes depicting people kissing in public, that Ugandans may find culturally offensive. Ugandan filmmakers' motives are a bit more complicated. They accuse VJs of copyright infringement, though they aren't trying to defend their foreign competitors; their goal is to prevent VJs from making foreign films more popular than locally produced ones. "The producers and writers of Ugandan films say that translated films consume their market," VJ Mun observed. "We invest little compared to them, but in the market, translated films are bought instead of theirs."

The solution, VJ Mun argues, is for government to establish guidelines for acceptable content in films. Without such regulation, he warns, moral standards and cultural values, which already are declining, will deteriorate further. "In Uganda today, or the world today, you see a youth of 16 years fantasising about a forty-year-old woman, Sheeba (a popular local artist criticised in the past for dressing skimpily and immorally in her music videos and concerts)." So far, the government has shown no interest in getting involved.

While VJs get involved in a wide range of issues, VJ Mun says the underlying issue is language. It is the conduit of expression, which effectively defines what is moral and what isn't. Thus, a decline in language translates into the decay of cultural values. "What they [foreign filmmakers] want is to promote their language," he argued. "If you start muting their dialogue and inserting yours in Luganda, you undermine theirs." He summarised the problem succinctly: "Okuwabba kw'olulimi" – a phrase that implies "language going astray," but also implies "degradation" or "distortion" of language. "I blame the government," he says. "The government has not done its job to help us protect our norms."

In fairness to the government, Uganda's linguistic landscape is so complex that it's hard to imagine how any centralised authority could control it. And even if it were possible, I'm not sure I would want to see such a concentration of power. It's better to leave the mixing, merging, invention and preservation in the hands of all Ugandans acting collectively.

VI

Ugandans are rightfully proud of their linguistic agility, which often showcases their strong sense of humour, although the situation leads to some bittersweet moments too. I experienced one recently when I ran into one of my old friends from our childhood days in the place we called Obara.

> *"Eh, you man! You disappeared! You're lost," he said as we embraced and shook hands. I hadn't seen him in years. His voice was different; it rumbled words that used to sound like sirens back in the day when he was the lookout for our neighbourhood squad. The small boy with the shrill voice had grown into a statuesque manliness.*

"Atte you?" I replied, using an expression that indicated inquisitive surprise. "You know bouncing from Obara then shule [school], then campu [university], and now me, I am here in the struggle."

"Waa. Which struggle?" he said, patting me on the back. "You look kawa."

"Man, you guy, the struggle, it is taking me."

He laughed and said, "What's up, man? What plan?"

"I'm going downtown to buy a trouser. But this kasana is too cos, I might just take a jaj."

"Let us foot, and I push you there. It will be chap-chap."

We continued our conversation. He spoke more animatedly and burst into sudden laughter when I mentioned the day when the Amudat boys surrounded him, and we had to rescue him. I found out much about his life. Before I knew it, we arrived downtown. Throughout our conversation, I wondered how our speech had become so foreign to how we used to speak in Obara.

"Throw me your digits, man," he said, pulling out his phone and handing it to me. "We need to link up properly." I punched in my phone number and handed it back. He said, "Kawa. Let me flash you." My phone vibrated once in my pocket. "That's my line."

We said our goodbyes and promised to keep in touch. As I pulled out my phone to save his number, I realised I couldn't remember his name.

We were speaking Uglish, a lingo born of complex interactions between English, Uganda's indigenous languages, and pop culture, all creatively mixed by a people whose experience living in a multilingual society has made them skilled at adapting, borrowing, translating and inventing words to meet their needs.

Indigenous languages, of course, are a big influence on Uglish. For most Ugandans, the mother tongue is still the first language children learn, so its speech patterns are deeply imprinted. This explains why a Ugandan might say, "Your sister Jackie, I saw her there yesterday," or "That car, it is ugly." Linguist Jude Sempuuma explains that in at least three major indigenous Ugandan languages, words surrounding nouns must be brought into agreement with them through the use of what are called "concord prefixes." In the Luganda phrase, "Abantu" (the people) balikisoma (will read it), the "ba" in front of the likisoma is a concord prefix. Literally, it is translated as "they," so the full phrase translated literally to English is, "The people, they will read it." Almost like a habit, many people hold onto that speech pattern after they have learned English, even though the result is an improper English sentence.

Uglish sometimes turns English notions of singular and plural upside down. In English, words like trousers, scissors or shorts are plural, even though they refer to single items; a "pair" of trousers is, in fact, just one item of clothing, for instance. But in many indigenous Ugandan languages, if a person wants to describe a single pair of shorts or scissors, he calls them a short or scissor. On the other hand, when one asks, "What is your name?" a native English speaker would answer, "My name is Mutumba Jacob." In the local languages of Uganda, each name is treated as its own, so Mutumba Jacob are two names and not just one name. In Uglish, the correct question is, "What are your names?" and the answer is, "My names are Mutumba Jacob."

While indigenous speech patterns live on in Uglish, Ugandans also change a wide range of English words to suit their needs. Sometimes they even apply English speech patterns where English speakers don't. For example, the Uglish verb, dirten (to make dirty), closely resembles English causative verbs like tighten, stiffen, sharpen, weaken or strengthen. Other times, Ugandans use English words more creatively. Consider the Uglish adaptation of the simple word "beep," which the English use to denote the sound of a car horn. In Uganda, beeping means to call someone, allow the recipient's phone to ring and then hang up before he answers. This indicates that the caller doesn't have enough credit for the call, so the beeped one should call back. The more times one beeps, the more urgently he needs a response. The Uglish verb "flash" describes what happens when a person hangs up so quickly that the phone only has time to light up, without making a sound, before the caller hangs up.

Even more imaginative is the word "rolex," which to a Ugandan is not a fancy watch but rather a type of street food consisting of fried eggs rolled in chapati – in other words, "rolled eggs." Another street food, kikomando, which consists of chopped chapati and beans, is a favourite of tough men with big appetites – construction workers, for instance. Kikomando literally translates to "for or by commando," a term any Schwarzenegger aficionado would immediately appreciate.

Like English, Uglish includes some brand names for items that are so heavily advertised that they become common nouns. "Colgate" means toothpaste, "Blue band" refers to margarine, and "Kiwi" has become a generic name for shoe polish. Other derived Uglish verbs include louse (to idle around), cowardise (to behave cowardly), vibe (to court/woo), and chuck (to reject, divorce, break up, or cut off communication).

Since Ugandans often alternate between two or more languages in a single conversation, they sometimes add English words to local languages. This is especially common when describing something with no local-language translation, such as lockdown, quarantine, and technology. Other times, the borrowing comes out as a blending of English into local languages. For example, "okukomplaininga" is a localised way of saying "to complain."

Borrowing words also works in the opposite direction, with Uglish speakers inserting local-language terms into English sentences when English doesn't quite capture the contextual meaning they want to convey. Common among these are askari (security guard), mukolo (event), kwanjula (a ceremony at which a potential husband is introduced to one's parents) and lumbe (funeral or memorial). A Ugandan might say, "Me, I was the askari at the mukolo. My boss' daughter was kwanjularing her boyfriend, but it was like a lumbe. No one was happy."

Ugandans also sometimes coin their own English slang. They have mined the English expression "The early bird catches the worm" to say one "early birds" when he does something ahead of schedule. The act is described as "early birding." The individual is called an "early bird."

Uglish also lends a local flavour to English by literally translating colloquialisms from indigenous languages into English. Take for example, the expression "to eat money," a direct translation of a Luganda expression, "kulya sente," which also appears in Runyakole, Acholi, and Lango, among other Ugandan languages. The meaning of the expression, translated into English, is "to spend money or to embezzle funds."

The Luganda word "kubula" or "kuburaa" in Runyankore and Rukiga literally means "to be lost or to have disappeared." But when a Ugandan greets another person by saying, "You're lost!" he just means he hasn't seen you in a long time.

Because cousins are considered siblings in most Ugandan tribes, Ugandans often say "cousin brother" or "cousin sister" to mean cousins to accommodate English speakers.

Linguists would say Ugandan English is undergoing a process of "nativisation" in which Standard English is blending with indigenous languages to produce a new vocabulary and grammatical structure. But the process has not reached a stage of "differentiation," in which an even more distinct and stable new language emerges – as, for instance, creole emerged in West Africa. Some forces could push Uganda toward this stage of linguistic development. One is democratisation; while education during the colonial and early post-colonial years was the province of upwardly mobile elite people who attended private schools where the Queen's English was strictly taught, the expansion of schooling has led to the employment of many teachers not so strictly trained or inclined to promote orthodox English. A teacher I met in rural Mbale may typify the new breed. Distracted from our conversation by a student who had been playing in the distance, he shouted, "You girl, you stop. You will dirten yourself. And me, I will punish you." When asked about his command of the English language, he said, "Superb!"

Ugandan language is being shaped by so many crosscurrents it would be foolhardy to predict how it ultimately will evolve. Pop culture is introducing phrases into Uglish at an accelerating rate. One such phrase, "love nigga," a term for a lover who refuses to marry, was popularised in reference to Eddy Kenzo, a popular singer who refused to marry a long-time partner. The phrase was taken up by tabloids and gained popularity via social media. Another popular new Uglish phrase is "in the struggle," which means working hard to make money. A popular TV presenter, known to move from one rich man to another, posted a picture of herself with a rich new boyfriend on Instagram with the caption containing the phrase tuli mu struggle ("we're in the struggle"). It was perceived as indicating she was using him for money, not love. Crystal Panda, a popular artiste made a song, Tuli mu Struggle, which popularised the phrase even further.

Many such additions to Uglish don't go further than the central region of Uganda, however. When I asked about these new phrases, many Uglish speakers in Mbale (East), Gulu (North), and Ibanda (West) weren't even aware of them. Social media, meanwhile, have drawn Ugandans a step further from their roots and closer to the world where English is pervasive. And with apps teaching a multitude of foreign languages but no indigenous Ugandan language, local languages are becoming less and less useful in the day-to-day lives of Ugandans. Their words are becoming foreign to the tongue.

When I met my childhood friend amidst the hubbub of Kampala, I tried to recall the conversations we used to have. I remembered what we discussed, but I could not recall much of how we spoke. Years spent away from Obara – in schools, in new communities, and in cyberspace – introduced us to new languages, but the Obara words, like many others we have learned or coined, have died in our mouths.

Radio Katwe, From Drums to the Internet

By Joachim Buwembo

CENTURIES BEFORE THE COLONIAL takeover brought European "modernisation" to Uganda, our ancestors had an unsophisticated but effective communication system. If, say, a hunter saw signs of small deer or a big buffalo near his village, he would use a horn to alert people in neighbouring villages scattered across the sparsely populated countryside. His counterparts would soon join the hunt, using horns to share intelligence until the animal was cornered and killed.

Kings and chiefs had more "bandwidth." If a king wanted to hold a meeting, he would use human couriers to carry his announcement to chiefs in charge of various localities within his realm. From there, the information would be relayed to scattered villages via messengers or encoded so it could be sent to the most outlying areas by drums and horns. The system worked well, and the right people would soon answer the call (with greater punctuality than we see today). In no time, individual homesteads would be busy carrying out assigned tasks related to agriculture, food, sanitation, flood control, road maintenance, emergency responses or other issues.

In times of war, pre-colonial Africans had another communication tool at their disposal: Smoke signals. Human networks, drums, and horns couldn't carry important messages fast enough or far enough to warriors operating over large areas. Since the eye can see farther than the ear can hear, smoke was a better option.

This early-day communications network was a model of efficiency – one built on tightly-knit social networks and, except in wartime, general social consensus. But then came colonialism, which substituted oppression for love, and fear for respect of authority. Communications networks continued to evolve, but they became a tool for control or opposition, not cooperation. They have continued that way ever since.

Under colonialism, Kampala developed a dual identity as the commercial capital of colonial Uganda and as the kibuga, or capital city, of the Buganda kingdom. The city's population became segregated, with enclaves for Europeans, Indians and Africans. Local artisans congregated in the settlement of Katwe, next to the palace of their leader, the Kabaka. There, they fabricated tools and goods ranging from newspapers to guns – all generally called magezi ga Baganda or "Ugandan wisdom." They also built resistance to colonial rulers by churning out anti-government news that quickly spread by word of mouth.

As the nineteenth century gave way to the twentieth, the radio emerged as a powerful new communications tool. Colonial authorities maintained strict control over broadcast facilities, but the informal and uncontrolled networks became more robust. Eventually, this unofficial source of news came to be called "Radio Katwe," Uganda's first alternative to mainstream news media. The system had no studios, no broadcast towers, and no sets around which listeners would gather to listen. But it had a tool almost as effective: Kampala's emerging local transportation network. Built from the ground up without central planning or finance, the system had become Uganda's best-organised industry, its buses, minibuses and small cars crisscrossing the city and reaching into outlying areas. Anti-colonial activists found they could quickly disseminate their unsanctioned version of news simply by sharing it with taxi drivers.

Radio Katwe made no claim to providing detached or objective journalism. It often dealt in propaganda, rumours and speculation. But the people who strained under the yoke of British colonialism turned out to be savvy news consumers. They did not always believe the news Radio Katwe brought them. "Radio Katwe was not official," explains Ssonko Lule Frederick, who has been a radio journalist for half a century. "Whenever people had something unofficial to say, they would start by saying, 'I have heard from Radio Katwe . . .' That would mean it was a rumour and could, therefore, be true or not."

"Nevertheless," he adds, "people lapped it up for a simple reason. Radio Katwe encouraged people who were losing hope."

Journalism practices have improved tremendously since those days. I have witnessed great change in the tools of the trade since 1989 when I typed my first story on a manual typewriter and hand-delivered it to the editor in the next town 40 kilometres away. Today, reporters digitally transmit their stories to editors who may be far away or seated on the next chair. Although they are guilty of frequent lapses, they go about their jobs with more professionalism – more commitment to bedrock standards of objectivity and balance – than in years past. Today, journalism is a job, not part of a political struggle as it was in the days leading up to Uganda's independence in 1962.

The changes since colonial days haven't been all positive, though. Today's journalists have become detached from the communities they serve. That hard-to-measure quality called passion has become suppressed in the name of objectivity. Call it the price of "modernisation." Today's messengers often appear to lack the sense of purpose that gave Radio Katwe its popularity. They sometimes seem motivated only by the desire to make money – a preoccupation that has grown as digitalisation has undermined the economic foundation on which objective journalism organisations have been based. As in many other places, the mainstream media have responded to financial pressures by cutting staff and holding salaries so low that many journalists leave the trade at an age that their contemporaries in other societies are just coming into their own. Those who stay in the business struggle to make ends meet.

Radio Katwe's reporters never worked for money. Their cause was opposition to colonialism, and they pursued it with determination. Before independence, one nationalist, pan-Africanist dissident John Kale, spent more time training artisans to handle modern weapons in Katwe (he is believed to have stolen them from a high school cadet training armoury at Kisubi) than he did in his studies of veterinary medicine at Makerere University.

Radio Katwe recruited anti-colonial fighters and mastered clandestine activities. It also organised and coordinated boycotts against Indian traders, reporting "traitors" who bought goods from Indians or drank European beer. One of their leaders in the 1950s was political activist Augustine Kamya, a resident of Kampala's Makindye suburb. He lived to see the end of colonial rule, but, in a sad testimony to the enduring strength of Radio Katwe, he was killed in 1972 by the then ruling military regime.

Radio Katwe went into a brief hiatus when Uganda achieved independence. But the independence government soon turned dictatorial, and the underground communications system once again became a force for political resistance.

When military strongman Idi Amin toppled President Milton Obote in a 1971 coup, Radio Katwe entered its golden age. As self-appointed president, Amin proved to be an effective rumourmonger, hiding behind aliases like "the Defence Council," "the Military Spokesman," or simply "the Government" to spread tales that helped confuse his opponents and keep himself in power. Using state radio, television, and newspapers, the "Military Spokesman" convinced many people that powers as big as China were helping Tanzania (where the man Amin overthrew had taken refuge) to invade Uganda.

Tanzania is a multiracial society with many citizens of Arab and Indian descent. Once, when Amin's troops killed a brown-skinned Tanzanian, they brought the body to Kampala and paraded it in the city square for the public to see a "Chinese colonel" killed by heroic Ugandan soldiers. But the dead man's skin quickly turned black in Kampala's heat and the display was abruptly discontinued.

In those days, it is hard to say whether the government or Radio Katwe, was the bigger merchant of what we now call "fake news." As the president churned out his propaganda under different guises, Radio Katwe spread rumours that the military regime was weak, along with exaggerated stories about acts of insanity by government leaders.

War broke out on October 9, 1978, which happened to be the anniversary of Uganda's Independence Day. After weeks of incursions by Amin's troops into Tanzania territory, Tanzanian troops started fighting back, blowing up an armoured personnel carrier deep in Tanzanian territory and killing some Ugandan soldiers on board. Amin's propaganda machine went into overdrive, decrying a "massive" invasion by Tanzania and proclaiming that Uganda would repulse it.

For the next eight months, government media pumped out full-blown lies. As the war progressed onto Ugandan territory and Tanzanian troops approached Kampala, the stories became laughable.

To persuade his citizens of Amin's prowess, the "Military Spokesman" broadcast graphic descriptions of Tanzanian troops as "so exhausted most of them dressed in rags, with no boots and their feet bleeding." When Ugandan troops were forced to retreat into the capital and beyond, the president described the situation as a "tactical withdrawal." To explain why he was not repulsing the supposedly exhausted and bleeding Tanzanians, Amin said he was "still watching the situation with a keen eye." Radio Katwe promptly called his "keen eye" a "closed eye."

Even after Amin and his troops were dislodged, they used advanced mobile communication technology – possibly with collaborators in the transmission unit of the national broadcasting organisation – to interfere with broadcasts for another day or two. He told "his people" that he was "leaving the country for a while to bring reinforcements" and warned people that upon his return, there would be "dire consequences" for those who fraternised with the invaders. That day never came. Amin died in quiet exile 25 years later, leaving behind a population inured to fact-free news.

Uganda did not know peace in the years after Amin's departure. Successive governments were too weak to take effective control of the country, and a civil war raged for five years. It was a hard time for Ugandans, but Radio Katwe was re-energised. One president, who ruled for only 11 months, mockingly renamed Kampala, which is known as the city of seven hills, the 'city of seven daily rumours.' Bus and taxi drivers played a key role in spreading these daily tales.

When Yoweri Museveni's National Resistance Army seized power in 1986, Radio Katwe went into limbo again. The NRM had grown up from the grassroots, and many people in Kampala and the surrounding central region embraced it. But despite growing demand for political pluralism, the government soon clamped down on opposition political activities. Dissent started to stir again.

For a while, radio – the kind that actually used the airwaves – became an outlet for public frustration. In the mid-1990s, the government started licensing private radio stations. Competition for audiences was fierce, and although programming at first was heavily entertainment-based, political talk shows sprang up and quickly gained popularity. Soon, every new radio station had a political talk show. Kampala became a gab fest. Then the creative producers took the shows a notch higher by holding Ugandan versions of town hall meetings, called *bimeeza*, after the wide tables where people typically sat to debate. The public flocked to the events.

Enthusiasm for political debate grew further after a 2005 referendum broke the single-party monopoly on power, restoring political pluralism and freeing parties to compete for power. But the government evidently decided this was too much freedom. It seized a technicality to silence the *bimeeza*: Radio licenses apparently did not permit stations to engage in such activities outside their studios. Modern technology offered a way around the crackdown, though. The mobile phone was no longer a prestige item available only to the rich; ordinary people could call the studios. They did just that. The *bimeeza* moved from public meeting places to the airwaves. Curbing freedom of expression was proving to be difficult.

As radio phone-ins became the in-thing and political contests gathered momentum, the state became smarter. It joined the radio battles, using its greater resources to line up well-coached callers to fight back against its critics over the airwaves. Some people became professional, full-time callers, giving the state's side of the story to every argument.

The state also started using its licensing authority to ensure radio stations would take a friendly stance toward the government. Today, most of the 300 active stations in the country belong to politicians of the ruling party or businesspeople who align with it to protect their investments. During peak campaign seasons, opposition politicians have reported that they often find themselves denied access to the airwaves, even when they have booked and paid for time slots.

With the police working overtly to crush opposition demonstrations and the state gaining control of the mainstream media, Radio Katwe returned in full swing. A new century had dawned and with it came the digital era. Government critics soon popped up online to spread their reports and opinions. They launched a website, aptly called Radio Katwe, but the digitally superior state security apparatus crushed it, apparently by using a virus to bury the website under millions of messages per second. The opposition didn't mourn for long, though. The rapid spread of digital media gave it alternative networks that proved impossible to silence.

One of the first stars of this new communication system was a mysterious cyber character who called himself Tom Voltaire Okwalinga. He popped up on Facebook and soon had a big following. The state couldn't crush TVO (Tee-Vee-Oh), as he (or she) came to be known. To this day, nobody knows his identity. Some suspect that TVO is actually a pseudonym used by a clandestine group. TVO harassed the government with unwelcome news and accusations, some of it appearing to come from very well-connected sources in high government offices. He published sensational claims about the goings-on in the State House and other sensitive government institutions, triggering many manhunts for him. But these always ended up targeting or netting the wrong people.

Once, a couple of suspects thought to be TVO were arrested, but the online hero proved their innocence by continuing to operate even while they were in detention. Later, a private lawyer, whom TVO accused of abusing a client who was a political opponent of the government, filed a lawsuit in Ireland to force Facebook to reveal TVO's identity, but he lost in court. TVO performed his greatest feat in March 2017. While President Museveni was addressing mourners at a vigil in the suburban home of a slain senior police officer, the cyber rebel went live, using the then-new Facebook Live feature to broadcast in real-time from inside the venue. The public wondered how he did it. People assumed he was on the scene. But there also was live television coverage of the event, so TVO may have managed to position his own computer or phone camera in front of a TV screen and obscure the station's logos. However he did it, the image of a dashing figure outsmarting the authorities and broadcasting from a ruling party inner sanctum increased his notoriety. To many, he was a dashing rebel, always a step ahead of his flat-footed enemies.

TVO's success may have emboldened a new kind of media-savvy rebel. Stella Nyanzi, a fiery post-doctoral researcher at Makerere University, attacked the state and its top leaders on Facebook in a way that made TVO seem as gentle as a Sunday school song. Unlike TVO, Nyanzi never hid her identity; in fact, she used her celebrity stature to draw the state into a fight. When she was made to surrender her office space at the university, she protested by stripping for the cameras outside her office in a well-staged publicity stunt (she probably limited her access to mass media, though, by voicing feminist passions in lurid language that is unprintable in "family" news outlets). She was thrown out of her university job, arrested, arraigned and kept in Luzira prison for a month without bail, but she ultimately won her battle with the university and was reinstated. Her next forum for fighting the establishment was Facebook, where in 2019, she attacked dead relatives of the people in power. That earned her a couple of years in jail under laws banning cyber harassment and offensive communication, but she was acquitted on a charge of abusing the president; ironically, she expressed bitter disappointment at this, saying her intention had been to annoy the president with her insults since she had no other way of hurting him. Much as the (social media) public cheered Stella on, the conservative psyche of Uganda culture led many people to disapprove of her explicitly sex-laden language; this probably explains why she lost a 2021 bid to win a parliament seat to a virtually unknown lady who picked the right political team – a very young party that did most of its campaigning on . . . that's right, social media.

In 2018, the state came up with a partial solution to its frustrations with the democratised communications system. Without hiding its objective, it imposed a tax on the use of social media, ostensibly to curb *lugambo*, or "rumour-mongering." No amount of protest from social media users could deter the state from this policy. People had to pay 200 shillings per day to use digital media. The fee – equal to five US cents a day – was not enough to deter Stella Nyanzi and her like, but it did cut a few million Ugandans off from social media. Before the tax became effective, clever people found a workaround; they started using virtual private networks (VPNs), which enable people to gain unfettered (encrypted) access to the internet and social media. Many people lacked the technology, know-how or funds to avoid having their use of social media curbed, but VPNs gained popularity as Chinese-made smartphones became cheaper.

Today, the Ugandan corner of cyberspace boasts hundreds of local "news" websites and millions of social media accounts. Participants in this media melee are not burdened with professional journalism standards requiring verification of information, objectivity, balance and fairness. But they aren't shackled by the financial and business problems that plague the mainstream media either. Of course, social media is cluttered with junk globally, and Uganda is no exception. A post by a top Ugandan researcher fighting malaria or sickle cell anemia might not get ten "likes" or even two "shares" or "retweets," while one by a socialite may get a million views. But that seems to be the story of cyberspace everywhere.

In Uganda, the noise generated in cyberspace may be masking a more profound development, though: Radio Katwe is going online. In its new form, it is young, technologically sophisticated and mostly urban. It lacks a unifying purpose like opposition to colonialism and thus is less cohesive. But it nevertheless may be changing Ugandan politics once again.

For one thing, it has unleashed passionate debate among Ugandans about what kind of society they want to be. To cite just one example, a group of young women who have found each other on Twitter and Facebook now use the platforms to espouse strong feminist ideals. Among other things, they have engaged government officials regarding oppressive and unlawful actions by those in positions of responsibility. At one point, for example, some women spoke online about police officers who had raped them or asked for sex in return for various favours. To speak openly about such matters required courage in a society used to women's silence, and their comments provoked some rather intemperate – or, to put it more bluntly, misogynistic – responses that have drawn the online battle lines sharply.

The freedom of the online world also is unleashing potent social commentary that is missing in the "mainstream" – that is, "old" or "legacy" – media. Some smart journalists who have fled – or been pushed out of – the mainstream media are finding a new home online. One effective polemicist is Timothy Kalyegira, who has gone farther online to provoke the powers-that-be than he could during his print media days. In his digital life, Kalyegira no longer confines himself to attacking political leaders; now he provokes all Ugandans – and African society in general – for what he sees as a lack of inspiration and discipline, which he says keeps the continent lagging behind other countries, including those with whom it was on the same development level in the sixties.

The new, iconoclastic breed of Radio Katwe "broadcasters" are a varied group; if they have a unifying worldview, it is outrage about government corruption, self-dealing, incompetence and efforts to stifle democratic freedoms. Among the latest breed of online fighters is Joseph Kabuleta, once a top sports journalist who in 2018 started making online dispatches that pushed daringly provocative theories accusing authorities of plundering national resources. Kabuleta often lacks all the facts that would make his commentary more interesting and credible, but as Radio Katwe did in its earliest days, he weaves what is known about contemporary affairs into a fabric that often seems to make sense of what otherwise would be confusing. And he does it in his own name. Kabuleta eventually stood for president in a pack of eleven in 2021, running on an interesting proposition: He pledged to "put money in everybody's pocket" and went ahead to show exactly how the money would be generated. He ended among ten "also-rans," but his bid showed that with digital media, a person could have an impact even if he doesn't have money.

So far, the new, digital Radio Katwe caters largely to the small, educated and mostly urban middle class. Until 2021, it posed little threat to President Museveni, who had endured to become one of Africa's longest-serving leaders. A highly skilled politician, he watches the media closely, but he doesn't depend on it. Instead, he maintains close contact with the masses, constantly traveling to far-flung areas and deftly using local languages to win the affection of people in whatever corner of the multi-ethnic country he visits. He also uses patronage effectively to cement his power, sometimes dispensing largesse in large bags filled with hard cash. He even once regaled the Uganda Journalists Association with a large gift, ostensibly to build a new centre. Not surprisingly, the facility is yet to see the light of day, more than a decade later. The money is nowhere to be seen either.

With his mastery of politics, patronage and, if all else fails, the police and army, the president seems to face no serious threat from the old political parties that sprang into existence at independence six decades ago. In fact, the opposition is losing ground as fast as old-technology media. Opposition parties have always had a tenuous hold on the imagination of Ugandans. There are few deep ideological rifts in Ugandan society to exploit, and it is impossible to distinguish between parties based on ideology, philosophy or policies. While the modern economy has spawned a small business elite and a restless urban middle class, they are too few to swing elections.

Still, the new Radio Katwe is making its presence felt. In 2021, a new kind of politician assumed the opposition mantle. Robert Kyagulanyi – better known as Bobi Wine – seemed in ways a direct offspring of Radio Katwe. Like Radio Katwe's founders, he is an artisan – but a distinctly modern one; before launching a career in politics, he was the most successful and wealthiest pop singer in the country. Also, like his predecessors at Radio Katwe, he has proved adept at using social networks. When authorities stopped granting him permits to hold concerts, he started posting his music and politics online. His unofficial manifesto came in the form of a music video that showed him singing and directing scores of extras in a new version of *Engule*, a hymn that traces its origins to 1700s England and took root in Uganda in the 1970s as a rallying cry for Pentecostals rebelling against Idi Amin and the stodgy church establishments of his day. With new lyrics by Kyagulanyi, the song featured people singing and dancing in celebration of hoped-for freedom from discrimination, corruption, heavy-handed policing, land-grabbing, tear gas, dictatorship, and embezzlement of public funds along with lower taxes, good markets for farmers' produce, freedom, and fully functioning hospitals. Its refrain: "When the struggle is over, we will wear the victor's crown and walk with swag in a new Uganda." Mainstream broadcasters shunned the video, but it could be seen and heard – where else? – on YouTube.

In its early days, Kyagulanyi's "People Power" movement had no formal organisation – no headquarters that could be closed, no staff that could be arrested, and no political registration that could be denied or revoked. But it attracted a wide range of followers, including some members of Parliament from the ruling and opposition parties and some people, mostly young adults, from no parties at all. Eventually, Kyagulanyi formed a political party, the National Unity Party, and in 2021 he was its standard bearer in the national elections.

The ten or so weeks of campaigning before the January 14 voting were unprecedented, first because they occurred at the height of the COVID-19 pandemic. The Ministry of Health issued guidelines, enforced by the Uganda Police Force, that prohibited public rallies involving more than 70 people, who had to be spaced two metres apart and wear face masks. And the rallies had to be authorised according to a schedule issued by the Electoral Commission. The rules were flouted daily, especially by parliamentary candidates. But the police blocked Kyagulanyi wherever he went. There were some violent incidents; in the worst, after authorities had arrested Kyagulanyi, 54 people were shot dead. Videos captured on phone cameras and shared widely on social media showed that some bystanders were shot by security forces.

In this volatile situation, Kyagulanyi's strongest tools became Facebook Live and YouTube.

A week or so before the 2021 presidential and parliamentary polls, the government inadvertently confirmed the potency of a digitised Radio Katwe. It formally asked the big global platforms to shut down the accounts of persons who were abusing cyberspace. Facebook reacted, and, no doubt to the government's surprise, it shut down a few hundred accounts run by pro-state players, apparently because the government's fans were the worst violators of its policies. A small number of individuals, for instance, had established multiple accounts to make it appear that their views were held by hundreds of people. Among other things, their posts accused Kyagulanyi of "crimes" like being supported by American gays.

The state's anger was swift: Facebook was officially blocked. So were other social media platforms, including Facebook's WhatsApp. Many users just switched to VPNs. But days before the election, the government shut down the internet entirely. Needless to say, that disarmed Radio Katwe. An online tool Kyagulanyi had just launched to show voting results at polling stations was rendered useless.

With the return of the internet some days after the elections, VPN users started sharing videos of alleged ballot abuses at polling stations, but it was too late. Results showing Museveni winning by a 58%-to-34% margin already had been announced and could only be challenged by a judicial petition supported by evidence. Still, Kyagulanyi probably shocked even himself by garnering more than a third of the ballots cast. The ability of someone who joined politics only three years earlier and whose political party was barely a hundred days old can mostly be attributed to the use of social media – the digital Radio Katwe – to reach the public despite physical obstacles.

What's next? Does Kyagulanyi have a political future? Will social media become a durable *bimeeza* or a political instrument for a new generation? I am loath to venture any predictions, but looming demographic changes just may favour youthful, Internet-savvy candidates. The number of young voters is certain to surge in the years ahead. In 2019, almost half of Uganda's population was under age 14. By the time of the next presidential election in 2026, candidates may be vying for the support of as many as five million first-time voters, many of whom have grown up with the Internet. Kyagulanyi has already used social media effectively, and he is almost 40 years younger than Museveni, who had to persuade Parliament to lift the constitutional retirement age of 75 so that he could seek re-election in 2021 when he was 77.

Somchow, Radio Katwe keeps evolving in response to changing circumstances. As we in the news business used to say, stay tuned.

Wakaliwood: Uganda's Answer to Hollywood

By Stephen Ssenkaaba

JUST WEST OF KAMPALA in Wakiso District, a massive rock rises above the verdant landscape to tower over the tin-roofed mud and wattle houses 40 metres below. This is Kkungu. In folklore, the imposing butte was said to have been the home of a powerful spirit who sometimes took the form of a short, stout but agile man called Kigaanira. Dark as night and known for his long unkempt hair and shrill voice, he would appear in khaki shorts and a sleeveless shirt to greet worshippers. On occasion, he would ascend to the peak of the rock to make dumfounding pronouncements – sometimes predicting war and disaster and other times foretelling peace. His female partner, Nampyangule, often appeared nearby in the form of a beautiful stream. Traditional lore holds that her waters were blessed but warns that people who want to draw from the stream should first seek permission from a snake that lies in wait near the stream, where it feeds its young at midday.

Many people still visit the rock of Kkungu to receive blessings and celebrate the great lore that surrounds it (rock climbers also come to climb its steep cliffs). Newspapers, blogs, travelogues, and television documentaries still relate its legend. Since the early 1950s, Kkungu has been an important place for divination for people of the Mpeewo (bushbuck) totem. One person who heard such stories from his grandmother is Isaac Godfrey Nabwana, who has become a legend in his own right as an artist who combines elements of traditional storytelling with modern social commentary in a new and distinctly Ugandan genre of movie making.

From the dusty paths and lush green of rural villages to the shanties and slum neighbourhoods of cities, Nabwana's movies evoke places where Ugandans grew up, played, and worked. They also tackle beliefs that were handed down from earlier days and endure to this day. In a society where some people go to church by day and consult traditional medicine men by night; where others carry good-luck charms from their jajjas (local diviners) in their handbags; where some people never embark on a journey without first sacrificing a chicken to appease the gods; where tycoons have been known to sacrifice goats and sometimes even humans before undertaking major financial projects; where business competitors place bad luck charms on each other's doorstep, Nabwana's movies are a mirror through which many of his fans can see themselves – their trials, triumphs, joys and sorrows, as well as their doubts, fears and foibles. Along the way, the movies give people a chance to laugh at the folly of some aspects of their society.

On a slow, dreary Saturday evening, I meet Nabwana at his home and studio in Wakaliga, a shanty town on the southwestern edge of Kampala. Rickety video halls boom with life as I navigate the narrow mud paths of the famous slum. Sounds of kung fu kicks and talk of thieves escaping from a shrine emanate from a rusty structure made of iron sheets. These whet my viewing appetite, but also my eagerness to meet the filmmaker who has won the hearts of many Ugandans by producing raw, mostly low-cost films amid the one-room tenements, muddy paths and open streams of sewage here. A slum might seem a surprising place for a movie studio, but Nabwana wears his roots with pride. He calls his studio Wakaliwood, linking it both to his immediate surroundings and to another centre of film-making half a world away – Hollywood. The similarity ends with the name, though. Nabwana's company, Ramon Film Productions, doesn't celebrate itself with glamorous starlets walking on red carpets or depict the lives of the rich and famous. Instead, its gritty output reflects the lives and daily struggles of ordinary Ugandans, often packaged in popular Buganda myths, folktales and wry humour.

Wakaliwood is the size of about a quarter of a soccer field. When I visit, it is a beehive of activity. Young men and women scurry from a rehearsal room to Nabwana's house, collecting cameras and recorders to film a scene. Makeshift sets, a prop room full of movie guns and even a life-sized model of a helicopter made of scrap metal all attest to the filmmaker's commitment to capturing the trappings of modern life while exploring traditional themes.

Nabwana is a soft-spoken man with a round mane of kinky, dark hair that is starting to show strands of grey. During our first meeting, he wears a loose blue t-shirt emblazoned with the phrase "Wakaliwood" on the back. When we sit to talk, he has just taken a break from a gruelling rehearsal for a new film project. He knows what movie I heard when I walked in to meet him. "It is called *Ejiini ly'entwetwe* (The Spirit of Ntwetwe)," he says. "I shot it right here."

Ntwetwe is a rural enclave in Buganda that, for many years, was the site of myths about witchcraft. The movie explores the turbulent lives of the residents and their attempts to justify their ways to outsiders – all with a good dose of satire aimed at well-off people who view the place with a mixture of fear and disdain. In Nabwana's Ntwetwe, dead bodies walk, as do beer calabashes. One does not offend an elder and get away with it. When a group of arrogant young city dwellers (Bannakampala) mess with a local resident, every scary story they have heard or imagined about the village comes to life.

The story begins when the urbanites, driving to attend a burial in the village, offer a lift to an elderly man who happens to be going to the same ceremony. He carries a calabash full of local brew. Some of the drink spills in the car, prompting the young men to throw him out. As they pour his beer on the ground and throw insults at him, the embarrassed older man grumbles a promise to pay them back. Soon after they leave him, their luck changes. First, their car breaks down. After they solve that problem and are ready to resume their trip, they find themselves in a thick forest. That obstacle eventually clears away, but when they reach the burial site, they are surprised to find the elderly gentleman already there. After the burial, the vehicle once again refuses to start. When it finally starts, they can't leave because one of them suddenly disappears. They finally find him brewing beer at the elderly man's brewery. He eventually releases the young man, but only after being satisfied that he has paid the young men back for their rude behaviour.

Ntwetwe is a village of powerful spirits, where no sin goes unpunished. In a subplot of Nabwana's movie, a group of young men who stop on their way to buy some yellow bananas take more than they had paid for. As they leave, a wine calabash starts chasing them and does not stop until they return what they had stolen.

While toying with ideas about witchcraft and its impact on society, the movie adds traces of contemporary life. At one point, a white missionary finds himself in the way of the calabash as it chases offenders. In another, several characters employ kung fu tactics to ward off their enemies, Jackie Chan style. And an episode of gunfire mimics scenes from Sylvester Stallone's Rambo. With this clever blend of elements, Nabwana gently pokes fun at Ugandans, westerners and Asians alike.

"Of all movies that I have made, this is the best-selling, but also the most pirated," Nabwana tells me. He accepts his losses with pleasure rather than anger. "Wherever I go, people ask me about this movie. More than five years since its release, I still get calls from people as far away as Soroti in eastern Uganda asking if they can get a copy," he says. He notes that the movie has done particularly well among petty traders in Kampala's second-hand markets, taxi drivers and newspaper vendors. But many members of the so-called "corporate class" who hold 8-to-5 office jobs buy it too.

Ugandans love the movie partly because its scenes are familiar. But uncomfortable subjects are a Nabwana speciality. At the time of our interview, he and his team are working on *Eaten Alive*, a movie about cannibalism – another topic rooted in folklore that continues to have a hold on the Ugandan imagination. In some communities, people, especially the less educated, believe it really occurs – a notion so powerful that some people have exploited it as a scare tactic. *Eaten Alive* is about a man and his expectant wife who travel to attend a burial in the town of Masaka in southwestern Uganda but later fail to find transportation home. They end up spending the night at the house of the Local Council chairman, who, during the night, hatches a plan with some of his relatives and friends to eat their visitor's wife and her unborn baby.

This story was triggered by a real-life news event that was first reported in Bukedde – a newspaper published in Luganda, the predominant native language in central Uganda. For dramatic effect, Nabwana introduces a white man (muzungu) who later visits the village and is eaten. The filmmaker agrees that the story speaks about some people's obsession with cannibals and what they do, but says he also just wanted to give his audience a good laugh.

Nabwana tapped mythical stories he heard in his own childhood for a movie he called *Bukunja Tekunja Miti* – a title used figuratively to mean that cannibalism really is practiced in Bukunja, a village in central Uganda. He recalls growing up hearing that people had to look out for their safety when visiting the place lest they would be eaten. "We were told some residents would dig deep pits inside their houses, place sharp spears in them and cover them with mats in order to trap visitors for dinner," he explains.

Nabwana's film showcases children from a modern Ugandan family who live and study abroad but visit their uncle's ancestral home in Bukunja. Though warned not to go out of the house at night because cannibals would eat them, they tempt fate one night by sneaking out to go to a disco hall, only to be waylaid by "night dancers" – cannibals who dance around their victims' homes in the dark of night before dining on them. The story is shown to be a fantasy when the children wake up in the morning only to realise it was all a dream.

Nabwana was born in 1972 in Mpigi, about a 45-minute drive southwest of Kampala. His mother was a young school dropout when she gave birth to him. He was raised by his paternal and maternal grandmothers, from whose first names, Rachel and Monica, he derived his studio name – Ramon. Nabwana spent part of his childhood in Wakaliga on a large piece of family land that is now the home of Wakaliwood. "We grew up in a culture of superstition," Nabwana recalls. "A lot of what we did had a superstitious explanation to it. Dogs and women were associated with bad luck, while mice were believed to be a source of blessings. Whichever of these you encountered on your way to work or school determined your fate for the day. If you found a woman or a dog as you set out for school or work in the morning, it was a premonition you would have a bad day. It was your cue to cancel the journey or change routes. On the other hand, if you met a rat as you left home early in the morning, that was a sign of good luck and fortune." Such beliefs were far from universal. Other Ugandan communities had different ideas; the Bakiga, for instance, thought that mice were related to poverty and girls to good luck.

Nabwana saw the story-telling potential in folklore as a child when one of his grandmothers told him the story of Kkungu. Forty years later, he is a father of three, but he bounces with excitement when he remembers her accounts of the spirit of the rock and his wife, the stream Nampyangule. "My grandmother told me so many stories about those rocks – some scary, others funny. She told me that Nampyangule, the stream, was generous but strict – that before drawing her water, one had to dance and sing." As he speaks, he smiles and throws his hands in different directions to underscore his points.

His brother, Robert Kizito, introduced him to the world of film. Kizito worked as a narrator of foreign action movies for audiences who didn't understand English. In the days before Ugandans used English widely, narrating foreign films was a true art form; clever narrators not only translated and explained the stories to viewers but creatively embellished them, frequently adding satirical commentary about how the stories reflected "strange" muzungu beliefs and customs. Nabwana does the same by aping foreign film styles, including martial arts, which he first saw depicted in Chinese sports magazines when he was still in primary school. He and Kizito practiced kung fu by sparring with each other as boys.

After graduating from Old Kampala secondary school, Nabwana worked as a welder and later as a bricklayer before founding Ramon music studio in 2005. In 2007, he moved to Wakaliga and established Wakaliwood. At first, the company consisted of just Nabwana, his wife Harriet, and a few young men. They were energetic; the studio produced more than 40 films in its first 13 years. While Nabwana is distinctly Ugandan, his movies now attract viewers as far away as Europe and America.

Nabwana applies the sense of imagination, gift for story-telling and deft mix of horror and humour that he learned from Ugandan folklore to address contemporary issues.

In a film called *Once a Soldier*, for instance, he tackled the issue of corruption. Agubiri, who deserted the army for reasons that aren't given, works diligently in a factory until one day, officers from the National Anti-Smuggling Unit (a now-defunct government agency) connive with army officers to steal merchandise from the plant. They stage a bombing as a diversion, and then accuse Agubiri of planning the attack. After escaping, fleeing and engaging in a trademark Nabwana brawl, the hapless hero finally manages to convince the factory earners that he is innocent. His tormentors end up behind bars while he is set free.

Justice is more elusive in *Who Killed Captain Alex?*, one of Nabwana's first movies. The titular captain, a senior soldier in the Ugandan army, is on a mission to neutralize "Tiger Mafia," a clandestine gang of thugs terrorizing the city. After a bitter battle that leaves many people dead on both sides, the head of the outlaw group sends a female spy to infiltrate Captain Alex's camp. She successfully befriends Captain Alex, who is later found dead under mysterious circumstances. The killer is never found in this not-so-subtle dig at government incompetence.

Ani Mulalu (The Crazy World) uses the story of a madman to question our society's rationality. It is a dryly funny story with sub-themes involving child sacrifice, blood money and the greed and foolishness of the rich, who in this movie engage in witchcraft to increase their wealth. *Operation Kakongoliro* (The Ugandan Expendables) delves into the plight of girls abducted during the war. The bitter topic is made a bit more palatable to audiences through exaggerated antics, but it still pointedly questions the commitment of those in power to protect vulnerable children.

While Nabwana has a wide range of themes to work with as a social critic, his perspectives are consistently rooted in his home base – Wakaliga, or as he unabashedly puts it, "the ghetto." Slums have become an increasingly large part of Kampala as people have fled troubled regions or decided to look for new economic opportunities.

People may debate whether these urban immigrants have found better lives, but people still come. Kampala has now joined other nations, developed and not-so-developed, in having large, economically segregated neighbourhoods.

The day I interview Nabwana, a makeshift sign over the entrance to his studio proclaims that visitors have reached the "Ghetto Republic of Uganja." The pun on "Uganda" may capture the sense of rebellion in slums, or perhaps it's just another example of Nabwana's wit. Not surprisingly, it also is a backdrop for a film in progress at the time of my visit. *Ghetto Republic* explores life in run-down neighbourhoods through the eyes of a young boy from a Kampala slum who somehow visits the United States and returns with a load of cash. On his return, the boy goes around his neighbourhood, giving out money to the local people and spending lavishly on food, nice clothes and alcohol. His followers start to call him "King of the Ghetto." As his spending spree continues, word goes around that an undercover American detective has come to Uganda on the trail of a Ugandan youth who committed murder and stole money in the States. The story ends with the arrest of the errant "king." Nabwana is not simply denouncing misdeeds like theft, though; his movie speaks to increasing materialistic tendencies – an inclination his ghetto community shares with the larger society.

Nabwana's art imitates life again in *Bad Black*, a film named for one of Kampala's most notorious "socialites." The real story on which the movie was based was sordid, but in this case, the filmmaker was idealistic. The real-life Bad Black seduced and lived off a wealthy British businessman until he accused her of defrauding him. She was found guilty and given a four-year jail term, but in the process, became a heroine of sorts in Kampala. On the day her trial ended, she was hailed in an impromptu parade through downtown Kampala, a heroine among those at the bottom of the socio-economic ladder who know it takes luck and street smarts to beat the rich and powerful.

Bad Black the movie tells the story of a young girl who is driven from home by a cruel uncle following the death of her father. Destitute, she starts living on the streets and scavenging for food. When she turns 18, she visits her childhood home, where her grandmother tells her about a suitcase that her father bequeathed to her. It contains her birth certificate and a stash of cash. This girl returns to the streets and starts dishing out her money to fellow street children. She also gets involved in some shady business. In one scam, she secures visas for people desperate to travel abroad. In another, she steals money from a British tourist. Then, on a visit to her childhood home, she finds an old man and starts an affair with him, only to learn that he is her grandfather, whom she never knew. A scuffle ensues, and the young woman's family takes her to court. During the trial, she divulges the details of her birth based on what she learned from the suitcase. Then, in a surprise turn of events, a woman who is in the courtroom turns out to be the young lady's real mother. They embrace and start a new journey together. In Nabwana's telling, ghetto life may force harsh choices on people, but wholesome values sometimes prevail.

Nabwana's irreverence has won him criticism at times. Some church and school leaders say his films promote violence. He argues differently; he says it is Hollywood movies that promote violence, while his teach children about death as one of the real consequences of violence. Nabwana says he decided long ago that stars would die in his films, even if that might displease the audience. The director's willingness to acknowledge the reality of death is on display in a room at his Ramon studios, where an entire wall is covered by the names of scores of his actors who have "died" in his movies and the dates of their cinematic deaths.

The wall reflects Nabwana's sense of humour, but he is serious about young people, who he believes represent a bright future for Uganda's movie industry. He argues that older people are too taken with

Western movies to see the potential for Ugandan people to create good movies on Ugandan themes. "By the time we entered the market, older people were used to Arnold Schwarzenegger, Rambo and the rest," he says. "Our work looks amateurish to them. But younger people are more attuned to the potential of movies to recreate Ugandan culture, with its unique folklore, current events, language, style and people." In deliberately aiming his movies at young people, he says, "we are grooming tomorrow's audience."

He is also cultivating tomorrow's filmmakers. I return to Wakaliwood on another day to see Nabwana and his team hard at work. Actors and actresses, film crew, make-up artists, and assorted technicians are busy filming one of the director's trademark martial-arts scenes. Actors meticulously plan their every move, act them out in slow motion, and run through countless rehearsals until they are punching, kicking, falling and running at full speed. Finally, they are ready. Nabwana breaks away from our conversation to begin filming. Their performance looks flawless to me from the outset, the actors moving with such speed I am surprised they don't hurt themselves. But the director orders them to act out the scene over and over. It takes almost two hours to film the scene, which will be less than a minute in the movie. The work is so strenuous and time-consuming that it seems a football match would be less physically demanding.

Most remarkable is the crew's dedication. They work this hard for almost no pay. Almost the entire creative team – actors and actresses, film crew, set designers and technicians – are, like Nabwana, school dropouts who have no formal training in the arts. That doesn't matter to Nabwana. "Art is not so much a matter of what you learn in art school as how you creatively express yourself," he says. "It is a talent given to some people by God."

The creative spirit expressed in Ugandan folklore is alive and on the move. It will be interesting indeed to see what Nabwana's apprentices produce in the decades to come.

Isaac Nabwana – In His Own Words

My career started in 2005 when I decided to venture into music. I opened a small music studio in my house in Lungujja, just about a 20-minute walk from Wakaliga. As I set up the studio, I enrolled in an editing and computer graphics course. I brought many young boys to my studio facility – including a few people who are now famous musicians: Eddy Kenzo, Master Parrot and others.

In 2007, I thought about buying a camera. I identified a video camera, approached the guy who was selling it and asked him to allow me to pay for it in instalments as I didn't have enough money to pay at once. It cost me 700,000 shillings. Before that, I had started making music videos using a Samsung Video Camera that I would borrow from my neighbour, Shafic. Every Saturday, I would shoot videos capturing performances by young musicians like the now famous Kenzo. After some time, I thought about shooting short martial-arts skits. Soon, I put together a team of young men in my neighbourhood and interested them in acting martial arts. We would feign kung fu plots, imitating Bruce Lee, Jackie Chan and John Rambo.

In 2008, one of the young men introduced me to a gentleman called Isaac Ssempijja who had some acting experience. When we met, he said he was planning to turn a folktale into a film. He was happy to take me on, and I agreed to work with him.

The movie was called *Ekisa Butwa* ("Kindness Begets Bitterness"). It was about a conflict in which a young Muslim lady fell in love with a Catholic man, but the bride's parents objected to the union. We introduced a ghost that comes to haunt the man and his girlfriend, tormenting their lives and scaring friends and family away. The ghost appears several times in the couple's dreams and later as hallucinations that become the talk of the neighbourhood. The couple see a witchdoctor. Eventually, they break up. The film was very popular. People in the communities around Lyantonde, where we shot it, asked us to do more such films. They were impressed by the way we built tension in this movie, bringing to life something many of them had grown up hearing about but never quite experienced.

After that, I got a team of young men together to work on a new story that we called *Byabuuka* ("Everything Flew Away"). The story is about a rich man who starts an affair with another man's wife. When the jilted husband learns about this, he consults a witchdoctor, who asks him to take a charm and place it somewhere inside his house. One day, as the rich man is having a good time with the jilted man's wife, his property suddenly starts flying out of the house – the fridge, sofa sets, cooker, television set, even the family car. The rich man is so scared that he seeks help from an evangelical pastor, who prays for him. Thanks to the churchman's intervention, the things that had flown away start to return. People enjoyed the movie very much, and this gave me the courage to continue.

I committed myself to continue making movies that reflected our own realities. I knew traditional folklore and all the themes surrounding daily activities in our society were going to be a huge part of my work.

Some of the things that I portray in my movies have a lot of bearing on experiences that I went through as a child. For instance, when my grandfather died, no one could find his will. The entire family went into a frenzy. Suspicions arose that perhaps some selfish, greedy family members had stolen the will to have it manipulated. It was a stressful moment for the family. Then one of my uncles told the distressed family that my grandfather had appeared to him in a dream and had told him where to find his will: in a black book kept by a certain lawyer in town. When the family checked with the lawyer, they found that the dream was exactly right.

I was only a young boy when this happened, but something about it stayed with me for a very long time. Do dead people return in dreams and talk to some people? So many of the movies that I have made have scenes that depict the deceased returning to speak to the living about something. Many of us have grown up around such narratives. This was my way of preserving them and giving Ugandans something to enjoy and identify with.

This – for me and, I believe, for many people – is an important way to preserve our culture. Even though we have gone digital as a society, these old, traditional myths and ways of seeing and appreciating our society need to be maintained. And this is what I have tried to do. In order not to alienate modern culture, I have modernised these tales and stories by portraying them in film and showing them on high-definition screens. That enables me to bring a modern touch to these stories.

However modern we become, superstition and belief in supernatural powers remain a huge part of our society. Look at the items people carry to football games whenever the national team or other local clubs are involved in big matches. Some people go with chickens to spell good luck to their team. Others carry calabashes. Some of our opponents know this, and they exploit our superstitious nature. Do you remember the African soccer qualifying match against Rwanda's national team in 2004? How the Rwandan goalkeeper kept a stash of what looked like herbs folded in a piece of cloth by his goalpost? Remember the frenzy that followed when a goal scored by Ugandans was disallowed? Ugandans quickly attributed it to witchcraft. It was hard to convince them that it was a questionable goal.

My desire to reflect us – the things that define our beliefs, our ways of life, perhaps even our biases – inspired me to reflect mythical, superstitious and sometimes ghost-filled themes in my movies. I love to portray these in film because film has an interesting way of modernizing these rather old-fashioned themes.

I was raised in a slum and my heart beats for Wakaliga and other such run-down places. For me, it is home. It is where my heart is, but it also has provided rich fodder for incredible storylines that have won many hearts. The storylines in my films reflect the struggles of ordinary people who live in run-down places like Wakaliga. They show poverty, desperation and wealth, thereby reflecting the poor-rich divide in our society. My films also reflect how superstition and belief in indigenous traditional practices transcend class and other boundaries, especially by depicting rich and poor people visiting traditional healers or mythical places for solutions to their problems. You could say that my work meets different people of different classes at their different points of need. While the poor love my work because it reflects their world and speaks a language that they understand (a language that is unsophisticated and reminiscent of school dropouts), for the elite, my films are parodies of their follies and hypocrisy. They mirror social iniquities.

Doing this work has been an important part of my life because through my films, I not only entertain people, I also document culture and its impact on Ugandans and people abroad. I have been privileged to serve my community and to have had a positive impact on the lives of many people.

At some point, I got an idea of building a school because of my own education experience. I went through much trouble going to school that I didn't wish anyone else to go through. I used part of the family land and some of our structures in Wakaliga to set up Crane Education Centre. I tried to start an education foundation to support children from poor backgrounds to get an education. I named it Ramon Foundation after my two beloved grandmothers who raised me – Rachel and Monica. I used to support so many children from poor families to go back to school. While I didn't have much money myself, I used some of the profits that I got from making bricks to raise money to buy scholastic materials for these children and pay the teachers. Sometimes, well-wishers contributed to the initiative. I later established Nateete Mixed Academy. This, too, worked for some time, but it didn't go well, so I abandoned it. I consider helping disadvantaged children important because of my own experience growing up. I was abandoned at an early age but survived by God's grace and the kindness of my poor grandmothers. They didn't have much, and yet they supported me. I have since felt the need to carry on the love by giving back to those in need.

I have always wondered how different Wakaliga would be if all its children had a chance at education.

A Healing Tradition

By Flavia Nassaka

MY MOTHER SUDDENLY STARTED weeping. She cried so hard that I had to stop the car just as we started driving out of the parking lot. It was early afternoon. We had been at Butabika National Referral Mental Hospital since early morning. Waiting in long queues to refill her prescriptions had become a monthly routine since she had been diagnosed with depression a year earlier.

But that is not why she was weeping. "These are tears of joy," she said. Struggling to control her emotions, she thanked me for understanding that she had suffered for many years. We had never spoken about her condition outside of the psychiatrist's office. "I constantly felt trapped," she stammered. "I always feared that my children would abandon me. I was so scared. Yet I could do nothing about it. It has been too dark. All I wanted was to leave, to die." Like many other people, I did not know how to handle this topic, so as usual, I gently coaxed her to refrain from starting such conversations.

My mother's struggle began more than 20 years ago. I first became aware of it as a child one evening when our family had just finished prayers and gathered on the mat so she could serve dinner. Suddenly, instead of serving us, she dashed to the bedroom without explanation. Father rushed after her. He reappeared minutes later. "They are back," he announced, before quickly returning to her. I did not know who "they" were, but I feared the worst; could "they" be some malevolent beings from the spirit world? Worry gripped our uncle's face. The silence was loud. Then, Mother began shouting at the top of her voice. As Father pled with her to calm down, our uncle herded us children to our bedroom. When we arose the next morning, father told us mother would be away from us for some time. She was sick, he told us. We knew Mother had "run mad."

When my mother fell ill, people with symptoms like hers typically visited traditional healers, who usually said they had been possessed by evil spirits or were being harassed by deceased ancestors. Treatment ranged from herbal remedies to animal sacrifice. But my mother went to a facility. That may sound like progress, but it is less impressive when you consider that the place was little more than a warehouse for people. When our father took us for a visit one Sunday afternoon, I saw nothing in the compound except a small hut and a few goats grazing on overgrown grass.

I was just 11 years old – too young to understand what I was seeing. I did not ask any questions – even at the sight of my mother's bloodshot eyes and unkempt hair. I remember her wearing a floral dress during one visit. She was sitting on a small mat when we entered the hut where she was staying. She looked up, but her gaze seemed uncomprehending. She never said a thing – not even later, when she finally returned home. Dad warned us to keep her condition a family secret – to deny knowing anything about her whereabouts if anybody inquired. Mother's younger sister was told to report anyone who disobeyed this directive.

Mental illness continues to be a subject of shame and fear to this day, partly because it is poorly understood. Psychiatrists use terms like schizophrenia, bipolar disorder, mania or depression, but these remain alien concepts to most Ugandans – and, indeed, to most

Africans. Our languages generally have no word for them; in my native tongue, Luganda, it is difficult to say anything more than "eryo ddalu" – one "has run mad."

Treatment options are still limited. Uganda, a country of more than 40 million people, had just 49 psychiatrists as of April 2021. Until recently, Butabika Hospital, which was established in 1955, was the country's only mental health facility. The government recently established regional mental health referral facilities to ease pressure on the hospital, but they fall far short of meeting the need. Many people still do not believe in modern, science-based treatment. Yet traditional treatments are losing favour too, mainly because many people consider them barbaric. Seeing no options, some families lock up their mentally troubled members and keep them out of sight. Some let healers see their afflicted loved ones, but only secretly.

In this void, superstition prevails. When a person has attempted or committed suicide, for instance, people will summon the most energetic youths in the village to whip him (or her) severely (or the body if the suicide has been completed) to please the gods. The body can never be buried in a family cemetery, and villagers cleanse themselves in baths of herbs to protect them against bad things they fear may happen because of the act.

It wasn't until years after my mother's breakdown that I started to understand what had happened in my family – and in the process to see mental health not as a reason for shame but as a public health issue. I had become a health journalist, and during the course of my work, I happened to meet Dr. Emilio Ovuga, a psychiatrist, educator and indefatigable advocate for better mental health services. I developed a sense of kinship with him when, to my surprise, he told me that his mother had suffered much the same way my mother did. Then came a bigger surprise: His mother was a traditional healer.

How does the son of a traditional healer become a modern psychiatrist? How does a person who grew up in the care of a woman who belongs to a profession that is widely denounced as unscientific reconcile his upbringing with his professional training in science-based medicine? The answers, I would learn, add up to a rich Ugandan story.

Dr. Ovuga grew up in a small village called Nyangiri in northern Uganda's Moyo District, just south of Uganda's border with what is now South Sudan. Six siblings who preceded him had died in infancy, and a sister 12 years his senior gave him the name "Ovuga," which means "for the grave" in the language of his people, the Madi. But despite her grim prediction, he survived. He was with his mother when she first got sick and later when she was initiated into the healing practice. He remembers seeing her roll on the ground crying whenever her illness set in. She got better after a traditional healer called Opoka treated her. Opoka taught her about emotional problems and how to solve them. Eventually, she started treating patients herself. This was not unusual. The World Health Organisation estimates that 80% of Africans who have suffered from mental illness have sought help from traditional healers. Studies also have shown that many healers experienced emotional problems themselves before being treated and subsequently recruited into the healing profession by other healers. The experienced healers believed that their patients' mental disorders arose from the spirit world and that their contact with the spirit world would enable them to help others.

The doctor described his childhood observations in a wide-ranging discussion I had with him at his quiet home in Luzira, on the shores of Lake Victoria. In those days, he said:

> *The most common explanation for mental illness was that*
> *it is a form of punishment for the family of an ancestor*

who committed a wrong and that it is caused by bad spirits that linger in the community. Some people believed that spirits who did not have family members to take care of them would jump into a victim and make him mentally ill; if the family of a mentally ill person sought the help of a traditional healer, the spirit would express through the healer its wish for a human home. The healer might expel the spirit, or the family might accept the spirit into their home; either action would cure the mentally ill person.

Severe forms of mental illness would keep recurring, though. When that happened, the person would be considered beyond cure. Such people used to walk freely in the villages. They were not harmful because nobody provoked them. If they came to a home, the mother in the home would give them water and something to eat. Occasionally one of them would wander into the bush and not return; if that happened, community members would mount a search and bring the person back. But unfortunately, most of them ended up disappearing into the wilderness and dying. I remember an age-mate who was brought back several times. He was not harmful or violent. One day, he disappeared again. As usual, the community looked for him but failed to find him.

After I went to secondary school, a classmate of mine who had gone to Israel for training came back mentally ill. He, too, started wandering in the community. One Saturday when I was home during vacation, he came to my hut. We talked for almost two hours. He never came back. He might be dead now.

Dr. Ovuga's mother told him she had been possessed by Mulai, an

Acholi spirit that enlisted her to work as an herbalist and spiritual medium. One evening, the spirit was unusually aggressive. Mr. Opoka, the traditional healer, was there. The young Ovuga watched as the spirit made his mother bounce on her knees and bum to the front of the hut where a treatment session was to be conducted. She danced until the spirit left her. Soon after that, people started flooding our home for treatment.

She cured people of afflictions ranging from fevers to evil spirits, from natal or neonatal teeth in babies (a rare condition of uncertain origin) to infertility in adults. She even helped hunters who were failing to kill any game. The young Ovuga, who was close to his mother because he was the only child still at home, developed a soft spot for these troubled ones, perhaps because he otherwise might have been lonely since there were no other children in the home. He described how she interacted with her many patients.

> *She would make physical and behavioral observations and then talk with them so she could understand the origin of their distress. She used to take their histories to identify cultural, social and traditional explanations for their maladies. Some of her patients were young women who had failed to become pregnant. Such women often would present with physical signs of depression and worry. My mother would inquire into their marital situations – whether their marriages were polygamous, whether they were under pressure from their husbands' families or their own families to get pregnant. She might ask such a woman to return with her husband, and she would make herbal preparations for them to drink once a day for three days. During those three days, the couple would be given their own hut – we had at least two huts where clients could sleep. To my surprise, many couples who received this treatment reported pregnancy a few*

months after the visit. I do not know who gave her the knowledge about which plant materials to mix; she never explained anything to me.

I pressed the doctor to explain why he thought his mother's treatments worked. He said faith, belief in the competence of the therapist and hope that her herbs would work all could have led to positive outcomes. Also, herbs she used to address infertility may have contained chemicals that increase ovulation. He didn't rule out the possibility that modern science might be able to validate some of her practices; after all, scientists have developed chemicals that increase ovulation and ease anxiety. And there is evidence that high-quality interpersonal interaction between a therapist and a client can explain what researchers call a "placebo effect" – a scientifically unexplained improvement in health that sometimes occurs when participants in studies are given pills that have no medicinal content.

Looking back, Dr. Ovuga says his mother probably suffered from depression or a dissociative disorder – a condition in which a person becomes disconnected from her thoughts, feelings, memories or surroundings. Her personal history would help her understand other patients similarly afflicted. To help them, she would put cowry shells in a calabash, seal it and shake it. Next, she would rub it on the face of the depressed person and then move it downward, hitting her patient's chest. Depending on the severity of the problem, she might continue this treatment downward all the way to his feet. She would repeat the procedure for three days for a man and four days for a woman. She explained that depression makes a person's heart fall out of its place. She had a way of measuring how far. When she found the heart in the top parts of the body, the hitting would not continue downward. For people with the most severe depression – ones whose hearts had dropped all the way to their feet – the treatment would follow its course all the way down. She also would tell some people to perform animal sacrifices to appease the ancestors.

Dr. Ovuga still wonders whether the spirit Mulai diagnosed patients for his mother or she came to these conclusions based on her own experience as a patient. He told me:

She could observe clients and know that they were suffering from worry, anxiety or depression, for instance, and tell them they were under the influence of a spirit that needed to be expelled or appeased. That's not so different from what some Ugandan doctors do today.

Science shows that mental illness is caused when levels of one of several biochemical neurotransmitters become imbalanced under conditions of stress. Neurotransmitters are chemicals in the brain that transport nerve impulses – electrical messages – within the brain and between it and other parts of the human body. Some researchers still use cultural explanations for these imbalances – blaming the symptoms on evil spirits associated with traumatic experiences, homeless spirits or spirits of people who were killed unjustly. So now you hear a mix of scientific and cultural explanations.

Dr. Ovuga could offer no explanation for a prediction his mother made about him, though. Despite the history of infant deaths in his family and the grim name his sister gave him, she told the boy his only health problem would come from the heat of the sun. She turned out to be right. His only health problems growing up came after long trips he frequently took under the scorching sun.

While Dr. Ovuga says his mother's theories became entrenched in his worldview at an early age, his interest in science and psychiatry also took root when he was young. The two worldviews coexisted side by side.

When I was a young boy, probably between age 3 and 5, there was a lot of sleeping sickness in my community, so health workers came once a year to examine people for signs of the disease. They would palpate people in the neck to check for swelling, the first sign someone has the disease. When a medical assistant palpated me, I thought I wanted to be a doctor like him.

When I was in Primary Six, I went into the care of my maternal uncle, who paid my school fees. He and his wife were both teachers. I was an avid reader of newspapers, magazines and books. One day I found a small pamphlet: 'Psychiatry for the Layman.' I did not even know how to pronounce 'psychiatry.' I used to call it 'p-s-chiatry.' But I read it from cover to cover. It intensified my earlier feeling that I should pursue a career in understanding human behavior.

Dr. Ovuga was a good student. He went on to study at Kings College Buddo, a secondary school set up by Christian missionaries to give free education to promising students.

In secondary school, my interest wavered between engineering, law, electronic technology, architecture and medicine. One day, I went to my headmaster, Brother Howard of the Congregation of the Sacred Heart, and I said to him, 'Brother, I want to be a doctor.' I mentioned the other professions that interested me as well. He asked me: 'Are you not afraid of blood?' When I instantly said no, he said: 'In that case, go for medicine.' When he left, he was replaced by the first African Headmaster, Mr. Henry Omwony, who also said I should go for medicine. This encouraged me a great deal.

Dr. Ovuga took their advice. And when he was admitted to medical school at Makerere University, he opted to seek a degree in psychiatry. But even at the university, he sometimes encountered unscientific thinking.

> *When we were in year two, I asked to spend my free time observing a senior lecturer help people in Butabika National Mental Teaching Hospital. He thought I was crazy and asked me, 'Do you have episodes of anxiety?' That question made me stop dealing with him. Sometimes even mental health professionals stigmatise psychiatry and persons who suffer from mental illness.*

Many of his peers expressed fear that dealing with mentally ill patients would make them become mentally ill themselves. This myth may help explain why very few students chose to pursue studies in psychiatry or psychology. Dr. Ovuga was one of only two students in his class who decided to specialise in psychiatry. There were no Ugandan professors of psychiatry at the time, so the two were taught exclusively by foreign professors. Dr. Ovuga's psychiatry classmate now lives in the UK. The situation hasn't changed much. Even though recent studies suggest that up to 30% of Ugandans suffer from some form of mental illness, the problem hardly gets any public policy attention. Mental-health care accounts for less than 2% of the government's health budget.

Makerere had few resources for students – Dr. Ovuga even had to teach himself how to conduct research – but he earned his degree and went on to teach mental health there. Later, he taught at Gulu University in northern Uganda, where he ultimately became Dean of the Medical School.

Having observed both traditional and science-based medicine in practice, Dr. Ovuga believes there should be a place for traditional healers in today's health-care system. Indeed, he believes doctors today could learn a few things from traditional healers.

My mother did not have labs or imaging facilities, and she never went to school. But she was very observant and a very attentive listener. She used the information she got to formulate care plans, just as I was trained to do in medical school. She talked with clients and their caretakers – and paid attention to what they said. She never got tired of listening and holding conversations with her clients.

What disappoints me most with some doctors today is their impatience in handling patients. When I go to see a doctor today, I am eager to explain in detail what I experience. But he or she turns to the screen and types the prescription without even looking at my face and before I have even finished saying what I want to say.

Another difference is that [modern doctors] do not ask clients to come back for reviews more than once. My mother always used to tell her clients to come back – most of the time without charging them. People she helped often would bring her cocks and millet flour. Our home was always full of people – clients and relatives alike. We did not lack food at home, even to feed clients. She told me that she could not charge for her services because God gave her the skill to help people. Today, people in modern medical practice sometimes charge very high fees. When I suffered a stroke, I was taken to a city hospital, and my family was told to pay ten million shillings as a deposit. Fortunately, the University Secretary heard that I was in the hospital. He came just in time. He said I was their professor and that the university would pay. But they still made him sign a commitment form before the doctor would start investigating the cause of the stroke.

The aloof stance western-trained doctors take toward patients reduces their effectiveness, according to Dr. Ovuga. For one thing, he says, Ugandan psychiatrists are too prone to prescribe medication rather than build human relationships with their patients.

We (Africans) are biological psychiatrists. African psychiatrists want to find a biological reason for mental health problems. They are more likely to prescribe medication, and the doses can be quite heavy. Patients can be harmed; after taking medicines, it can take them at least eight hours to start to wake up, and even then, they feel drowsy. Most western psychiatrists are more likely to combine medication with psychotherapy. Very few Ugandan psychiatrists conduct psychotherapy.

A good psychiatrist should take time to understand clients and help them understand the source and nature of their problems, formulate a treatment plan with clients and the caregivers, and be available to tutor and mentor junior doctors. These days, psychiatrists do not seem to have time to teach those below them, even though graduates in any field of medical practice are expected to transfer knowledge and skills to those below them so that there will be people to continue the work after they leave.

Dr. Ovuga believes that traditional healers could hold an answer to Uganda's chronic shortage of mental health professionals.

Traditional healers could be invited to address minor mental disorders as my mother did. Their involvement could reduce the government's medical burden. They can address anxiety and mild cases of depression because they live in the community and know the people who come for help. They know what troubles each neighbour. My mother asked her clients about their marital situations or

*family relationships because she had at least some vague
ideas about what might be going on.*

*Traditional healers have been recognised by government.
The problem is that government is not in control of
monitoring and regulating their activities. Government
needs to develop a policy to bring the traditional healers
under the control of the Ministry of Health so that they
can work with them, monitor and regulate their
activities.*

Some healers set high ethical standards for themselves, while others
fall short, according to Dr. Ovuga. He recalls some people used to ask
his mother to help them pursue "evil intentions."

*They would say, 'My neighbour so and so has done this to
me, so I want you to perform magic so that this person
dies.' I would hear her reply, 'My spirit is not for causing
harm. It is for helping people in distress. If you want that
kind of service, you go elsewhere.' She was quite firm.*

*We as humans want to understand the basis of our
experiences, and one of the easiest sources of
understanding is to lay blame on neighbours or evil
spirits. When I was a young child, there were many
traditional chiefs. They were believed to be rain makers,
so when rain failed to come, one chief or the other got the
blame. The chiefs would pray, and rain eventually would
come. No harm was done. But it is counterproductive to
blame a neighbour for one's troubles. That just leads to
enmity, which causes more stress and more trouble.*

Healers have a professional association, the doctor notes, but it lacks
authority, even to prevent abhorrent practices.

Unregistered healers include some people who practice human sacrifice. They tell clients to bring them the eyes, head or genitalia of a person, maybe a child, for instance. You cannot bring these body parts without killing. When I was still young, I wrote two or three articles about this. I said there was no scientific or religious basis for killing people. The official association for traditional healers always says they are not practicing human sacrifice, but almost every month, sometimes every week, the papers report cases of human sacrifice.

Dr. Ovuga has sought to put his ideas to work by enlisting not only traditional healers but lay people to screen people with troubles, help ones with relatively minor problems and refer those with more serious problems to professionals.

I was asked to help address a surge of suicide in my district, Adjumani, in 2002-2007, and in Gulu district in 2015-2017. The population in Adjumani had fled to the present South Sudan following the fall of President Idi Amin Dada's eight-year rule. In Gulu, people had been displaced during the long Lord's Resistance Army insurgency and then returned to their ancestral homes without adequate preparations. Each family came back with just a panga – machete – to clear their homes that were overgrown, a hoe, a basin, a bucket, and a few plates and saucepans to cook in. It was a stressful time. Each family found itself on its own; the previous collective way of addressing community problems was left to each individual home. Every district had welfare offices, but most officers were not trained or equipped to provide psycho-social support services.

I worked with clinical officers and village chairpersons to hold village meetings and to select one or two volunteers per village or parish based on whether they were liked in their communities, were approachable, friendly, trustworthy and able to keep secrets. In training them, I did not refer to mental illness as 'madness.' I used the term 'distress.' People easily came to appreciate that mental illness is not due to witchcraft or evil spirits but because of experiences we all could address collectively. In our sessions, volunteers identified the warning signs themselves: alcoholism, poverty, failed crops, marital disharmony, living in polygamous homes and so on. Then we discussed how to support people who were sick and help them learn how to perform within their households and communities.

The only problem was that there was no funding. Originally, I told the volunteers, 'You are doing voluntary work because suicide is robbing our districts of human capital.' For three years in each district, they did the voluntary work. But it was a big commitment, and people could only give so much time. We hoped to get some resources, but government money went to hospitals, which served only those in severe distress. The need was mainly at the village level. Even though Adjumani District Local Government recognised mental health as one of the district's health priorities, the money did not trickle down to support the volunteers.

We had discussed so many things. I asked the doctor to summarise his thoughts. Have conditions for the mentally ill improved? Dr. Ovuga, always the reformer, said he is still not satisfied.

I think the level of communal support when I was little boy was a lot higher than it is today. Now we are more individualistic. We do not want people's problems to spill over the fence. When I was growing up, everybody was concerned about other people's problems; people were willing to intervene – even without being asked.

Also, we do not have time today for our children. We are busy running up and down in search of money. Some people leave their homes before the children wake up and get back after the children are in bed. Some children, with tongues in cheek, see their fathers so little they refer to them as uncles. The children end up being influenced by their peers, and they get hooked on drugs, alcohol and other forms of social evils such as pornography or crimes.

Imitation, peer pressure, and lack of control, supervision and support from busy parents – not just the fathers but also mothers – is a big, big problem [leading to] alcohol and drug abuse. There are counseling homes for rehabilitation of those who are addicted to drugs and alcohol dotted everywhere in Kampala. People who go there do not want the centers where they go to be known as rehabilitation centers. They call them 'health spas' or something like that.

Such comments may be controversial. Ugandan parents traditionally ruled their homes with a firm hand – often one that yielded a cane to punish children for misbehaving. Today, parents are less powerful. In many households, both parents are away from home much of the time because they must hold jobs to make ends meet. At the same time, universal education, television, social media and entertainment have all exposed children to influences from outside of the home. Who's to blame when children stray? Many parents feel unfairly accused when they are held responsible. Some even suggest that children deliberately try to excuse bad behaviour by pointing a finger at their parents. It's a tough issue – one of many challenges for people in the mental health profession and in many other walks of life. As the doctor puts it,

Psychiatry must do a better job explaining itself. One way is by providing a type of mental health service that delivers effective, positive outcomes. This requires taking time with clients and their families, listening carefully, formulating treatment plans with families and sick people, providing the right medication that achieves rapid resolution of symptoms, keeping clients long enough in the hospital and following up to make sure they get better. We are always in a hurry. We do not take time to listen. We do not take time to explain. Ugandans come from multiple ethnic and cultural backgrounds, so we often do not communicate effectively. We cannot claim to be better than traditional healers. The only complaint I have against traditional healers involves ones who engage in harmful practices like human sacrifice. But otherwise, they have the time medical professionals could use to listen to clients and make sure they understand how to help them get better.

The doctor ended on a note of optimism. People at least are starting to realise that mental illness can be treated, he said. In his view, it has been a slow and still incomplete transformation, but indicators of change are multiplying. On that, I can offer one piece of evidence. When my mother recently showed signs that her depression was recurring, family members called a psychiatrist at Butabika Hospital. No one in the house frowned at the idea. No silence gripped us when it was suggested. And no one warned anybody else to keep it a secret.

A Bright Gold Ray

By Edna Namara

I LEARNT THAT I was human from my grandmother. She gave me my name and everything else that pertains to humanity and culture. I was satisfied. I never wanted to know why I lived with her because I needed no other place. Nothing felt more perfect. Years later, when I learned that my parents, both civil servants living in Kampala, had sent me to live with her because they wanted me to be raised in the ways of our culture, my only reaction was utter gratitude.

Grandma taught me to greet every person I met. "Never pass by people without greeting them – it's a law of culture," she would say, noting that only animals do not greet, although they do acknowledge kinship.

She reinforced her teaching by having me join church groups, including a philanthropy club. Every Sunday after mass, my peers and I would visit old women in the village to wash their food pots, fetch their firewood and water, and clean their homes. We did this with diligence. In fact, we punished members who didn't join in our labours with enthusiasm, blocking them from participating in our activities the following Sunday, much like footballers get suspended from their teams for misconduct.

We would record what we had done in books we kept as part of the club. The priest, Father Andrew Bakeihahwenki, had said God attends to many people, so we decided to aid his memory in case He forgot about us. We thought God was a human being who would sit with us at table and ask us to explain how we used our time on earth. My grandmother never said much about my expectation that I would meet God someday, but I am thankful for this elementary practice in record keeping and team spirit.

Grandmother bathed me up to the time I became conscious of the need for privacy. Then she loosened her grip and allowed me to move with other girls. For us, collecting firewood or swamp reeds was an adventure. We would feed many curiosities on our expeditions. I especially enjoyed looking for gooseberries or strawberries. My love for candy began on one such outing when we chewed on the sap of Burikooti trees. The stuff was a delicacy.

We sometimes painted our faces with volcanic soils that local painters would dig up to paint their homes. We put the paint on our faces so thick we looked like muzungus. We thought we looked so beautiful. I was afraid Grandma would reproach me, but she was delighted, although she advised me to apply the soil sparingly and use it not to change my colour but to create beautiful patterns. Later, when we learned that an African girl had to have a gap in the centre of her dental array to be beautiful, she introduced me to a beauty specialist she trusted to chip my teeth with a knife, creating a gap we would stuff with sizeable sticks to keep the teeth apart. I eventually abandoned that practice, trusting my instincts but confident that Grandma would stand by me.

When the time came to attend school, Grandmother emphasised swiftness. She taught us to run to and from school quickly because that would show people that we were serious about our business. One must always show your commitment to doing something, my grandmother stressed, because this would earn us respect.

She also advised us to listen to people entrusted to direct us because they never go wrong. But her opinion changed after our head teacher once meted out a harsh punishment to me and my colleagues. He had sent word for all Primary Seven members to come to school during a holiday. We rushed to heed his call, anticipating tips on how to pass our national exams, which were in the offing. But after we had assembled, the teacher, a slender man with a sharply ironed trouser and a spotless sky-blue shirt, told us he wanted us to climb uphill to harvest his two plots of sorghum. "It is only three days' work," he said.

This was such a letdown. The big boys in class decided to stage a rebellion. Our ringleader, Byensi, told him that we were not willing to go uphill during a holiday to harvest his sorghum. The headteacher listened intently to the reasons Byensi gave and shook his head. Later, we all applauded Byensi for taking a strong stand, the stronger boys lifting him shoulder high. "Our hero," we all shouted.

Our sense of triumph gave way to anxiety at church the following Sunday, when the catechist announced that every parent with a P-7 child should come with them to school the next day. I sheepishly went, following grandmother, who was worried stiff about what might happen to us. When we arrived, many parents already had gathered. Some, including my grandmother, discussed going uphill and harvesting the sorghum on behalf of the children. But the head teacher did not want to hear that. He asked every parent to come and witness a correction of stubborn minds. He then called us to the cleansing arena and administered ten lashes to each of us. After the beating, each child rolled in the grass, pressing hard and rubbing our burning bums. During my turn, at the seventh blow of the cane, grandmother could not hold her pain anymore; she burst out crying. That prompted the head teacher to take a break, during which he gave me bonus lashes in the back and neck, each lash attached to words of reproach: "You, you! . . . *lash lash* . . . it is your stubborn . . . *lash lash lash* . . . little spirit . . . *lash lash* . . . that is making your . . . lash lash

lash lash . . . loving and caring grandmother cry loudly . . . *lash lash lash lash lash lash.*" The pain was too much. I was cursing the person who invented adjectives. After my bonus, I dashed lamely to join my classmates to cool off. When I reached home, my grandmother was ready with steamed herbs, which she pressed on the lesions so I could catch some sleep. I was better in three days.

Grandmother was a databank of traditional health treatments. Her pharmacy was the wilderness. She knew herbs to cure wounds, to heal a bad stomach, to make women in labour produce quickly, to clear running tummies and constipation, to help little babies with breathing difficulties – she had a remedy for any ailment.

"We are part of this system," she said.

"What does that mean?" I asked her, and she told me of the days before white medicine was introduced.

"We were able to live on herbs and grow up to great ages," she said.

"Maybe there were no diseases like now," I challenged her.

"Far from it. There were diseases, but we had our own means."

"Take me through the means at that time," I implored.

She noted that community involvement and service were the norm in the early days. If someone complained of a headache, people would tie a piece of cloth around his or her neck until the veins bulged. Then they would look for the most prominent vein and cut it, using a special knife. When hot, black blood shot out, it would be aimed at a small hole dug in the ground. When the hole filled with the blood, they would untie the client, who would be up and about in a matter of hours.

The logic was that the headache arose because the person had too much blood in the head. The blood-letting outlet would return the person to normalcy.

When I reached high school, my family decided to move me to Kampala, where schools were better than in the village. Grandma was excited at the wider experience this would give me. I returned home each holiday, and she was eager to learn what secondary school was like. On one such visit, I told her the story of the *River Between* by Kenyan writer Ngũgĩ wa Thiong'o. We noted that the description of two villages divided by religious differences put into perspective a conflict in our area between peoples of different religions who lived on two opposite hills.

Another time, I recounted lessons I learned about a time European countries fell into a conflict so big it was called a "world war."

"Wait a minute," she cut in. "When did this happen?"

"1940-45."

"Are you talking about the Abaseveni?"

"Who are they?" I asked.

"The African men who took their youthfulness to war. They fought at some big-water place. Some went further to distant places called Burma."

It's true. During Uganda's colonial period, Abaseveni, a group of Ugandan soldiers known as the King's African Rifles, had fought in a global conflagration. It turned out that my grandfather and his brother both fought on the side of the British. I asked how my grandma knew about this.

"My dear, not only did I hear about them, but I lost my life partner to that war. There is no way I can forget it."

My grandfather's brother ultimately returned from the war, but my grandmother said he and my grandfather had been separated at some big sea. My grandmother said the family kept hoping for years that my grandfather would reappear, but he never did. To contain her changed mood, I helped her with her headscarf. But a sudden silence fell between us, an invisible vacuum filled by her memories and my deep curiosity. My grandfather's death closed the door for my grandmother to have more children. As we talked, I felt like more than a grandchild; I was Grandma's confidant and friend. None of my siblings ever learned the truth about the effect of the world war on us.

In the discomfiting emptiness, I soliloquised, asking about what else this war brought to us apart from misery. It was the birth of African will to fight, my grandmother said. "Nationalism" was how our history teacher put it. Those who fought for independence got their inspiration from that war; if we fought *for* the British, they reasoned, we also could fight *against* them and have self-rule.

With such conversations, Grandma became my student but also led me in connecting the dots between now and the past.

Later, we discussed another literature text. I narrated the story of a little orphan girl who went through trying times. She was mistreated by her aunt and cousins and harassed by her patrons in an orphanage. Later, she took to the road alone and found another country where she got her new relations. But again, she left.

"Was something chasing her?" Grandma asked. "How could she leave her relatives who were warm and caring?"

"A cousin wanted to marry her, but she did not feel his love for her."

"Oh no. Love grows, she should have waited. But in this case, this would have been incest. Cousins carry the same blood in their veins, they don't marry."

"What happens if they do?"

"Another rule of culture: The products of such a marriage would be cursed with unexplainable diseases. Did she eventually get married?"

"Yes."

"How?"

I explained. The two of us were amazed that from miles apart Jane Eyre and Rochester shared important feelings. We discarded it as an untruth – a literary invention.

Until a similar situation happened to us . . .

The clock of our lives kept ticking and after a while, with each tick, the distance between us grew wider. I got married. I became pregnant. One day, my grandmother asked her niece to write a letter for her to me. It took two weeks to reach me. In it, she instructed me to listen for the heartbeat of the baby.

"Lie on your bed, stay clear of any interruptions and noise, and listen for ten minutes. If there is no movement, give it more time until you feel some movement. Then write back." I wrote back, and a month later she received the letter. She was so happy. She would soon see her great grandchild.

Slowly, I became older, and she became frail. I now had a job and responsibilities. The distance stood between us. As my grandmother became weaker, my siblings and I decided on a plan. We found a young girl to live with her. We supported her so she could continue going to school. In return, she prepared Grandma's meals, leaving them on a table near grandmother's bed so she could get them easily when she became hungry. My grandma would move to the brook with a one-litre jug in case she wanted drinking water. Her friends tilled her land and in turn sent her food.

Most times the girl found Grandma's meals untouched. She would say food only makes sense when one is with company. This became a challenge. If any of us visited, she would eat. That would give her more strength; she would hobble and check the store for something to cook, asking, "Waryaki mwana wangye? What do I offer you, my child?"

We thought she needed more company. We raised the possibility of taking her to a home for the elderly in Mbarara, the largest nearby town. More Ugandans are resorting to this strategy for keeping their elders safe and healthy; the demands of work life make other solutions increasingly difficult. But we also thought being with friends and age-mates might lift her spirits.

She was unpersuaded and asked, "Is that a boarding school like where you people used to go?" We explained how they would just let her be, with routine walks and people to help her with life, food, bathing and sleeping. She wondered why we would take her to a place where people walked aimlessly. "What would I be doing in such a place?" she quizzed.

Then she shocked us with a question, "Am I so burdensome to you that you think of throwing me to some far-off place with new people to learn their ways and unlearn mine?" She explained how life to her meant looking at familiar faces and features in the environment. She also wondered what would become of her home when she left. She quickly answered her own question. "The house will crumble before I die, the footpath will grow into weeds and my home will turn into a bush."

We couldn't convince her to join a home for the elderly. Time and again on a surprise visit, I would find her napping in a nearby garden with a handful of weeds. I worried about the dangers she could face – snakes were on top of the list. She spoke of a time when a snake had climbed over her legs as she lay basking in the sun. She had felt the cold reptile on her skin and decided just to lay still so it wouldn't be startled and bite her in self-defense.

"Don't you see you are in danger?" I asked. "You need to be free of such life-threatening creatures."

"But why am I telling you this story?" she answered. "It's only God who protects us."

I found it impossible to shift her from a home she had known for more than six decades. She just could not leave the place unless she was leaving the world. Eventually, that is what happened.

Her home never turned to bush while she was still alive because we hired people to keep the compound tidy, neighbours visited her frequently, and the five of us children would come home monthly in turns.

Eventually, she became ill so she agreed to leave home, but only to go to a hospital, not a home for the elderly. She stayed for three weeks, often half awake and half afloat. She periodically would laugh in response to some voice only she could hear.

Despite her age, she still managed her affairs. There was a community group called "Let's Bury Each Other." She was the treasurer. She would keep the members' money, mats and pans. After she died, we found some money wrapped in a cloth in a hole in the floor of her bedroom. When we consulted, we were told that at the time of her death, she was keeping that money for the group, but the group had written it off as a bad debt since they could not ask any of us for it. We were proud to turn it over to them.

The cultural group could not buy our idea of burying her in a foreign coffin. "She has been our committed member so we must bury her in our own coffin," the chairman said.

They nailed pieces of wood together and made her coffin. This is what she had wished. We could not go against her wish.

Today, funeral homes are starting to appear in Uganda. They are meant to ease stress for the grieving relatives. They handle the rites, bathe the body, dress it, and buy flowers and caskets. This is becoming a new normal, although it still isn't universally accepted. Many people feel the new way of burial estranges them from their loved ones. They want to participate in sending off their beloved. Relatives deserve each other's presence, dead or alive. "You don't celebrate someone's life by paying people to bury him for you," says a senior citizen from Rukiga. He adds that actively participating in the rites of passage gives some satisfaction and helps one accept that a person is gone.

My grandmother, who had guided me through many of life's most important moments, concluded her responsibility by easing her release for me. She helped me understand and accept her own death.

A few weeks after she had been in the hospital, she came to me in a dream. She was close to me, near enough for us to exchange words. We were separated by a bright gold ray. She was strong. She was dancing and happy. She told me she was feeling rejuvenated. "Please tell your siblings not to care anymore about how I feel because I am happy."

This made me happy too. I kept on looking at her. I had never seen her with such a glow. I had never seen her so strong. Our conversation went on to one other sentence.

"Look, the nurses have moved me off the bed." she said.

"Really Grandma? This is so good," I answered her.

A phone call cut short my dream. My cousin George, who had been taking care of her, was on the line.

"Edna, grandmother has breathed her last."

"What did you say, George?" I asked, throwing back my covers.

"Grandmother died a moment ago. The nurses are removing her from the bed right now."

I wanted to return to the dream, but I could not. I wanted to ask more questions, but what for? What was important was her message – she was happy, and she wished us all to be happy. She gave me the means to let her go because she knew it would be hard for me.

My grandmother, who introduced me to a culture of humans also gave me a sneak peek into the culture of life after death. There is a rebirth, a rekindling, a rebranding and perfect bliss in the spirit world after our mission on earth is accomplished.

RIP, my best friend, Grandma.

Authors

Linda Akoth Orando was born and raised by Winifred Akello Orando and Mercellus Orando of the Goria clan of the Jopadhola tribe in eastern Uganda. She has lived most of her life in Kampala. She received a Bachelor's degree in architecture from Makerere University and has practiced architecture for 10 years as a project manager, interior designer, furniture designer, and contractor. She performs social work to empower a group of the urban poor in Kampala through skills training and literacy learning.

Wobusobozi Amooti Kangere, a writer, publisher, and artistic director, runs the publishing enterprise Ibua Publishing, which was established to promote reading and writing in African societies with oral traditions. A lover of literature, history, theatre, film, debate, expressive art and learning, he defines his mission as documenting and preserving African history, lore, culture and knowledge systems, and seeing Africans assume

their place as equal players at the global cultural table. His poems appear in two anthologies – *Broken Voices of the Revolution* and *Streetlights at Noon Eclipse.* He contributes essays to www.journal.ibuapublishing.com

Edna Namara is a news reporter for Global Press Journal, an international online publishing House. Born in Kampala but raised in Rukiga district, she attended Old Kampala secondary school and received a BA degree in Education and a Master's degree in Education Management and Policy Planning from Kyambogo University. Her undergraduate research was on The Force and Literary Merit of Oral Literature among her people, the Bakiga. She has loved storytelling since her early childhood.

Joachim Buwembo is a distinguished Ugandan journalist and social commentator. He has served as Sunday Editor for the New Vision newspaper and as managing editor of the Daily Monitor newspaper. In 2004, he became the founding editor of The Citizen newspaper in Tanzania, which is owned by the Nation Media Group, the largest media group in east and central Africa. He

also created *Kilimo Kwanza* ("Agriculture First") – an agriculture supplement that focuses on poverty and development issues in Tanzania. Buwembo won acclaim for his book, *How to be a Ugandan* (2002), which deconstructs Ugandan society in a series of profiles of social types. He followed that with *The Ugandan Paradox* (2012), which describes Uganda as "a rich country of poor people" in addressing varied topics.

A.K. Kaiza is a Ugandan writer and journalist, who joined the media in 1994. He has worked at the former Uganda Television and at The East African newspaper as a reporter at large and pioneering art and literary journalism and critic. He has worked in Kenya as literary editor for the magazine Kwani? and as editor of the online arts magazine, AfricanColours. He is currently involved in arts and cultural development.

Caroline Ariba is a journalist, researcher, and media consultant. A graduate of Makerere University and former Global Health Scholar at the Queen Mary University of London, her passion for culture and social justice has informed her reporting, winning her multiple awards both locally and internationally.  She has worked with the New Vision media group in Uganda, the Guardian and The Times in the UK, and City Press in South Africa. She also contributed to several media outlets across the globe. Caroline was part of the eleven women authors of *Crossroads: Women Coming of Age in Today's Uganda.*

Joseph Elunya Sr. was born into a peasant family in Oderai village in eastern Uganda's Soroti District. He spent his early life helping his parents cultivate food crops and raise cattle for the family's subsistence. At the age of nine, he assumed responsibility for raising money to pay his school fees by selling vegetables. After high school, he joined Voice of Teso radio station as a newscaster and later as News Editor. He also has worked as Bureau Chief for the Institute of War and Peace Reporting at Uganda Radio Network. He is co-director of the Centre for Investigative Journalism in Uganda. He holds a Diploma in Journalism, a Bachelor of Ethics and Development Studies, and a Master of Science in Monitoring and Evaluation.

Regina Asinde is an activist, facilitator, trainer, publisher, editor and author who passionately believes in stories as a powerful tool for social change. She is the Managing Director of Wordsmith Publications Uganda Limited and the author of *Shards of Brokenness* (a poetry collection) and *Sullied Threads* (a short story collection). Her other works have

been published in a number of anthologies and various online magazines. She lives in Tororo, Uganda, with her husband and children.

Aliker P'Ocitti is a poet, author of two books – *My Mayor: The Political Campaign Story of a Poor Elite and Rich Illiterate* and *Even Female Dogs Hunt* (publication pending) – and a collection of poems in the book *Hidden Scars*. He also is a blogger and online news editor, and he has served as a local television talk show host. He has contributed opinion to major Ugandan newspapers and online publications and has published literary works in the African Book Collective: *Best "New" African Poets Anthology 2020* and other books. He holds a B.A. Education and has earned Master's Degrees from Makerere University and the University of San Diego.

Achelam D. Kinyera was born in Northern Uganda and grew up in Kampala. He completed secondary school at Uganda Martyrs Secondary School, Namugongo, and then joined Makerere University and trained as a medical doctor. A member of the Lantern Meet of Poets, he has written poetry, performed all over Kampala and played numerous roles in theatre productions. His poetry was published in an anthology, *Streetlights At Noon Eclipse*, and he has published short stories, essays, and reviews online in the Ibua Journal, for which he is a regular contributor and part of the editorial team. He lives in Kampala and is eternally haunted by manuscripts he hopes will one day see the light of day.

Stephen Ssenkaaba, an award-winning features writer and editor, was a contributing editor for The New Vision, where he specialised in covering arts and culture, education and development issues. As a 2018-2019 Knight Wallace Journalism Research Fellow at the University of Michigan, he studied the role of online technologies in journalism in Africa. He subsequently helped establish the New Vision's first-ever podcasting platform. He has taught undergraduate courses in online and digital communication, editing, feature writing and contemporary issues in media and society at Uganda Christian University. As this book went to press, he was a PhD student in Communications and Media Studies at the University of Oregon.

Flavia Nassaka is a journalist based in Kampala. A graduate of Makerere University, she currently works with Uganda Radio Network, a news agency that offers hard news, documentaries, and magazine stories to subscribing newspapers, radio stations, and online media outlets. She is a mother of two boys, Jamal and Jibril. Flavia developed a passionate interest in health science as a print journalist for the Independent Magazine. She has won two awards for excellence in health journalism. Her greatest fulfillment comes from comprehending scientific issues that often tend to be complicated to non-scientists.

Editors

Christopher Conte is a writer, editor and journalism teacher based in Washington, DC. A former reporter and editor for the Wall Street Journal, he has trained journalists on health, economic, and social issues, and writing. He has worked with the International Center for Journalists (which introduced him to Uganda) and the World Association of Newspapers and News Publishers. He also has consulted and edited for a number of nonprofit organisations, including the World Bank, the International Finance Corporation, and Gateway House – the Indian Council on Global Relations.

Hilda J. Twongyeirwe is a writer and book editor from Western Uganda. She works with FEMRITE – Uganda Women Writers Association, and has coordinated writing projects for women in Uganda, South Sudan and the United States. She is a member of the Lions Club of Kampala Central and The Graca Machel Trust – Women in Media Network. She serves on the International

Advisory Board of African Research Universities Alliance – Makerere University. A Fellow of the USA International Visitors Leadership Programme, she received the Uganda Government National Medal and the Uganda Registration Services Bureau Award for her contribution to Uganda's literary arts. She is a mountain climber – a sport that has taken her to places like Mount Moroto, which is mentioned in *Remembering the Future*.

Ibua Publishing: Re-framing the African narrative

Ibua Publishing is a digital brand on a mission to promote African storytelling. We produce and distribute African stories in diverse forms – literature, audio, video, and live performance – to keep the art of storytelling relevant in changing times.

As we celebrate, preserve and transfer to the next generation the continent's storytelling heritage, we also strive to empower Africans living on the continent to tell the stories of our time while honouring the new ways in which modern audiences consume content.

Our effort to reframe the African narrative involves four primary initiatives: Ibua Journal, an online multimedia magazine featuring essays, short stories and poetry; Ibua Labs, training spaces for writers and editors working with the written word, theatre, and film; Ibua Series, an imprint that produces fiction, creative nonfiction, and poetry; and Ibua Productions, a unit that produces audio, visual, film, and live performances.

Our publications include *Streetlights at Noon Eclipse*, an anthology of poems celebrating 12 years of the Lantern Meet of Poets; *Why do Sunflowers Follow the Sun*, a children's book on community and generosity; *Still Blossoming*, a collection of poems on mental wellness and becoming; and *Mighty Angwech and Other Stories*, a collection of three stories based on female legends from Ugandan folktales. All are available on our webshop and at select stores.

We also have produced *Killing Time*, a two-person satirical play about the pursuit of happiness, which we also produced as an audio drama, along with a second audio drama entitled *Virus in Baghdad*. The audios are available on the music streaming service SoundCloud. We also have a short film, *Sunflowers*, which can be streamed off our YouTube channel, ibualounge.

We have published three anthologies in Ibua Journal – *Pack Light: Memories of Growing up in Africa, Bold: Imagining a New Africa, and Bold: Food (in Africa)* – as part of our themed annual continental call with submissions from African writers living across the continent.

Our training spaces, designed to equip writers and editors with the foundations for storytelling and the tools to improve the editorial quality of works produced on the continent, run annually. The facilitators for both are practitioners and academics in the literary field.

Visit us at www.ibuapublishing.com to learn more about our initiatives and coming events. You can buy a copy of our books through our webshop too.

Ibua Publishing was started in 2018 as an initiative of the Lantern Meet Foundation.

Karungi Charity Kwatampora
Publisher

Acknowledgments

More people participated in the in the preparation of this book than we can list. Our heartfelt thanks to the many family members and friends who have helped and supported us in so many ways over so many years. For this particular project, special thanks go to:

Kwara Thomas Odoi, Fred Obbo and Jane-Frances Alowo for sharing with Linda Orando the wisdom of a patriarch; Egrance "Chaachi" Katanywa, Godfrey and Christine Katanywa, Derrick Aruho, and Mr. Kibeherire for helping Wobusobozi Amooti Kangere uncover the story of a Ugandan matriarchy; Sokodina Bagirogwabusha, Gaudensia Tumwesigyire, Prisca Kyindimugura, and Kacanga Vian for explaining to Edna Namara in words and song the bittersweet lives of women in an earlier time; Mr Ssonko Lule Frederick of Kiwatule village in eastern Kampala for supporting Joachim Buwembo's account of changing communications technology; John Napua, Tolim Lomer and Paul Otyang, who figured prominently in A.K. Kaiza's probing story of colonial and post-colonial history as lived by the Karamojong people; Suleiman Kairugala Etembeya, Ibrahim Khaima, Juma Kafafa, Fredah Kafafa, Musa Kafafa, Wilson Kategere Ngobi, Charles Dikan, Gemma Ahaibwe, Paul Lakuma, Christine Naisiko Omongole, and Margaret Asekenye Ogwang for their contributions to Caroline Ariba's portrait of hardship in rural Uganda; Peter Esimu, Bishop Justine Edweu, James Prince Eparu and Peter Esimu for making possible Joseph Elunya's description of genuine and phony traditional healers;

Ogomba Lawrence of Iyopok, Mulanda sub-county, Tororo, and Awori Evelyne of Mulanda Central, Mulanda sub county, Tororo for their support of Regina Asinde's reporting on traditional religion and Christianity; Okello Johnson, Komakech Henry Kilama and Otim Ocogo for the parts they played in Aliker P'Ocitti's powerful reflections on traditional Acholi justice and "modern" western notions of justice; David Orach, Mugoda Gordons Good ("Wake"), Kawaabi Bukenya Herbert ("VJ Mun"), Agaba Alfred, Eric Atuda, Isaac Kwizera, and Bwojji Elijah who gave Achelam D. Kinyera fodder for his review of Uganda's rich linguistic heritage; Isaac Godfrey Nabwana, the film maker who, in Stephen Ssenkaaba's telling, uses folklore to entertain and enlighten; and Dr. Emilio Ovuga for explaining continuity and change in the healing arts through his personal and professional experience.

As editor, I would like to give special thanks to Hilda Twongyeirwe for co-editing many of the stories, and Karungi Charity Kwatampora and Wobusobozi Amooti Kangere, at Ibua Publishing for their support and management of the publication and marketing effort – and especially for helping a muzungu keep his preconceptions about Uganda in check; Nandini Bhaskaran Jai for giving me much needed cross-cultural advice and support; Lydia Namubiru, Samuel Gummah Nabaasa, Benon Oluka, Danson Kahyana, Beatrice Lamwaka, Kagayi Ngobi, Daniel Kalinaki, Esther Nakkazi and Florence Kyohangirwe for sharing their talents, enthusiasm and wise advice; Sean Conte for devoting many hours of hard work and loving care to develop the web site for this book; and last but definitely not least, Kristen and Lauren Conte, who have helped me in more ways than I can count.

Christopher Conte

www.ingramcontent.com/pod-product-compliance
Lightning Source LLC
Chambersburg PA
CBHW071144130626
46553CB00004B/1510